CRUISE VACATIONS WITH KIDS

Candyce H. Stapen

Prima Publishing

To my favorite traveling companions: Matthew, Alissa, and David. And to Grandma Edith, who made our cruise to Costa Rica so memorable.

PRIMA PUBLISHING and colophon are trademarks of Prima Communications, Inc.

Library of Congress Cataloging-in-Publication Data

Stapen, Candyce H.
  Cruise vacations with kids / Candyce H. Stapen.
    p.   cm.
    "Inside tips, including: choosing the right cruise for your family; getting the most for your money; finding family-friendly ships around the world; discovering eco-adventures, sailing expeditions, and more!"
  Includes index.
  ISBN 0-7615-0320-X
  1. Ocean travel. 2. Cruise ships. 3. Family recreation.
  I. Title.
G550.S78 1995
910.4'5—dc20   95-23780
                                                 CIP

96 97 98 99 00 DD 10 9 8 7 6 5 4 3 2 1
Printed in the United States of America

How to Order:
Single copies may be ordered from Prima Publishing, P.O. Box 1260BK, Rocklin, CA 95677; telephone (916) 632-4400. Quantity discounts are also available. On your letterhead, include information concerning the intended use of the books and the number of books you wish to purchase.

Contents

iii

Acknowledgments

I thank my editor Alice Anderson for her patience and assistance, and my agent Carol Mann for her support. Special thanks go to Carol Eannarino, whose fine writing contributed much to this book. I appreciate the help of my editorial assistants Valerie Bandura and Virginia Campbell.

Introduction

Before our first family cruise, my husband and I wondered whether seven days in the same cabin with our children was sane or sadistic, if the kids could forgo T-shirts and sibling rivalry at our formal dinner seatings, and if we would return home fat, bored, and broke. Instead, we had one of our best family vacations ever.

Since then (more than ten years ago), we've been on many cruises together. Cruising frees us from the usual family nemeses—packing, unpacking, schlepping suitcases, and dealing with cranky children in a hot car. We find that the up-front price, the variety of on-shore and on-board family fun, and the children's and teens' programs make a cruise a something-for-everyone vacation and a family favorite.

In the next five years, forty-four million Americans are expected to go on a cruise. And why not? On a cruise, no generation has to sacrifice vacation fun so that others can enjoy themselves. Kids from tots to teens keep busy with creative programs that often include beach parties, computer games, on-deck Olympics, and after-dinner shows. Parents and grandparents enjoy a diverse array of on-board classes such as bridge and skeet shooting, putting tournaments, big band dances, and a host of shore choices from shopping to sightseeing to relaxing in the shade of palm tree-lined beaches.

Cruises also give families lots of opportunities to enjoy activities together. We always team up for sports trivia and bingo on board, and on shore we enjoy snorkeling trips, beach hopping, and shopping excursions together. For all these reasons, cruising creates the kind of memories that your family will talk about forever, but only if you choose the right cruise. Because programs and amenities vary from cruise line to cruise line and among ships within a line, the key is to select a cruise that meets your family's needs.

This book is full of the kind of advice that should enable you to make the most of your cruise vacation. To help guide your family, each chapter in this book lists family-friendly beaches, outdoor activities, historical sites, and natural attractions as well as shops and restaurants (children will want snacks or lunch in town).

We organized this book the way we, and many people, pick cruises: by destination. Chapters focus on the popular cruise spots—the Caribbean, Bermuda, Mexico, the Bahamas, Hawaii, and Alaska—as well as such popular ecological destinations as the Galápagos Islands and Costa Rica's Pacific coast. We've also covered windjammer cruises along the coast of New England and river trips in the heartland along the Mississippi and its tributaries. Options such as barge trips on European canals and rivers are described as well. Because of space limitations, however, we have generally not listed repositioning cruises, special one-time-only sailings, or traditional cruise destinations that are less family-oriented, such as Panama Canal cruises and European cruises.

Chapter one offers suggestions on how to choose a family cruise and save money. Chapter two presents a detailed explanation of the children's programs and the personalities of the top ten traditional cruise lines for families. These choices are based on extensive research and my personal observations, experiences, and analysis of the lines' programs and itineraries. The main choices of ships and their itineraries are listed first to give you a quick-and-easy look at your top options. Then, descriptions of the ships are followed by our shore picks. We've created lists of best bets for ship and for shore and have also highlighted tips designed to make your cruise easier and more enjoyable.

We hope you find this book helpful and come to enjoy cruising as much as our family does. We look forward to hearing about your experiences both on board and on shore. This will help us provide the best possible service to our readers in the future. Please share your experiences by writing to us care of Prima Publishing and Communications, attn: Alice Anderson, editor, P. O. Box 1260, Rocklin, CA 95677-1260.

Thank you so much and *bon voyage!*

Note: We've listed the primary fall/winter and spring/summer itineraries for the top cruise lines. Cruise lines often reposition ships and change itineraries with little notice. The itineraries listed are accurate as of press time, but it's likely that one or two will have changed by the time this book is printed.

1

The Dollars and Sense of Cruising

How to Choose a Family Cruise and Save Money

The key to a great family cruise is planning ahead. First, pick the ship and the itinerary that meets your family's needs. Consider the entire spectrum of cruising options, which ranges from traditional cruise ships to windjammer sailings, steamboats, mini-cruise ships, barges, and ecological and eco-educational cruises. Then you need to assess the family-friendly quality of each ship and destination to find the best combination for you and your children. Children's programs and services vary not only with cruise lines but also among ships and sailings on the same line. Planning ahead also allows you to save a significant amount of money on both the cost of the cruise and the cost of shore tours.

HOW TO CHOOSE A FAMILY CRUISE

Discover Your Fantasies

Begin with your family's fantasies. After all, a cruise more than most vacations floats a dreamlike aura. Part of the fun of cruising is getting what you wish for, so be honest about both practical issues and preferences. Does your family want the never-ending activities that come with a big cruise ship, the intimacy of a small ship, or a bit of both afforded by a mini-cruise? Does your first-grader want friends to play with and swimming in every port? Does your teen vote for a beach itinerary so she can party with other teens and also try parasailing and Jet Skiing? Does your spouse crave golf clinics on board and tee times in every port? Does your mother-in-law want bridge tournaments in the afternoon and big band dances at night? Does your dad prefer professional entertainment and elaborate shows to lectures by wildlife experts? Do you long for a luxurious course of facials, aromatherapy treatments, and therapeutic massages? Are you looking for a luxury, moderate, or budget ship? Consider the personalities of each cruise line, which are discussed at length in chapter two.

Also, consider the alternatives to traditional cruise ships. If the wildlife on shore is more important than the nightlife on board, then your family may prefer to go on an ecological voyage where you can observe sea lions resting belly-to-belly on beaches rather than coeds sunbathing in bikinis. Are your children studying nineteenth-century America? If so, a trip down the mighty Mississippi River on a gingerbread-trimmed steamboat or a hands-on adventure under the billowing sails of a windjammer makes the era come magically and memorably alive.

Decide on a Length

Do you want a short, sampler trip or a longer voyage of seven to twelve or fourteen days? Three- or four-day outings offer cost-effective ways to taste ocean life and a chance to learn whether you really can stomach those undulating waves. But with a port each day and a party each night, you're likely to disembark happy but tired. You won't, however, have experienced one of cruising's great allures—the relaxed pace of lazy sea days. There's something to be savored about a deck chair and a limitless horizon. With a longer itinerary, your children will also have time to become involved in a creative kids' program that transcends baby-sitting.

Assess the Children's Program

Consider the following when choosing a children's program:

1. Frequency: Be certain the program operates for the sailing you've booked. Avoid cruises that only offer children's programs when a minimum number of kids sign on. This requirement could leave your children without activities or shipboard friends.

2. Ages: Make sure the program functions for your children's ages. The best programs employ enough counselors to separate children into several age groups. When a four-year-old is grouped with a ten-year-old, neither one has a good time.

3. Hours: Find out whether counselors supervise activities for blocks of time or intermittent activities are scheduled at selected intervals throughout the day. The latter works better for teens who want to join in a Nintendo game competition in the morning but also want free time to hang out by the pool. However, if children's bingo runs from 10 A.M. to 11 A.M. and the next event for junior cruisers is a 3 P.M. scavenger hunt, your children may become bored, and you won't have free time to play bridge or read your novel.

4. Evening hours: Without an evening program, you must either book a private baby-sitter for an extra fee, take your child to the nightly shows (children are not welcome in the casinos), or return to your cabin when your tot tires at 7 P.M.

5. Facilities: A designated children's and/or teen center is a definite plus. This not only indicates

the ship's commitment to children but also provides a much-needed focus. Children know where to go to join activities and to meet others, and parents know where their children are. A separate teen center encourages participation by teens, many of whom wouldn't be caught dead fraternizing with a five-year-old.

6. Staff: There should be enough counselors to adequately divide the children into workable age groups. The counselors should have been trained by a supervisor with a background in childhood development and/or recreation. A plus: counselors who are certified in CPR and other emergency medical techniques.

7. Safety: Check out the ship's safety precautions. Areas for toddlers and pre-schoolers should have gates so that curious little ones cannot wander. There should be a definite sign-in and sign-out program for young children to prevent an unauthorized person from taking your child out of the program and to prevent a fast-talking first-grader from convincing her counselor that "Mommy always lets me walk around the ship by myself."

8. Port hours: Some programs operate when in port but others do not. A port program offers flexibility. You can spend the morning exploring the sites with your children, return to the ship for lunch, and then happily go scuba diving or shopping without your children, who would much rather play on board with their newfound friends.

9. Shore programs: Some cruise lines offer special tours for teens and programs for families. These

Splashing in the pool on board. Photo © Celebrity Cruises.

help shy teens develop shipboard friendships, and families have more fun together.

10. Cruise rhythms: On a three- or four-day cruise that leaves in the afternoon and arrives the next morning in port, there's little time or reason for children to use the kids' program because they are too busy in port or playing by the pool. If the day at sea is the cruise's last, fewer kids participate in the organized program because they've already made shipboard friends.

Look for Family-Friendly Amenities

1. Equipment: Can you reserve a high chair, booster seat, or crib ahead of time?

> **TIP:** Teens often turn up their noses at organized activities, pronouncing themselves "too cool" for any kids' program. However, you should encourage (bribe?) your teens to attend the first meeting of the teens' group and the first few activities since cliques form quickly on board. Activities offer a great way for your teen to meet others to "hang out" with, which goes a long way toward making the cruise a success for your teen.

2. Food: Do the dining rooms offer children's menus? (While grilled salmon with mango sauce sounds superb to you, your five-year-old smiles at the thought of pizza and hamburgers.)

3. Room service: Some ships will serve full meals in your cabin, but others offer only limited snacks. Room service meals give you the option of enjoying such conveniences as in-cabin breakfast or a full meal for a toddler too sleepy to eat in the dining room.

4. Informal eateries: Many ships offer a range of informal dining options, including pizza parlors and pasta stations. Not only do these please picky eaters but they also enable parents to get food for their children at any time, even if they come back from shore tours after lunch has been served.

5. Cabins: Although five-berth cabins are a rarity, some ships, such as the Big Red Boat's *Oceanic*, do offer them. These are a blessing for families with three kids or a grandparent who wants to take the grandkids and their parents along but can't afford two cabins.

6. Single parent pricing: Because children (and others) receive significant discounts when they travel as third or fourth passengers, single parents must often pay the adult rate for the first child in the family. Some lines reduce or eliminate this penalty. On the Big Red Boat, single parents pay 125 percent of the adult fare and pay the typical children's rate for their kids. Celebrity Cruise Lines charges parents, even if there's just one in the cabin, the regular adult rate and allows children to cruise for the children's rate.

HOW TO SAVE MONEY

In most situations, no one pays the full brochure rate for a cruise—you shouldn't either.

A prime reason for that in 1996 is the major expansion of the cruise market. "From 1995 through 1996," says Larry Fishkin, president of the Cruise Line, Inc., a high-volume cruise agency in Miami, "three of the major cruise lines, Carnival, Royal Caribbean, and Princess, are each expanding by 20 percent. In the short-term, supply is outstripping demand." So if you've only dreamed of taking a cruise but thought the cost floated this wish out of your realm, think again. This year cruising is not only more affordable than ever before, it's one of the best vacation buys around.

As cruise lines battle for passengers, a trend that is likely to continue in the near future, the rates will continue to come swirling down. Lines lure voyagers by offering such special promotions as two-for-one deals and low rates or even free fare for third and fourth passengers in a cabin. While these tactics aren't new, the choices are. Instead of applying primarily to older vessels sailing shoulder seasons on less desirable routes, these discounts are now available on some of the spiffiest ships during peak seasons on sought-after itineraries. So, if you need a financial incentive to take your dream vacation, this is it. Booking a cruise now is likely to save you and your family more money than ever before.

Another reason not to pay the brochure rate is early booking plans. The earlier you book, the more money you save. Some lines still use standard formulas in which you can book a cruise six months in advance and pocket between 10 and 20 percent of the fare depending on the ship and the departure date. Many lines also use price incentives to encourage early bookings. Carnival calls their plan "SuperSavers"; Royal Caribbean labels theirs "Breakthrough Rates"; Norwegian Cruise Lines dubs theirs "Leadership Fares"; Princess has "Love Boat Savers"; Holland America offers "KIS Rates"; and Costa has "Andiamo Rates." Whatever the name, these programs can save you from 20 to 50 percent off the brochure rates. The catch: these rates are capacity controlled (only a limited number of cabins will be sold at this price) and can be withdrawn at any time. The earlier you book, the more you're likely to save. If the rate drops after you book but before you cruise, the line should honor the lower fare. You may, however, need to point out the lower rate to your booking agent (although a top agent should call you with this good news).

Another reason families should always book as far in advance as possible is to secure their first choice of cabins and dates. To save money, families should bunk together, but ships offer a limited number of three- and four-berth cabins. The third and fourth passengers in a cabin cruise for significant reductions, but in most

Young passengers enjoy a game of ring toss. Photo courtesy of Royal Caribbean Cruise Lines.

instances, if children share a separate cabin, they must pay the full adult fare. Booking early assures you one of the limited number of four-person cabins. The deeply discounted berths for third and fourth passengers enable you take along kids and grandparents at a fraction of the individual fares. Also, booking early gets you the dates you need—the ones that coincide with school vacations.

Another good way to save money is by booking with a reputable high-volume, cruise-only agency. Because these agencies buy large blocks of cabins from the cruise lines, the agencies are able to pass along substantial savings to their clients. The Cruise Line, Inc., for example, advertises saving customers from

$600 to $2000 per cabin depending on the cruise and the date. World Wide Cruises Inc. lists discounts between 25 and 60 percent. Obviously, the cruise-only agencies don't offer these savings on already reduced book-ahead fares and special promotions, but sometimes the agencies can offer a small savings. Even on two-for-one deals, the Cruise Line, Inc. often has discounts of 5 percent or more.

In addition to saving you money, high-volume cruise agencies do two important things: offer information and monitor your fare. Although any travel agent can book a cruise, an agent who deals exclusively with cruises is much more likely to know the distinctions among the different lines and ships. Because these agents book only cruises, they preview the ships and can describe their nuances. This information is crucial because your dream voyage starts with the ship that's right for your family. Also, because cruise-only agents are constantly involved with the industry, they know when regional deals and special promotions are offered that will reduce your already booked fare. A busy agent who only does a small amount of cruise business may not pass on a fare reduction to you simply because he or she may not know about it.

How to Pick a High-Volume Cruise Agency

Many large agencies offer savings for most ships, sailings, and dates, but often with the exception of the heavily demanded Christmas, New Year's, and holiday sailings. But choosing an agency requires savvy. Look for an agency that is a member of the National Association of Cruise Only Agencies (NACOA) and find out if the agency has a master

---

TIP: No matter which agent you use, keep informed
of price fluctuations. Read the newspaper ads and
check with the cruise line just to be sure that you
are not missing out on a promotion that would cut
your price.

---

cruise counselor, an agent who has taken courses to
be certified as a specialist.

Make sure your agent listens to your needs and
doesn't just try to push you into his or her pre-booked
inventory. "The most frequent sin," says Fishkin, "is
one of omission. The person selling the cruise is just
featuring what they have instead of what is best for
the client." Your agent should fit you to a cruise by dis-
covering what vacations, ports, and places you and
your family like.

Find out with which cruise lines the agency does the
most business because the agent may have better savings on these sailings. Also ask if the agent has been on
board the ships he or she recommends.

Remember, you don't need a cruise-only agency in
your neighborhood to book your cruise because you can
call many large agencies toll-free. Cruise-only agencies
include:

- The Cruise Line, Inc., 150 N.W. 168th Street,
  North Miami Beach, FL 33169; (800) 777-0707;
  (305) 653-6111;
- World Wide Cruises Inc., 8059 West McNab Road,
  Fort Lauderdale, FL 33321; (800) 882-9000; (305)
  720-9000;
- The Cruise Center at Leaders In Travel, 200 Middle Neck Road, Great Neck, NY 11021; (800)
  477-4441; (516) 829-0880.

FIFTEEN TIPS FOR SAVING MONEY ON THE SEAS

By booking smart, you will save money and enjoy the cruise that's right for you. To get the best deal possible, follow these fifteen tips.

1. Book ahead. Book six months ahead to secure the ship, sailing, and cabin of your choice. While cruise lines do offer last-minute deals, the best buys come with an early purchase because cabins are discounted and you can reserve what you want, not just what's available. Some lines also offer such bonuses for early booking as cabin upgrades or free lodging on shore to facilitate extending your stay.

2. Share a cabin. Although the first two passengers pay full fare, the third and fourth persons—children or adult—cruise for as much as 70 percent less. But be aware: some third and fourth person rates don't include airfare.

3. Choose a less expensive cabin. Cabins located inside and lower down mean savings. Surprisingly, the higher priced cabins—outside on upper decks—sway the most, while midship cabins are the best for those prone to seasickness.

4. Sail the value season when rates run 10 to 15 percent less. The Caribbean shoulder season is usually summer and November to mid-December. These early winter departures are dubbed "Christmas shopping cruises" because bargains on leather, china, and jewelry combined with duty-free shopping make these attractive buying trips. But shoulder seasons vary. For Royal

Caribbean Cruise Lines, some ships' rates dip in the summer, but summer is peak season for Carnival. Read the brochures carefully.

5. Book with a high-volume cruise agency. These cruise-only agencies can offer you significant savings.

6. Use frequent-flier mileage. This allows you to pocket the $250 often deducted per adult cruise passenger if you book your own air.

7. Consider a less expensive ship. The flagships of the fleet, like Royal Caribbean Cruise Lines' *Legend of the Seas*, cost more, but a voyage on an older ship will give you the same RCCL service. Decide whether you want to pay for top-of-the-line amenities, such as a television in your cabin, celebrity entertainment, and glitzy lounges. A dash less panache saves money.

8. Research special promotions. Cruise lines offer special promotions to lure passengers. For example, this year American Hawaii Cruises lets children age sixteen and under cruise for free in certain cabin categories with two full-fare adults.

9. Check newspapers for regional specials. Several lines cut cabin prices from specialized cities of departure.

10. Find children's rates with airfare. A low children's rate with low airfare is a great bargain.

11. Use single parent rates. Find a line with a single parent rate that lets kids sail at the reduced children's rate instead of being bumped to the adult fare.

12. Use seniors plans. Some lines offer discounts for passengers age sixty and older. This makes it

An artist's computerized impression of the Sun Princess *in the Caribbean. Photo courtesy of Princess Cruises.*

especially sweet for grandparents to travel with their grandchildren.

13. Join or create a group. Check with your alumni, retirement, and professional organizations for discounted cruise bookings or create your own group (especially easy for large families arranging reunions). With fifteen full-fare bookings (7½ cabins), travel agents commonly book the sixteenth person free. A few agents will work a deal with ten full-fare cruisers. Ask.

14. Consider a repositioning cruise that takes a ship from a winter port to a summer port. Savings on these twice yearly trans-Atlantic, trans-canal, or

coastal cruises can be significant. But go only if you like sea days because these voyages usually have few ports.

15. Use land packages. Extend your vacation by taking advantage of well priced pre- or post-cruise land packages.

SAFEGUARD YOUR VACATION DOLLAR

With children, the unexpected often occurs. Without trip cancellation insurance, you could lose 50 percent of your fare if you must cancel your cruise within thirty days. If your child breaks out with chicken pox three days before departure, you would not only miss your vacation, you'd lose the entire cost of the trip unless you had purchased trip cancellation insurance. Families shouldn't book a cruise without also buying cancellation insurance.

Some policies also cover cruise and airline default in which you receive a refund if these companies go out of business before your trip, as well as trip interruption (the policy covers certain costs of returning early because of medical or emergency situations on board or at home). Also consider trip delay insurance. Several cruise lines make buying insurance especially easy by providing their own policies or referring customers to a carrier. Ask your travel agent. Travel Guard (800-826-1300) is one frequently used company.

SAVING MONEY ON SHORE EXCURSIONS

Before sailing, sit down and decide, as a family, what you want to do at each port. Then figure what it's going to cost. Although they are convenient, there's no doubt that organized shore excursions for a family of four can be costly additions to a cruise. As a general rule, for a family of three or more it's less expensive and often more fun to go off on your own, but there are some exceptions (see below). If you plan to book shore tours, resist the temptation to do so the first day because these are non-refundable. If you change your mind, you are still stuck with the fee.

You will save money and time and avoid the hordes of "boat people" by going to a beach (a different one than everybody else), historic site, flower garden, national park, or other such places on your own. Most group shore tours end up spending more time at gift shops and bathrooms than interesting sites. So be prepared. Buy a guide book and check out our brief picks in port in each destination chapter. Select a beach, museum, historic tour, or all of the above, and head off in a rental car or hire a cab. For taxi fare rates, check with your cruise director or shore activities office. Many times these are standard rates per destination, hour, or person. If you hire a cab for several hours you can sometimes negotiate a special rate. Also, consider sharing a taxi with another family. This saves money and is often more fun. But always establish the rate before you enter the cab, and always use a *legitimate cab company*. Do not go off with anyone in an unmarked car because this could be dangerous.

Avoiding organized shore excursions saves money. One gentleman who recently cruised with his wife and two children reported that while in Jamaica he hired a taxi on his own to Dunn's River Falls for $20. With the $20 per person fee for admission to the park, the total cost for his family of four was $100. The on-board shore tour price was $168. He saved $68.

This same passenger reported trying to book a shore excursion boat ride to Stingray City in Grand Cayman for his family of four at $31 per person (this was a Carnival cruise, but the price is typical of all cruise lines). However, because the tour was sold out on board, the family went ashore and booked a tour directly at the dock with a captain who owned his own boat. Price: $20 per person, "and there were only six of us on the boat, compared to hundreds on the Carnival tour." There was even time for the captain to take them snorkeling at another site for a half hour at no extra charge. He saved $44 and had more fun.

However, for small boat or plane excursions it's generally easier, though not necessarily cheaper, to go with the ship's group. As steady, big customers, the cruise lines are able to book the best boats and planes, sometimes all the boats and planes, available in small ports. While the cruise's shore tour fees may be higher than you would pay if you booked these water or air excursions yourself, the cruise ship's package is more convenient because it includes transportation to the airfield or small-boat dock.

TIPPING

While this is a personal matter, most cruise service personnel rely heavily on tips to supplement what are often meager wages. Your cruise director can tell you what's typical, most offering the following guidelines: $3 per passenger per diem ($12 per day for a family of four) to the room steward; $3 per passenger per diem ($12 per day for a family of four) to the waiter; and $1.50 per passenger per diem ($6 per day for a family of four) to the busperson. Deck stewards and room service waiters should be tipped about 15 percent at the time of service. Most lines suggest tipping the maitre d' and head waiter at your own discretion. (Have they performed any special services for you and your family?) Other lines suggest tipping the maitre d' $7.50 per passenger per cruise.

One category of service personnel most cruise lines routinely forget to remind families to tip are the children's counselors. Even though most counselors are paid regular wages, a tip is always appreciated. Counselors can make your child's cruise wonderful; this is especially true for younger children who may at first be hesitant to join their group. For example, perhaps the mother of a shy but curious six-year-old finds her child's counselor the first day and tips him or her $10 with the explanation that her child may require a little more attention. She follows this up with another tip at the cruise's end. Does this work? Yes. Would the child get the same supervision if his mother didn't tip on the first day? Probably. Are we advocating this? No, but we thought you'd like to know.

CABINS, CURFEWS, KEYS, AND FREEDOM

One thing young children relish about a cruise is the freedom. Often, in the safe atmosphere of a ship, parents allow their kids more freedom than they have at home. Some children join and leave the activities program on their own, freely moving about the ship. While your children treasure this privilege, it can make it hard for you to find them and vice versa. First, if appropriate, give each child his or her own cabin key. Then, keep a note pad in a designated, central loca-

> **TIP:** If you book an inside cabin, bring along a flashlight (always a good idea anyway). Without the natural light that outside cabins have, it's harder for children to see at night to go to the bathroom. With any cabin, you may want to bring along a night-light for the bathroom (we always do).

tion in the cabin (perhaps on top of the bureau) on which each family member—parents included—specifies his or her intended shipboard location and expected return time. That way your child can simply read "in aerobics class at the gym until 3 P.M." and easily reach you, and you can find your child too. Admittedly this, like most things, may be harder to do with a teen, but that's what curfews are for.

Always establish times to be in the cabin to dress for dinner, get ready for shore tours, and go to sleep. This eliminates many frantic searches and much worry.

2

✾✾✾✾✾✾✾✾✾✾✾✾✾✾✾✾

Ship Savvy

Cruise lines have their own personalities. In general, each of the cruise lines detailed below likes and caters to children, creating a family-friendly ambiance. Each line has its own style, strengths, and weaknesses. To book the perfect vacation for your family, you need to understand not only the distinctions among cruise lines, but also the various programs offered by ships on the same line because children's programs and services differ among ships on the same line. For example, even though a cruise line may offer comprehensive children's activities, the program may be offered year-round on some ships but only in summer or on holidays on other ships.

Modern cruise ships with all the requisite glitz, glamour, and programs aren't the only option for a family vacation on the water. Families should also consider what we call "alternative cruises." These voyages offer other ways to enjoy a water vacation with your family. Some possible adventures: Learn to navigate aboard a windjammer, get close to wildlife on an ecological voyage, relive America's river heyday on a steamboat, or travel on barges and river yachts through lush countryside to the heart of sophisticated European cities. Although most of these alternative cruises do not offer designated children's programs, some do. Some vessels feature special family sailings that have a children's program or selected activities for kids. Even without a designated program, your children, especially older ones, may enjoy the informality and adventure of these voyages. These alternative cruises are described briefly at the end of this chapter and in-depth in chapters nine through twelve.

In addition to the lines described below, watch for the new Disney Cruise Lines, which is scheduled to launch two ships in 1998—both are sure to be winners.

The first ship, *Disney Magic* (85,000 tons), is slated to enter service in January 1998. The ship will compete directly with the Big Red Boat by packaging three- and four-day cruises from Port Canaveral, Florida, with a stay at Walt Disney Resort.

Several cruise lines that offer children's programs were not included in this book, primarily because of space limitations. The editorial choice was for breadth of description, focusing on major cruise lines that are committed to families and children. We did not want to produce an all-inclusive listing that could overwhelm both novice and experienced cruisers.

We also chose to describe the lines and ships that feature the most popular family destinations. That's why our traditional cruise section focuses on the Caribbean, Mexico, the Bahamas, Hawaii, Bermuda, and Alaska, but not Europe. We do, however, include European canal trips as an alternative to traditional cruises.

The following are among cruise lines not described in this book that do offer a children's program on some or all of their sailings: Crystal Cruises (800) 446-6620; Dolphin Cruise Line (800) 992-4299; Fantasy Cruises (800) 423-2100; Royal Cruise Line (415) 956-7200; Seawind Cruise Line (305) 854-7800; and Sun Line Cruises (800) 872-6400.

TOP FAMILY CRUISE LINES (Alphabetical Listing)

American Hawaii Cruises
Big Red Boat (Premier Cruise Lines)
Carnival Cruise Lines

Celebrity Cruises

Costa Cruises

Norwegian Cruise Line (NCL)

Princess Cruises

Royal Caribbean Cruise Line (RCCL)

Two more lines—Cunard and Holland America—are worth noting for specific reasons discussed later in this chapter. Cunard's *Queen Elizabeth II*, for example, provides a unique service. The ship features a staffed nursery that takes care of children age six weeks and older. Holland America Line's Alaskan ships are another alternative for families traveling the famed Inside Passage.

BEST BETS FOR TRADITIONAL CRUISE SHIPS

While all of the above ships were chosen because they are child- and family-friendly, the following offer something special for children in specific age groups:

Best Cruise Ships for Families with Children Under Age Two

NCL offers a guaranteed baby-sitting service from noon to 2 A.M. Cunard's *Queen Elizabeth II* has a staffed nursery.

Best Cruise Ships for Families with Children Ages Two to Four

All Camp Carnival programs offered by Carnival Cruise Lines for ages two to four years (except aboard the *Festivale* and *Tropicale*, where camp minimum age is four) begin with a breakfast with the staff during days at sea and include pool fun and arts and crafts. Princess' *Star* and *Sun Princess* offer youth center activities for ages two and up (if a child is not toilet-trained, parents are responsible for diapering). The Big Red Boat's children's program also starts at age two, and the Looney Tunes characters on board win over this age group.

Best Cruise Ships for Families with Children Ages Five to Eleven

You really can't go wrong with any of our choices, but particular standouts include RCCL for its caring counselors and comprehensive program, NCL's "Circus at Sea," where kids learn circus skills, and Carnival Cruise Line's "Camp Carnival," with backstage tours and special entertainment performances.

Best Cruise Ships for Families with Pre-teens and Teens

NCL's *Dreamward* and *Windward* each feature a teen activity center, complete with jukebox and forty-five-inch color television. The *Star* and *Sun Princess* each have a special teen room for nightly movies and their discos open to teens early in the evening. RCCL's *Grandeur of the Seas*, *Splendour of the Seas*, *Monarch of the Seas*, *Legend of the Seas*, and *Majesty of the Seas* have teen centers as do all Carnival ships, which recently expanded their teen programs to include makeovers, fashion tips, and photography workshops. Carnival's *Holiday* sports a new $1 million entertainment center featuring action-packed virtual reality games, a surefire hit with pre-teens and teens. In season, Celebrity's ships present an extensive program for teens that includes midnight film festivals, reggae Jacuzzi parties, and Dating Game "shows."

CHILDREN'S PROGRAM REGISTRATION FORMS

First of all, there should be a registration form, and there usually is because most cruise lines have become increasingly savvy to children's and parents' needs. The forms, however, should go beyond merely requiring the child's name, age, parents' names, and cabin number. Feel free to add details *in writing*, especially if your child is too young or shy to tell the counselors themselves.

Writing down this information (ask for a sheet of paper if you need to) is critical, especially for the little ones. Even the most well meaning counselor can't possibly remember all the details of every child's preferred routine. Besides, the counselor you speak with when you register may not be the one who is with your tot during snack time when it's vital to remember that your child has a milk allergy.

So, what goes on the form? Whatever you think is important about or to your child. Some items to consider:

- The names and signatures of the *only* adults and/or siblings allowed to sign your child into or out of the program.

- A list of any food or drug allergies as well as a note about snack food preferences. Find out what snacks are planned and direct the counselors as needed. For example, if the day's featured treat is chocolate chip cookies but your child has a chocolate allergy, write this down. Also make sure that the counselors have a substitute snack ready so that your child doesn't go hungry or feel left out.

- The child's nickname. After all, a two-year-old in a strange place will be much comforted if the counselors and his new friends call him "J.D." just as his parents and friends at home do, instead of the more formal "Jonathan David."

- List names of special items. This includes bathroom terms and other situations. For example, if your toddler brought along "Amy," her favorite teddy bear who always naps with her, tell the counselors who Amy is and advise them of her importance. A tired toddler may easily turn cranky and frustrated if her calls for Amy go unheeded because the counselor on duty doesn't know that this refers to the bear stored in the cubby rather than a big sister lounging on a deck chair.

ABOUT CHILDREN AND CHILDREN'S PROGRAMS

Not every child wants to spend every minute in a program. Be sure to take time on the cruise to be with your children and teens. All cruise lines provide newsletters that detail the next day's adult and children's activities. These newsletters are slipped under your cabin door the night before. (One cruiser told us that he received so many pieces of paper that he began to think of his cabin door as a Xerox machine.)

Children's programs offer all kinds of surprises. Photo courtesy of Cunard.

Talk about the upcoming events over evening hot chocolate or morning coffee. Plan which ones your children want to do with their organized groups and which ones they want to do with you. Many activities offered to adults are suitable for kids of various ages. That's much of the fun of family cruising. For example, afternoon bingo is a popular cruise activity and a great draw for all ages. Another fun option is teaming up for sports trivia games, shuffleboard contests, and even the silly antics of deck and beach Olympics. These may seem hokey (because they are), but they are also lots of fun when you participate as a family. (We have great photographs and fond memories of us hopping around with volleyballs and jumping our way through sack races.)

In addition, nearly every ship has a game/card room stocked with board games (which often may be checked out) and a movie theater. If the weather's rainy or you simply want some off-the-beach fun, consider sharing an afternoon movie with your children. And don't forget about the simplest fun of all: find some deck chairs in a quiet corner of the ship and enjoy the view and each other's company.

DINING AND CHILDREN'S PROGRAMS

Most children's programs break for meals. This is generally not a problem for breakfast and lunch, but be sure to coordinate your activities with your child's schedule. Dinner, however, may require some planning. Many children's evening programs resume around 8 P.M., so you should usually choose the early sitting for dinner. That way your children will be happily full and ready for their evening activities. If the thought of dressing for dinner by 6:15 P.M. does not appeal to you, but your young children howl if not fed, look for a ship that features full-service cabin meals (such as Celebrity) or an eatery that meets your schedule and your kids' tastes. This solution accomplishes two goals: it lets you give your child a meal he or she likes, and enables you to linger over a romantic dinner with your spouse.

SHIP'S RULES

You should be aware of the shipboard rules and make your child aware of them as well. Every ship, for example, has age restrictions for certain public areas, rooms, and lounges. Generally, all ships restrict children age twelve and under from attending lounge shows unaccompanied by an adult. Ages eighteen and under are prohibited from the casino, and children under age sixteen are not allowed in the gym unless with an adult. There are also age restrictions for hot tubs (which is a good idea in light of the recent health concerns involving hot tub use).

While many of these rules are enforced, you will definitely find that some ships are more lax than others. You will find youngsters in the hot tub and unescorted pre-teens playing slot machines. Nearly every ship has a rule that unaccompanied children may not use elevators but this rule, need we add, is rarely enforced.

THE LINES

American Hawaii Cruises

American Hawaii Cruises is the only cruise line that offers weeklong cruises to the Hawaiian islands all year. These cruises are not only a good value but they also offer a great way to sample the islands, stopping at four islands in seven days. In the last few years, American Hawaii has increased its commitment to educating passengers about the Hawaiian culture. Each ship has a room devoted to Hawaiiana with displays and hands-on exhibits about the environ-ment, myths, early Polynesian voyages, the land, people, food, and arts. A "kumu," or teacher, offers workshops on island culture and history and often tells ghost stories and legends of Hawaiian gods and goddesses. This focus on getting to know Hawaii extends to the line's shore excursions, on which passengers can

TIP: Families should take advantage of American Hawaii Cruises' frequent specials, including land and cruise packages that offer free or reduced-rate stays in Waikiki. Great news for 1996: A special promotion allows children under eighteen to sail free when sharing a cabin with two full-price passengers except for the December 21 and 28 sailings.

explore the less-seen parts of the islands under the guidance of a "Kama'aina," one who knows the island. Last year, the cruise line added eight shore excursions to its already long list of forty. These include a rain forest walk on Maui, two hikes to explore Kilauea (the world's most active volcano), a historic tour through Hilo, a trip to Kona Village, a biking/hiking/snorkeling trip on Kauai, and a historic tour of Lahaina Town. Reduced excursion rates are often available for children.

Children's Program

The youth (*keiki*) program is offered during the summer months and on major holidays on both the *Independence* and the *Constitution*. The program, designed for ages five through twelve and for teens thirteen to sixteen, operates from 8 A.M. to 9 P.M. with breaks for lunch and dinner. Recreation coordinators organize and supervise activities for both groups. Children enjoy talent shows, pool games, pizza parties, and scavenger hunts. The program also teaches children about the Hawaiian culture through such typically Hawaiian activities as lei-making, hula demonstrations, and ukulele lessons.

Because American Hawaii picks its youth counselors from on-board staff, counselors do not necessarily have a background in child care or education.

Dining

Meals, especially dinners, offer a variety of Hawaiian-inspired dishes as well as many American favorites. There is a children's menu of typical kid-pleasing dishes.

The Big Red Boat (Premier Cruise Lines)

The Big Red Boat—actually the two "big red boats," the *Atlantic* and the *Oceanic*—caters mainly to families, which make up the majority of their cruisers. There are supervised children's and teens' programs, and Looney Tunes characters—Sylvester, Tweety, Bugs Bunny, and Yosemite Sam among them—frequently appear for photos and autographs. For an extra fee, they will show up to surprise your kids at breakfast or at bedtime, when the lucky tot being tucked in receives a character-printed pillow case, a plush character toy, and a tuck-in photo.

New for 1996, the Big Red Boat is adding a computer learning center with the latest PCs and CD-ROMs for children. The redesigned teen centers have state-of-the-art video, light, and audio equipment as well as karaoke.

TIP: Strollers for use during shore excursions are available for rent at the tour desk.

Children's Program

Both the *Oceanic* and the *Atlantic* offer children's programs year-round.

The programs operate from 9 A.M. until 10 P.M., and group baby-sitting for ages two through twelve is available for a small fee from 10 P.M. to 9 A.M. In addition, on the night of the Captain's Cocktail Reception, special dining for children is provided, so parents have the option of attending the reception and dinner without their youngsters.

The children's and teens' programs generally have eighteen to twenty counselors per ship. Children are placed into five age groups, including:

First Mates (two to four years): The cheerful playroom for this age group is stocked with slides, toys, and games. Counselor-led activities include treasure hunts, sing-alongs, and story time, as well as costume making for the ship's current play, sand castle building, treasure map drawing, and face painting. Children also get to "steer" the ship on a tour of the navigational bridge—a great photo opportunity.

Kids Call (five to seven years): Some of the highlights are ice cream parties, swimming in the kiddie pool, watching magic shows, and touring the bridge with the captain. Other fun includes finger painting, karaoke singing, and maybe even starring in the ship's current production

Starcruisers (eight to ten years): Children participate in their own Junior Pool and Beach Olympics, game-show activities, and poster-making competitions, There's also a shore-side scavenger hunt, video and board games, bingo, and—always an ice breaker—Twister.

Navigators (eleven to thirteen years): Ship charades and games follow a special Welcome Aboard party on the pool deck. Lively activities include "Go for the Gold" indoor Olympics, beach Olympics, beach football, and a Ping-Pong tournament.

Teen Cruisers (fourteen to seventeen years): After a "Sail Away" party, teens participate in pool and beach Olympics, play volleyball, and dance or sing at karaoke parties in their own nightclub.

The youth counselors all meet Florida's state regulations for child-care workers and have backgrounds in education or child care. All have CPR training.

Many of the on-board activities are suitable for the entire family, such as Family Feud, Name That Tune, or island beach Olympics. In addition to these activities, the Big Red Boat offers educational programs for the entire family. "Voyages of Discovery" revolves around four main aspects of the cruise experience: sea, sky, great ships, and the history of the Caribbean.

Dining

Children have their own menus, featuring such appetite pleasers as grilled cheese, spaghetti, cheese pizza, chicken nuggets, fish fingers, peanut butter sandwiches, hot dogs, and fresh fruit cups.

TIP: As the official cruise line of the Major League Baseball Players Alumni (MLBPA), the Big Red Boat offers a baseball fantasy camp one Saturday each month as part of a cruise package. Slugger fans practice and play with such players as Tug McGraw and Brooks Robinson. Cruise participants also receive a cap, T-shirt, ball, bat, and souvenir photo.

Carnival Cruise Lines

Carnival deserves credit for bringing cruises to middle America—the price is right and their SuperLiners, which roll out on a regular basis, are truly impressive, thanks to designer Joe Farcus' never-ending wealth of theme ideas. The decor generally fits the "glitz and glamour" category rather than conforming with understated elegance, although there are surprises such as the charming, sedate, and proper-looking wood-paneled libraries.

Carnival bills itself as having the "Fun Ship"—indeed, life on board sometimes resembles a nonstop party. This is not the line to take if you seek getting away from it all or crave peace and solitude. While you'll see all ages on board, families and young singles dominate the passenger list. And, yes, it can get noisy, even in the wee hours as passengers head back to their cabins, not always on tiptoes.

That said, for those who want nonstop activity, Carnival fulfills its promise of fun. There are lots of children's and family-friendly activities, though a noted exception is the beer guzzling contest.

Carnival has commissioned three new ships. The *Inspiration*, a 2,040-passenger ship scheduled to debut in March 1996, is a sister ship of the *Imagination*, which first sailed in July 1995. Like the *Imagination*, the *Inspiration* is slated to cruise the Caribbean. In December 1997, Carnival will launch a third (as yet unnamed) sister ship to the *Inspiration* and the *Imagination*. An itinerary was not available at press time.

The line's most anticipated ship, however, is the *Carnival Destiny*, a 100,000-ton, $400 million vessel with a 3,350-passenger capacity. Scheduled to sail its maiden voyage out of Miami in the fall of 1996, this ship heralds a new generation of extra-large mega-ships. *Destiny* will be the largest modern day cruise vessel ever built. Despite the ship's size, Carnival President Bob Dickinson calls the *Destiny* "evolutionary rather than revolutionary." That means, he assures cruisers, that such hallmark Carnival features as glass-domed atria, multi-deck showrooms, and expansive spas will be on board. New touches include more cabins with verandahs (56 percent of the 740 ocean-view cabins will feature private balconies), and an aft pool with a retractable glass dome. (No itineraries were available for the Carnival *Destiny* at press time.)

Children's Program

Carnival offers a children's program on board every ship and every sailing year-round. Infants must be at least four months old to travel.

In 1995, after hosting a record one hundred thousand kids, Carnival beefed up its children's programs, nearly doubling the number of full-time counselors. The line now claims the largest staff of trained youth counselors in the industry (more than fifty counselors). All counselors must have a bachelor's degree in an education-related field and experience in child care. Carnival has also added more activities to the Camp Carnival roster, including children's aerobics classes, karaoke parties, bridge and galley tours, and special performances by the ships' entertainers. The program expansion also included adding a new youth director position to each ship and giving each child a "prize" as a reminder of his or her cruise experience.

Moreover, a new kiddie slide has been added to the children's pools on all vessels to supplement the larger, and definitely intimidating, 114-foot-long, 15-foot-high water slides that older children adore (and sometimes simultaneously fear). Each ship also sports a playroom and an electronic game room.

Carnival's playrooms are fairly standard: small (about 625 square feet) and cheerful, with art supplies, books, games, and a slide with Ping-Pong balls to dive into (though the ball slide isn't always open). Sleeping pallets are used for naps and for late-night baby-sitting (slumber party) sessions. As one father of a Camp Carnival child who recently sailed on the *Sensation* said, "The playroom is your basic well-stocked pre-school gone to sea." Camp Carnival is offered to ages two to seventeen except on board the *Festivale* and *Tropicale* where the program begins at age five. Groups are divided according to age: Toddlers (ages two to four), Juniors (ages five to eight), Intermediates (ages nine to thirteen), and Teens (ages fourteen to seventeen).

Sea days feature a supervised breakfast for each group. In addition to fun in the playroom, a typical day includes:

For toddlers: Mousercize, cartoons, pool fun, talent shows, movies, and puppet making.

For juniors and intermediates: Arts and crafts, formal "Coketail parties," movies, puzzles, pool Olympics, and charades.

For teens: Ping-Pong tournaments, a pool party, pizza party, lip-synch contest, disco, and makeovers and fashion tips from the ship's beauty experts, as well as photography workshops. The

TIP: Children attending Camp Carnival are free to come and go as they please. Counselors won't encourage them to stay unless you specifically instruct them to do so. Be sure that you are comfortable with your children checking themselves in and out of the program.

Teen Club is open daily from 10 A.M. to midnight for that all-important teen activity—hanging out.

Baby-sitting

Group baby-sitting is available in the playroom of each ship. Formerly provided only from 9:30 P.M. to 1:30 A.M. (when pillows, blankets, and cribs are offered), group baby-sitting has been expanded to ensure that child care is also available when the ship is in port (when Camp Carnival activities are suspended) and at sea— twenty-four hours a day including mealtimes, if you like.

To schedule baby-sitting, sign up in advance at the purser's information office or see one of the counselors at any of the scheduled activities. Rates run $4 per hour for the first child in each family and $2 per hour for each additional child in the same family.

Dining

Children may breakfast with their camp group during days at sea. High chairs and booster seats are available in the dining room. A kids' menu is offered at mealtime with favorites such as hamburgers, ravioli, fried chicken, hot dogs, and fish and chips. The kids' menu, however, is not available through room service.

Carnival, recognizing that the majority of its passengers prefer casual eating options to the ship's main dining rooms, has upgraded the food and service offered in the Lido bar and grills. These eateries serve such kid favorites as hot dogs, burgers, grilled chicken breast sandwiches, fish and chips, chicken fajitas, and grilled Cajun sausages. Also, a juice alternative has been added to the complimentary beverage list. Made-to-order pasta stations in the Lido areas enable younger passengers to choose from a variety of pastas, sauces, and ingredients—kids can just point to what they want and the Carnival chefs prepare the dishes. In the afternoons, the Lido serves sweets such as cookies and brownies, and soft serve ice cream and frozen yogurt are available throughout the day. In addition, the new *Imagination* has a twenty-four-hour pizzeria.

Cabins and Pricing

Most staterooms designed for families consist of twin beds that convert to a king plus one or two upper berths. All quads with two uppers are large enough to accommodate a fifth berth in the form of a rollaway cot or a crib (both are available from the line). The cabin stewards go out of their way for kids, even making amusing arrangements (such as animals shaped from towels) to place on a child's pillow at bedtime.

TIP: Amenities, such as shampoo and hair dryers, are not routinely offered on Carnival ships, so be sure to pack your own.

Celebrity Cruises

Celebrity has a fleet of sophisticated, relatively new ships, most of which have a spacious feel. Spokespeople for Celebrity state that the cruise line "was established in 1990 with the targeted objective of creating the 'premium' cruise experience by establishing a high-quality cruise vacation offered at reasonable cost." To a large extent, Celebrity has succeeded while garnering numerous honors. Readers of the magazine *Conde Nast Traveler* have rated the cruise line one of the top ten, and the World Ocean and Cruise Line Society also ranks Celebrity high. *Onboard Service* magazine gave Celebrity the top service award, and an *Ocean and Cruise News* reader survey ranked it tops in cuisine.

The main restaurants and the observation lounges are two-storied, and the fitness centers and spas tend to be roomy. This line offers the usual evening entertainment from variety shows to jazz bands in the smaller lounges. Each ship also has a children's pool, which is unsupervised but located near the adult pool.

Minimum age to sail is one year old, and passengers under two sail free. Cribs are available upon request, but parents may also bring their own.

In late 1995, Celebrity introduced the *Century*, a 70,000-ton, 1,750-passenger ship. In 1996, the *Galaxy*, a 72,000-ton, 1,840-passenger ship debuts; and in 1997, a third unnamed 72,000-ton, 1,840-passenger ship will be launched. Both *Century* and *Galaxy* will cruise the Caribbean year-round by 1996, though the *Galaxy*'s complete itinerary was not available at press time. With these ships, Celebrity is hoping to literally take passengers into the new century. Besides more spacious cabins and public areas, these new ships also

feature state-of-the-art Sony audio and video systems
in the theaters and bars as well as in cabins with an
interactive guest services network. These new ships
also sport AquaSpa—a Japanese garden and bathhouse themed spa that offers traditional treatments
plus specialties such as Aqua Mediation and the Rasul,
a treatment based on an Oriental ceremony that
includes a seaweed soap shower, medicinal mud pack,
herbal steambath, and massage.

Children's Program

Celebrity's program is offered on all ships during
the summer months and during major holidays.
Check with your travel agent for times because we're
told that holidays do not include Easter or Thanksgiv-
ing. (Depending on the cruise destination, summer
months may be defined as May to October or June
to September.)

The children's program is divided into three age
groups. Ship Mates operates for ages three to seven,
Celebrity Cadets for ages eight to twelve, and Ensigns
for ages thirteen to seventeen. The program operates
from 9 A.M. to noon, 2 P.M. to 4 P.M., and 8 P.M. to midnight. The breaks enable children to dine with their
families, a program requirement, except breakfast,
which children may eat with their groups.

Ship Mates usually meet in the children's playroom
for dancing, games, finger painting, and storytelling.
The playroom, which is supervised by up to eight counselors from 9 A.M. to 5 P.M., is stocked with movies,
board games, toys, books, and arts and crafts supplies.
Children under age six who are not part of the program can enjoy these facilities, but they must be
accompanied by an adult. Ship Mates Fun Factory, the
playroom on board the new *Century*, is designed for

ages three to twelve, and children do not have to be with their parents.

Celebrity gives each Ship Mate a wristband to be worn for the duration of the cruise. This makes for easy identification during activities and also in the rare instance when a child might get lost. Ship Mates are signed in and out of the youth program by their parents, who must show their boarding passes as proper identification when signing children out. In season, some children's shore activities are offered.

Celebrity Cadets and teens gather in the ships' public areas before going off to enjoy movies, pool volleyball, and deck parties. Although there is no designated teen center, teens tend to meet in the video game room. Celebrity gets high marks for trying to engage this hard-to-please group with appealing programs such as midnight film festivals, reggae Jacuzzi parties, karaoke parties, and a Dating Game "show."

Baby-sitting

Private baby-sitting is available at $6 per hour with a minimum of two children, but this must be arranged ahead of time through your travel agent or through the ship's information desk. Free group baby-sitting—the nightly pajama party—takes place in the children's playroom from 10 P.M. to 1 A.M.

Dining

Food is part of Celebrity's "premium" service. Their menus feature heart-healthy and vegetarian dishes along with continental fare. Cruisers like both the quality of chef Michel Roux's cuisine and the line's extensive in-cabin service, which is not limited to pretzels, stale bologna sandwiches, and olives (the only

TIP: Why, with all the eateries and a complete dining room menu, would anyone want cabin service? Because it can be exceptionally convenient for feeding young children when and what they want, wonderfully indulgent for breakfast in bed, surprisingly relaxing for afternoon tea and fresh pastries, or sweetly romantic for candlelit dinners for two. After all, it's your vacation, too.

in-cabin food available for my then seven-year-old daughter on another line's ship).

Cabins

Also as part of its "premium" concept, Celebrity, starting with the *Century*, offers Sony state-of-the-art video, audio, and in-cabin entertainment systems. Most cabins are average size or bigger and all feature hair dryers and ample storage space.

Costa Cruise Line

Because Costa offers year-round children's programs on all its cruises, both European and Caribbean, this line offers an interesting option to families. Few lines feature supervised children's activities on European voyages. Families should note that while this Italian-owned line's Caribbean cruises carry large numbers of Americans, Costa's European cruises draw more Europeans, so the primary language is often not English. The *Costa Allegra* is specifically marketed to Europeans. Although menus and announcements are delivered in four languages, youth counselors often may not speak English, which could be a problem for some children. Most of the time, however, we've found that children adapt quickly, cutting through language barriers with smiles and games.

Costa's ships include the *Costa Allegra*, *Costa Classica*, *Costa Romantica*, *Costa Riviera*, *Costa Marina*, and *Eugenio Costa*. Two new Costa ships are currently being built. The *Costa Victoria*, a 1,920-passenger ship, debuts June 1996. This vessel will sail from Port Everglades to the Caribbean in winter and spring and to Greece in summer and fall. The second ship, as yet unnamed, is scheduled to enter service in June 1997. It is a 78,000-ton vessel with a passenger capacity of 2,100. This will be the largest ship in Costa's international fleet, sailing to the Caribbean in winter, and the Mediterranean in summer.

Three of Costa's ships—*Costa Romantica*, *Costa Allegra*, and *Costa Classica*—each feature a 6,500-square-foot fitness facility and a Caracalla spa that offers hydrotherapy baths, seaweed and algae treatments, and other pampering services.

Children's Program

Costa formerly provided activities for children only on Caribbean cruises, but they now offer the children's program year-round on all ships. On Caribbean cruises, Costa offers the Costa Kids Club for ages five to twelve (with possible age grouping for ages five to eight and nine to twelve, depending on the number of children) and Costa Teens Club for ages thirteen to seventeen. Kids Club participants enjoy Nintendo, face painting, arts and crafts, deck games, and Italian lessons taught by the counselors. There is always one full-time youth counselor on board. If more than twelve children are on board, additional counselors are employed. All counselors know CPR.

Note: Five is the youngest age for which there is an organized children's program. Parents may bring younger children aboard, but are responsible for them.

Hours for the Kids Club are from 9:30 to 11:30 A.M., 2 to 5 P.M., and 8 to 10 P.M. Children eat meals with their parents. While in port, the ships do not generally offer children's activities except from 8 to 10 P.M. It is possible for parents to request that a counselor remain on board while in port, but a counselor's presence is not guaranteed. Costa does accepts infants on some ships.

On European cruises, there are three children's groups: The Baby Club for ages three to six, The Junior Club for ages seven to twelve, and The Teens Club for ages thirteen to seventeen. Activities for Baby Club members include story hour, games, and ice cream parties. Activities for Junior Club members include mini-Olympics, treasure hunts, and aerobics. Activities for teens include a fitness program, guitar hour, video show productions, and more.

Baby-sitting

From 9:30 P.M. to 1:30 A.M., group baby-sitting is available upon request. In-port group baby-sitting from 8:30 A.M. to 12:30 P.M. and from 2:30 to 6:30 P.M. may be

---

TIP: Be aware that with only a handful of children on some sailings, a twelve-year-old could get put in the same group with a five-year-old, often not the best experience for either one. Check ahead to find out the number and ages of children that may be aboard.

arranged by request. Double-check with your travel agent and the line's information desk. Hourly fees are $8 per child or $10 for two children. Baby-sitting is always subject to the availability of personnel.

Norwegian Cruise Line

Note: At press time, Kloster Cruise, Norwegian Cruise Line's (NCL) parent company, was considering various strategies to refinance its debt obligation. NCL executives insist that Kloster's financial concerns will not change NCL's style or services. The following information is based on NCL's past performance and company policies, but please remember that, at this point, NCL could be acquired by another company, radically change its image, policies, and itineraries, or remain the same fine cruise line. Check with a cruise agent on NCL's status before planning a vacation.

Norwegian Cruise Lines truly offers something for everyone, and you'll see a wide spectrum of passengers on board. NCL ships are not from cookie-cutter assembly lines: passengers are offered distinctive choices, from the *Norway* (formerly the *France*) to the *Windward*, one of the newest in the fleet.

With a plethora of activities for all ages, NCL is noted for its theme cruises and sports-oriented cruises, both of which are scheduled throughout the year. Theme cruises include sailings with an emphasis on country music, comedy, the fifties and sixties, jazz, or big band. Most theme cruises in 1996 take place on the *Norway*.

"Sports Afloat" sailings feature celebrity athletes on board offering pointers and interaction with the passengers. Most of the Sports Afloat programs are also on the *Norway*. These popular voyages include basketball, football, golf, motor sports, skiing, volleyball, and hockey pros, but be sure to book well in advance. In 1996, the *Dreamward* hosts the skiing, motor sports, and professional beach volleyball cruises. NCL's Dive Programs, described in chapter three, are also extremely popular.

Some other popular NCL touches: a "chocoholic" buffet on every cruise, some smoke-free cabins, and a European bistro for dining in an intimate atmosphere at no additional cost. For adults, the *Leeward*, *Dreamward*, and *Windward* each feature a sports bar and grill.

Because NCL was the forerunner in what is known as the "mainstream" cruise market, they are very good at what they do—providing good service and a friendly cruise experience. It also helps that Adam Aron, president and CEO of NCL (and of Kloster Cruise Ltd., the line's parent company), is a youthful father of two small boys who can often be spotted aboard with his wife and kids. Obviously, this is a line well tuned to families.

Children's Program

NCL offers year-round children's programs for ages six through seventeen on the *Dreamward*, *Leeward*, *Norway*, *Seaward*, and *Windward*. Other ships offer programs in summer and during holidays.

NCL's Kids Crew program, created for ages three to seventeen, is divided into four groups. Junior Sailors (ages three to five) is limited to summer months and major holidays, and is restricted to the mornings of sea days only. The year-round groups are First Mates (ages six to eight), Navigators (ages nine to twelve), and teens (ages thirteen to seventeen). Children under three may participate in Junior Sailor activities, and those under six in First Mate activities if accompanied by a parent or baby-sitter older than the age of thirteen. While NCL does not have age restrictions, children under one year old must have a pediatrician's letter to come aboard.

Each program is supervised by youth coordinators, who (according to the line) are selected from leading universities and organizations throughout the United States. As part of their training, the counselors undergo a comprehensive course that covers building team confidence, designing activities, and working with special needs children. Dr. Peter Favaro, doctor of child psychology, has designed NCL's programs to meet the special requirements of the different age groups, which is a good indication of how sincere the line is about creating quality programs. Youngsters get their own "Cruiser News" brochures detailing the day's events. There are no activities when the ship is in port.

Program activities include sports competitions, dances, arts and crafts, and the very popular "Circus at Sea," in which children learn to juggle and perform as clowns for adult passengers. A sample day's activities might include: ages three to five—drawing ships, playing pirate games, watching cartoons, dancing, and performing in "Goofy Olympics"; ages six to nine and

---

TIP: Children six and older have an open-door policy, which means they can come and go from the program as they choose. If you prefer to sign your kids out, be sure to make this clear to the youth coordinator ahead of time.

> **TIP:** Your children may welcome the opportunity to
> participate as a family in the NCL Olympics or talent
> show, or in many of the other on-board activities suit-
> able for all ages.

ten to twelve—scavenger hunts, pajama parties,
snacks and movies, face painting, and bridge tours;
and teens—movie trivia, Ping-Pong tournaments,
dancing, junk food bingo, and Win, Lose, or Draw.
Teens are allowed in the disco during designated
hours.

Baby-sitting
The baby-sitting service on board NCL is open from
noon to 2 A.M. Rates for the first child are $8 per hour,
and an additional $1.50 per hour for each child in the
same family. The service has a four-hour minimum.
Remember to make reservations through the information desk twenty-four hours in advance. Rates double
on Christmas and New Year's Eve.

Dining
Booster seats and high chairs are available, as are
children's menus. All NCL cruises offer a chocoholic
buffet—truly a vision.

Princess Cruises

Princess—otherwise known as the "Love Boat"—is a
British-owned (P&O) cruise line that, while ranked in
the mass-market category, is more upscale than many
others in this group. Good service and understated ele-

gance are typical hallmarks of a Princess cruise. Part of the good service aimed at giving the cruise all the comforts of home has included live satellite programming of CNN and ESPN available on board. In 1996, Princess adds eighteen hours of selected Discovery Channel programming to the shows available for in-cabin viewing. This is a small touch, but television shows can be quite comforting to fidgety children waiting for mom and dad to dress for dinner or as a quiet bedtime option.

The line offers a mix of ships, from relatively small to the new SuperLiners. Two SuperLiners will debut soon, including the *Grand Princess*, which will be the largest vessel afloat (104,000 tons).

The median age aboard most Princess ships is somewhat older than what you might find aboard a Carnival ship, and unless you're cruising during a major school holiday you won't notice a plethora of children. However, after a few years of waffling, the line is again committed to providing children's activities. The ships listed here offer daylong activities programs at sea.

Perhaps the reason children aren't as visible on a Princess cruise is, according to a spokesperson, "We believe that we should keep children entertained and occupied, separate from the main passenger areas and activities." Princess accomplishes all this.

With the introduction of the *Sun Princess* in December of 1995 and the *Dawn Princess* and *Grand Princess* in May and October of 1997 respectively, Princess cruises is ready to handle the upcoming century. No itinerary or ship description was available about the *Dawn Princess* at press time, but see chapter three for ship descriptions of the *Sun Princess* and *Grand Princess*, which will sail the Caribbean year-round.

Children's Program

Each Princess ship has capacity limits for children on board, and no child under the age of eighteen months is permitted to sail. Princess also retains the right to limit the number of children under three years old. The youth program is offered for ages two (toilet trained or parents must diaper) to twelve and ages thirteen to sixteen from 9 A.M. to midnight, except during meals, which children eat with their parents. On cruises with fifteen or more teens (usually the holiday and summer cruises), the Princess Teen Club for thirteen- to sixteen-year-olds feature late-night movies, on-board Olympics, and karaoke. The kids' regular program does not operate when the ship is in port, but the youth center is open and staffed so that counselors can keep an eye on participants as they enjoy quiet activities, such as arts and crafts and board games.

Princess offers year-round children's programs and a designated youth center on all its ships. Youth centers are for younger kids; teen centers are places for ages thirteen to seventeen to meet and hang out. These generally feature juke boxes, flashing lights, and loud music. Those ships that have a designated youth and teen center are: *Dawn Princess* (to debut 1997), *Grand Princess* (to debut 1997), *Sky Princess*, *Sun Princess*, *Star Princess*, and, as of fall 1995, *Golden Princess*, *Regal Princess*, and *Crown Princess*. These ships also have a children's pool and video arcade near the youth center.

On other ships, including the *Royal Princess*, *Island Princess*, and *Pacific Princess*, which do not offer designated youth facilities, the cruise line will operate a children's program with a minimum of fifteen children ages two to sixteen. Day and evening activities are scheduled while these ships are at sea. While in port, some on-shore activities are scheduled but, unlike ships with a youth center, children may not stay on board with the youth coordinator while their parents are on shore.

Princess has three levels of youth staff: Youth Activities Coordinator (YAC), teen director, and youth counselors. The teen director and youth counselors report to the YAC. According to Princess, nearly all of the YACs have either a teaching or child development background and are interviewed and hired by "two experienced recruiting agencies that thoroughly research each applicant's credentials. We're proud to have an excellent track record with the quality of our youth staff." The teen director must have experience working with teens, but is not required to be a certified teacher. All youth staff have CPR training.

There is no individual baby-sitting available. Children eat with their parents in the dining room, but there is no special kids' menu. Princess has a limited number of high chairs and cribs on board.

Royal Caribbean Cruise Lines

RCCL offers a diverse fleet of ships that attract an equally diverse group of cruisers. While a mass-market line, the on-board ambiance is somewhat more sedate than what you might find on a Carnival ship. But don't get us wrong, there's plenty to do—virtually nonstop activity—but the pace, intensity, and noise level is generally less intense than on many Carnival ships.

The main drawback of many RCCL ships for families is the smaller-sized staterooms. Typical though, is the parent who, after a *Majesty of the Seas* cruise with her husband and fourteen-year-old son, proclaimed the trip to be "our best cruise ever," noting that the quality and volume of on-board activities more than compensates for the smaller staterooms. The *Majesty of the Seas* and *Monarch of the Seas* each have a six-person family suite consisting of two bedrooms, two bathrooms, a living area, and a verandah; however, such space doesn't come cheap.

A further indication of RCCL's popularity with families is the increase in the number of young passengers (those up to age seventeen) from about 4 percent of total passengers in 1986 to 7 percent in 1994. According to RCCL, "while this may not seem like a gigantic leap in percentage points, it represents a huge increase in bodies—6,964 youngsters carried in 1986, and 66,637 carried in 1994." True, some of this is due to RCCL's increased fleet capacity, but in the past ten years, RCCL has also been savvy enough to respond to the dramatic increase in the popularity of cruising as a family vacation.

Grandeur of the Seas, a 1,950-passenger megaship, is scheduled to sail its maiden voyage in December 1996. Year-round the ship will follow a seven-night Eastern Caribbean itinerary (see chapter three for itinerary and ship description).

Two other new Royal Caribbean megaships that are scheduled to sail in April and September 1997 respectively are *Rhapsody of the Seas* (2,000-passenger capacity) and *Enchantment of the Seas* (1,950-passenger capacity). In April 1998, an eighth Royal Caribbean megaship, *Vision of the Seas* (75,000 tons) will set sail. Itineraries and ship descriptions were not available at press time.

In the spring of 1996, Royal Caribbean will expand its European market with the introduction of *Splendour of the Seas*. Says the line's executive vice president of sales, marketing, and passenger services, Rod

McLeod, "Our commitment to Europe as an important Royal Caribbean destination has grown substantially since we offered our first cruises there in 1990 with the *Sun Viking*." With her home port in Barcelona, Spain, *Splendour of the Seas* will spend the 1996 summer season cruising the Mediterranean, Scandinavia/Russia, and North Cape/Norwegian Fjords. After that, *Splendour of the Seas* will join *Monarch of the Seas* for a winter season (1996–1997) on a Southern Caribbean itinerary. (See chapter three for more information.) *Splendour of the Seas* will offer the regular Royal Caribbean children's program throughout the summer.

European Cruises

With the arrival of *Splendor of the Seas*, RCCL promises to offer its excellent children's program on the ship's three-, six-, eight-, and twelve-night European voyages—a good choice for Europe-bound families.

Children's Program

RCCL offers children's programs year-round on: *Legend of the Seas*, *Majesty of the Seas*, *Monarch of the Seas*, *Nordic Empress*, *Song of America*, *Viking Serenade*, *Sovereign of the Seas*, *Splendour of the Seas* (to debut 1996), *Grandeur of the Seas* (to debut late 1996), *Rhapsody of the Seas* (to debut 1997), *Enchantment of the Seas* (to debut 1997), and *Vision of the Seas* (to debut 1998). The children's program operates only during the summer and holidays on *Song of Norway* and *Sun Viking*. The program operates from about 9 A.M. to noon, 1:30 to 5:30 P.M., and 8 to 10 P.M. Children eat meals with their parents.

RCCL offers an excellent children's program, which is divided into three basic age groups: ages five to eight, nine to twelve, and thirteen to seventeen. There is no minimum age for kids or infants. Children and teens receive their own "Ship Compass" activity schedule highlighting each day's activities, including scavenger hunts, seashell collecting, sand castle building, fun fitness walk-a-thons, and face painting. Teen activities include late-night dancing, teen trivia, and Night at the Teen Improv. Teens also congregate in their own disco at night and in a designated teen center on the *Monarch*, *Majesty*, *Legend of the Seas*, and *Viking Serenade*.

As any parent who has sweated out next year's class assignment knows, getting a child assigned to an exceptional teacher is dependent, in part, on luck. Chance also plays a role on board ships. Based on our experience, we remain impressed by the quality and exuberance of most of RCCL's counselors who bring a great deal of enthusiasm—a crucial attribute—to the job.

Baby-sitting

This may be arranged through the ship's purser for children ages five through twelve from 10 P.M. to 1 A.M. Book well in advance.

Dining

RCCL offers an eight-page "Captain Sealy's Kids' Galley" dinner menu for ages four to twelve that features tried-and-true kids' meals, including peanut butter and jelly sandwiches, burgers, grilled cheese, hot dogs, macaroni and cheese, personal pan pizzas, popcorn shrimp, pasta, salads, fruit, chicken nuggets,

Monarch of the Seas. *Photo courtesy of Royal Caribbean Cruise Lines.*

and homemade alphabet soup. The menu comes with a small pack of Crayons and features connect-the-dots puzzles, word searches, and pictures to color. The menu is not, however, available through room service, but high chairs and booster seats are available in the dining room. Although there's no pizzeria, RCCL ships feature buffet restaurants with pizza and other buffet foods.

Cabins

Although earlier we noted the small size of many RCCL cabins, the new ships that will be introduced over the next few years are said to sport larger cabins.

MORE FAMILY-FRIENDLY CRUISES

Cunard Cruise Line Limited

Cunard is a well-established line with a history of offering luxury cruises, particularly aboard the *Queen Elizabeth II*, a classic ocean liner that still provides different classes of dining service. The luxury liners *Sagafjord* and *Vistafjord* tend to draw older passengers who desire formal service. Cunard's Crown ships, *Crown Dynasty*, *Cunard Countess*, and *Cunard Princess*, offer less expensive and somewhat more informal voyages. Passengers on these ships tend to be younger than those on the *Sagafjord* and *Vistafjord*. The *Sagafjord*, *Royal Viking Sun*, and *Vistafjord* offer no formal youth program.

Cunard offers children's programs on only three ships, and only one of these, the *Queen Elizabeth II*, offers a year-round children's program. (See chapter six for this ship's description.)

Children's Program

There is a nursery on the *Queen Elizabeth II* that is open to toddlers of any age (even newborns) through age six. The nursery, which operates from 8 A.M. to 6 P.M., is staffed by two professional nannies. Refurbished in 1994, this room features a mini cinema and an extensive play area. After 6 P.M., child-care services are charged as baby-sitting.

For ages eight to seventeen, Club 2000 offers sports, scavenger hunts, parties, arts and crafts, and more. Organized activities take place in the youth center and throughout the ship from 8 A.M. to 6 P.M. The activities scheduled depend on the ages of the children on board. For example, with a predominance of eight- to ten-year-olds on board, the counselors would schedule few teen parties. Generally, there is only one youth counselor, but more staff is provided as needed. Board games and the latest videos are available at the library for in-cabin use. Club 2000 is open twenty-four hours a day, and is attended from 8 A.M. to noon, and from 2 to 6 P.M.

Two other Cunard ships, the *Cunard Countess* and *Crown Dynasty*, offer children's programs periodically. The *Cunard Countess* offers a children's program in July, August, and for Christmas cruises, but only for ages two to twelve. Two counselors supervise activities such as story time, scavenger hunts, and deck hikes. Although there is a teen center, there is no playroom, which means that children must meet in unoccupied lounges.

The *Crown Dynasty* only offers a children's program with a minimum of fifteen children on board. Check with your travel agent about your particular sailing. If a program is scheduled, only one counselor is assigned per cruise. Day activities are designed for children ages two and older. This could bore an active eleven-year-old who is confined to a room with a three- and four-year-old. Youth staff, whether part-time or full-time, all have backgrounds in day care or education, but not all counselors know CPR.

Baby-sitting

Cunard ships do not offer formal baby-sitting services unless specially arranged with a staff member. Depending on the ship, fees can be negotiated but are about $5 per hour. Make arrangements well in advance.

For dining and cabin information, see each ship's description. The *Cunard Countess* is described in chapter three; the *Queen Elizabeth II* and *Vistafjord* are described in chapter four; and the *Sagafjord* is described in chapter eight.

Holland America Cruise Line

As part of its commitment to establish Alaska cruises as a shared family learning experience, Holland America offers a variety of outdoor and wildlife excursions. A special bonus on these cruises is an educational program in which children learn about Alaskan wildlife with the help of on-board naturalists. In the Alaska Naturalist Youth Program, an experienced naturalist or ranger answers children's questions about whales, seals, and birds. On Inside Passage cruises, a ranger discusses the history and environment of Glacier Bay National Park. On European voyages, the line presents Flagship Forum—various lectures, primarily for adults, on such topics as finance, art, culture, and history.

Holland America's ships are equipped with outside swimming pools, saunas, and movie theaters for a relaxing cruise. Two new ships are scheduled to launch soon. The *Veendam*, a 1,266-passenger ship, is scheduled to sail its maiden voyage in June 1996. This ship tours the Mediterranean, northern Europe, the transatlantic, and the Caribbean. During the late summer and early fall of 1996, the *Veendam* offers a series of ten- and twelve-day eastern Canada and New England cruises. An as-yet-unnamed, 1,320-passenger ship is scheduled to sail October 1997.

Children's Program

Holland America's youth program is different from the others. Some activities are offered intermittently throughout the day for ages five to seventeen on all ships year-round. There is generally one activity in the morning, one in the afternoon, and one or two in the evening. This is not a program where parents drop off children for blocks of time. During Christmas and other major holidays, additional counselors and teen coordinators may be brought on board.

All ships except the *Rotterdam* are equipped with a children's activity room. Activities for ages five to eight include indoor games, arts and crafts, and ice cream parties. Activities for ages nine to twelve include disco parties, golf putting lessons, and scavenger hunts. For teens (ages thirteen to seventeen), Holland America offers a teen disco, arcade games, movies, and more. Programs such as Passport to Fitness and Chocolate Dessert Extravaganza are open to passengers of all ages.

If the number of children on board exceeds thirty, the line puts additional staff on board. Youth staff are not necessarily trained in CPR. Their backgrounds include either education, childhood development, recreation, or leisure.

Baby-sitting

Baby-sitting can be arranged, but it is not a guaranteed service. Passengers should check with the front office well in advance to schedule services. Fees are $5 per hour per child.

ALTERNATIVE CRUISING

Traditional cruise ships with the requisite glitz, glamour, and programs, aren't the only options for a family vacation on the water. Alternative possibilities are as varied as sailing on a nineteenth-century windjammer, reliving America's river heydays on a steamboat, floating on a European barge or yacht, or focusing on a region's natural habitat, wildlife, and culture on an ecologically oriented yacht or small cruise ship. Although many of these alternative cruises do not offer designated children's programs, some do. Some vessels feature special family sailings that may have a full children's program or selected kids' activities. Even without a designated program, children, especially older ones, generally enjoy the informality and adventure of these voyages.

The following are brief descriptions of these alternatives, which could provide just the right adventure for your family. For specific details, see chapters ten through twelve.

Steamboats

American steamboats evoke images of the heartland at the turn of the century—a time of bustling business in small towns and thriving ports. A steamboat voyage lets you commune with the river, experiencing the Mississippi as Mark Twain may have. Some ships are authentic vessels complete with crystal chandeliers and Victorian settees (refurbished with modern amenities), others are period reproductions, and still others are modern versions with swimming pools and other ship-board comforts.

The steamboat experience lets you enjoy the river and the river towns. American West Steamboats cruises out of Portland, Oregon, to America's northwest, a region rich in pioneering history, Native American lore, and beautiful wildlands. The Delta Queen Steamboat Company cruises the Mississippi River and its tributaries, places where steamboating as transportation once flourished. Ports, which vary with the itinerary, are such prominent river towns as New Orleans, Louisiana; Natchez, Mississippi; Memphis and Chattanooga, Tennessee; St. Paul, Minnesota; St. Louis, Missouri; and Cincinnati, Ohio. Besides the usual town tours, passengers visit nearby plantations and Civil War battlefields. St. Lawrence Cruise Lines, which uses modern steamboats, takes passengers on the St. Lawrence River to cities such as Ottawa (Ontario) and Quebec City (Quebec), exploring the scenery and heritage of Canada.

Barges and River Yachts

Barges move languidly along a river, carrying from six to fifty passengers, with an average ship holding twelve to twenty-four people. Because these vessels are smaller than big cruise ships, they can go where larger ones can't—through canals and along inland rivers. This means that, in addition to docking in cities, these ships float to regions less visited so that passengers can shop at local markets, wander through vineyards, bike along the towpaths, and hike the hillsides. The barges and yachts listed here travel through France, England, Germany, and Holland. (See chapter twelve for descriptions.)

Windjammers

Windjammers, those tall-masted sailing ships, evoke the feeling of the eighteenth and nineteenth centuries. Once aboard, you can imagine the captain of a ship whose hull is filled with exotic spices and teas navigating by starlight, or perhaps a crusty New England whaler searching the horizon for a breaching behemoth of the deep. Passengers aboard these ships embrace the feel of a historic journey and enjoy going where the wind blows them. Many windjammers sail the New England coast in summer. Most have passenger age minimums of twelve or sixteen, but some feature family voyages for children as young as five. Even without a designated children's program, pre-teens and teens often find the voyage exhilarating, especially enjoying the opportunity to learn some hands-on seamanship. (See chapter nine for more information.)

American Canadian Caribbean Line

American Canadian Caribbean Line offers still another option—mini cruise ships. These ships are larger than yachts but smaller than traditional cruise ships, although the vessels offer some big-ship comforts. Because they are relatively small, these mini cruise ships sail open waterways, such as the Erie Canal, and also anchor near off-the-beaten-path Caribbean beaches. In winter, the ships generally cruise the Caribbean, Belize, and Panama. The summer season takes the vessels to various ports in the United States, including Chicago, Buffalo, New Orleans, Niagara Falls, and more. American Canadian Caribbean Line, which does not have a children's program, generally caters to older clientele or to families with adult children (children under fourteen usually are not permitted).

The line has three ships. The *Caribbean Prince*, at 156 feet in length and with a 78-passenger capacity, entered service in 1983. The *Mayan Prince*, which entered service in 1992, is 175 feet long and capable of carrying 92 passengers; and *Niagara Prince*, which entered service in 1994, is 175 feet in length and has an 84-passenger capacity.

(See chapter three for itineraries in Belize, Panama, and other ports in the Caribbean. Itineraries in U.S. ports are in chapter twelve.)

ECOLOGICAL ADVENTURES

For those who *still* snub cruising, regarding ships as big, floating buffets (which of course they are not), there's yet another alternative: the ecological (eco-adventure) cruise. These voyages tempt cruisers with rain forests, remote rivers, and icy blue glaciers. On these journeys, the ship functions less as an end in itself, and more as a reasonably comfortable means of transportation to get close to wildlife and natural wonders. The ships, which tend to cruise at night, vary tremendously, ranging from 8-passenger yachts to 130-passenger vessels. Some are sleek and have teak-paneled cabins, polished brass, private baths, air conditioning, elaborate galleys, and sun decks with lounge chairs. Others offer basic bunk beds, shared baths, and simple meals.

These trips truly focus on the magic of the outdoors. You'll often hear exclamations like, "Mom [or Dad], look," and "Grandpa [or Grandma], did you see that?" By this standard—the number of times your children call on you to share a "wow" moment—eco-adventures rate near the top of any list. Take advantage of these cruises to teach your children more about the wonders of wildlife and wild places, and to treat them to some truly once-in-a-lifetime experiences.

The following is a brief list of some interesting eco-adventure cruises with family appeal. Chapters ten and eleven are devoted to the especially popular destinations of Costa Rica and Ecuador's Galapagos Islands.

Natural Habitat Adventures

These are more like expeditions than cruises. Expeditions have a definite goal, often nature oriented, and use the sea as a means of accomplishing this goal. Natural Habitat Adventures offers trips to the Caribbean, the Dominican Republic, the Baja Peninsula off Mexico, and the Bahamas. Each trip is a unique experience and an opportunity to interact with wildlife through means that were previously reserved only for researchers. The educational experience will definitely be memorable. Although Natural Habitat Adventures does not have a formal children's program, well-behaved children are always welcome to join the trips. Program leaders are highly skilled and experienced, and the strictest safety precautions are taken at all times during wildlife encounters. Inquire about the age requirements for each trip.

Dolphin Watch, Bahamas

Join the crew on board the *Jennifer Marie* (an 8-passenger, 70-foot sailing schooner) for a dolphin encounter. With the help of experienced program leaders, you sail to White Sand Ridge just north of Grand Bahama island to swim with dolphins who announce their arrival with high pitched whistles. The eight-day Dolphin Watch is offered about four times between June and August.

Caribbean Humpback Adventure, Dominican Republic

Whales, especially humpbacks, which are known for their gentle natures, have long fascinated wildlife enthusiasts. From the top deck of the ship or from the ship's launch, passengers can watch these whales interact during their mating and birthing season.

This area also sports bottle-nosed and spotted dolphins, plus an array of tropical fish. The program guide leads scuba and snorkeling trips. Scuba equipment is available free of charge, but you'll need to bring your own snorkeling equipment.

The motorized catamaran can accommodate twenty-eight passengers, but the ten-person crew limits the expedition to approximately eighteen passengers. *Bottom Time II* is 86 feet long and air-conditioned, with eight showers and four toilets across the hall from the cabins. Double and single cabins have personal storage space, a sink, and a vanity. This ten-day trip departs about three times from February to March.

TIP: American Wilderness Experience (800-444-0099), a clearinghouse for soft-adventure companies, represents several whale-watching and dolphin expeditions.

3

*The
Caribbean*

The Caribbean offers families the perfect tropical setting for a great vacation—miles of white sand beaches,
coral reefs for snorkeling, a gentle climate, and warm,
crystal-clear water. Beyond the beaches, the welcoming people of the Caribbean represent a rich diversity
of races and colors. There are also some important cultural lessons to be learned here since the island's history includes slavery and colonialism.

Children who cruise the Caribbean with their parents also learn that all the islands are not alike. Aside
from having its own special topography, flora, and
fauna, each island is unique in its history, people, customs, food specialties, and levels of prosperity. Cruising the Caribbean offers an ideal introduction to the
islands because a cruise allows children (and parents)
to sample a variety of destinations while learning
about each island's unique characteristics.

In 1995, hurricanes Luis and Marilyn hit several Caribbean islands. Hit especially hard were
St. Thomas, St. John, and St. Maarten. Cruise lines
temporarily rearranged their itineraries, substituting
other ports for those that suffered severe damage. The
itineraries listed here, however, are the original schedules because the cruise ships plan to return to those
ports by spring 1996. The section on shore attractions
contains a description of the best pre-hurricane sites
(the islands pledge to rebuild as soon as possible).

The most popular cruise lines are discussed alpha-
betically and are followed by a list of additional cruise
lines. The following information, current at press time,
is subject to change.

Note: Several of the itineraries below stop at Nassau and Playa del Carmen/Cozumel. For details on
these ports, refer to chapters five and six. Also, cruise

lines frequently reposition ships and make changes to their itineraries.

THE LINES

Carnival Cruise Lines

- *Destiny* will enter service in fall 1996 and will sail from Miami; the itinerary was not set at press time.
- *Fascination* provides year-round, seven-day southern Caribbean voyages from San Juan. Ports include St. Thomas, Guadeloupe, Grenada, La Guaira/Caracas and Aruba.
- Starting April 29, 1996, *Festivale* sails year-round on seven-day southern Caribbean voyages; round-trip from San Juan includes stops in St. Thomas, Antigua, Barbados, St. Lucia, St. Kitts, and St. Barts.
- *Imagination* offers year-round, seven-day western Caribbean trips from Miami, with visits in Playa del Carmen/Cozumel, Grand Cayman, and Ocho Rios.
- *Inspiration* is slated to offer year-round, seven-day western Caribbean voyages from San Juan, visiting St. Thomas, St. Maarten, St. Lucia, Barbados, and Martinique.
- *Sensation* sails year-round alternating eastern and western Caribbean voyages departing from Miami. The eastern itinerary includes San Juan, St. Croix, and St. Thomas. The western itinerary features Playa del Carmen/Cozumel, Grand Cayman, and Ocho Rios.

- *Tropicale* features seven-day cruises to the western Caribbean from Tampa and New Orleans, with ports in Grand Cayman, Playa del Carmen, and Cozumel (sails from fall to mid-spring).

Celebrity Cruises

- *Century* sails seven-night cruises round-trip from Ft. Lauderdale, visiting San Juan, St. Thomas, St. Maarten, and Nassau.
- Scheduled to enter service in the fall of 1996, *Galaxy* (at 72,000 tons) is probably going to sail the Caribbean year-round, but this is not definite. Check with your travel agent.
- *Horizon* offers seven-night cruises round-trip from San Juan with visits to Martinique, Barbados, Antigua, and St. Thomas (sails January through April).

Costa Cruises

- *Costa Allegra* features seven-night cruises to the Caribbean from San Juan with stops in St. Thomas, St. John, St. Maarten, Guadeloupe, St. Lucia, Tortola/Virgin Gorda, and Serena Cay/ Casa de Campo (sails November to April).
- *Costa Classica* provides seven-night cruises from Guadeloupe, visiting Barbados, Antigua, Tortola, Serena Cay, St. Maarten, and Martinique (from November through April).
- Five-, seven-, and eight-night cruises can be taken on *Costa Romantica* to tour the eastern and western Caribbean. The ship departs from Miami and stops in Cozumel, Montego Bay, Grand Cayman,

> **TIP:** *Costa Allegra* is marketed by Costa to Euro-
> peans, so the primary languages on board are Italian
> and French. Costa encourages Americans to sample
> their other ships on Caribbean cruises.

San Juan, St. Thomas, Serena Cay, and Nassau
(from November to April, with special Christmas
and New Year's cruises).

- *Costa Victoria* and a second ship (as yet unnamed)
  will debut in 1996 and 1997, respectively. Both
  have itineraries to the Caribbean. Check with your
  travel agent.

Generally, from November to April Costa ships sail
the Caribbean, and from May to October they are repo-
sitioned to cruise Europe and the Mediterranean.

Cunard

- *Cunard Countess* sails year-round, seven-day
  alternating cruises round-trip from San Juan. One
  departure visits Tortola, Antigua, Martinique, Barbados, and St. Thomas, and the following departure visits St. Maarten, Guadeloupe, Grenada,
  St. Lucia, St. Kitts, and St. Thomas.
- *Crown Dynasty* takes off on seven-day round-trips
  from Ft. Lauderdale, visiting Ocho Rios, Grand
  Cayman, Cancun, and Cozumel (only during
  December).

Holland America

- *Nieuw Amsterdam* offers seven-day cruises round-
  trip from New Orleans, with stops in Montego Bay,

Grand Cayman, and Cozumel (sails from January to April and October to December, and holiday cruises are available).

- *Noordam* cruises seven days round-trip from Tampa, with ports in Key West, Cozumel, Ocho Rios, and Grand Cayman (from January to April and October to December, and holiday cruises are available).

- *Ryndam* makes ten-day, round-trip cruises from Ft. Lauderdale and visits St. Maarten, St. Lucia, Barbados, Antigua, St. John/St. Thomas, and Nassau (from January to April and October to December with holiday cruises available).

- *Statendam* sails ten days round-trip from Ft. Lauderdale with stops in St. John/St. Thomas, Dominica, Grenada, Venezuela, and Curacao (from January to April and October to December with holiday cruises available).

- *Veendam* goes on seven-day cruises round-trip from Ft. Lauderdale, stopping in Key West, Cozumel/Playa del Carmen, Ocho Rios, and Grand Cayman (during October, November, and December).

- *Westerdam* offers seven-day, round-trip cruises from Ft. Lauderdale, with calls in Philipsburg, St. Maarten, St. John/St. Thomas, and Nassau (from January to April and October to December with holiday cruises available).

Norwegian Cruise Line

- *Norway* provides seven-day tours of the eastern Caribbean year-round from Miami (excluding two cruises in May, one in August, and one in

November when it follows a western Caribbean itinerary. The eastern itinerary includes St. Maarten, St. John/St. Thomas, and NCL's private island Great Stirrup Cay. The western itinerary includes Ocho Rios, Grand Cayman, Playa del Carmen/ Cozumel, and Great Stirrup Cay.

- Year-round cruises aboard *Seaward* travel round-trip from San Juan, and alternate between the seven-day Aruba series (which also stops in Curacao, Tortola, and St. Thomas) and the seven-day Barbados series (which also visits Martinique, St. Maarten, Antigua, and St. Thomas).

- *Windward* makes seven-day, round-trip cruises from San Juan to the southern Caribbean on alternating itineraries. One departure cruises to Barbados, Martinique, St. Maarten, Antigua, and St. Thomas. The other cruises to Aruba, Curacao, Tortola/Virgin Gorda, St. John, and St. Thomas.

Princess Cruises

- *Crown Princess* makes ten-day southern Caribbean round-trip voyages from Ft. Lauderdale, with stops in Nassau, St. Thomas, Guadeloupe, Barbados, Dominica, St. Maarten, and Princess Cay, Princess' private island.

- *Regal Princess* provides seven-day southern Caribbean round-trip voyages from San Juan. Ports include Barbados, Princess Cay, Mayreau, Martinique, St. Maarten, and St. Thomas.

- *Star Princess* offers seven-day eastern Caribbean voyages round-trip from Ft. Lauderdale, visiting Nassau, St. Thomas, St. Maarten, and Princess Cay.

- *Sun Princess* sails round-trip from Ft. Lauderdale on seven-day western Caribbean voyages with ports in Princess Cay, Montego Bay, Grand Cayman, and Playa del Carmen/Cozumel.

Royal Caribbean Cruise Line

- *Grandeur of the Seas* makes seven-day round-trips from Miami, visiting Labadee (Royal Caribbean's private island in Haiti), San Juan, St. Thomas, and the Bahamas.

- *Majesty of the Seas* travels seven nights round-trip from Miami, and stops in Labadee, Ocho Rios, Grand Cayman, and Playa del Carmen/Cozumel.

- *Monarch of the Seas* offers seven-night, round-trip voyages from San Juan, and ports include Martinique, Barbados, Antigua, St. Maarten, and St. Thomas.

- *Nordic Empress* makes three-night cruises from San Juan, with stops in St. Thomas and St. Maarten; four-night cruises from San Juan visit St. Croix, St. Maarten, and St. Thomas. The winter season for both itineraries begins in December.

- *Sovereign of the Seas* features seven-night, round-trip voyages from Miami, stopping in Labadee, St. John, St. Thomas, and Coco Cay, RCCL's private island.

- *Song of Norway* offers ten- and eleven-night cruises between San Juan and Miami during the winter.

- *Splendour of the Seas* makes seven-day, round-trip cruises from San Juan, visiting Aruba, Curacao, St. Maarten, and St. Thomas during the winter.

ADDITIONAL CRUISE LINES

American Canadian Caribbean Line

- *Caribbean Prince* provides twelve-day, round-trip cruises from Belize, with ports in San Pedro, Ambergris Cay, Goff Cay, Man-o-War Cay, South Water Cay, Laughingbird Cay, Placencia, Lime Cay, Pt. Icacos, West Snake Cay, Punta Gorda, and ports in Guatemala (Christmas cruise and cruises from January to February). Twelve-day cruises also go from Belize to Roatan (reverse itinerary also applies), stopping in Goff Cay, South Water Cay, Laughingbird Cay, Placencia, Lime Cay, West Snake Cay, Punta Gorda, and ports in Guatemala and Honduras (sails from March to April). You can find more information in chapters ten and thirteen. ACCL is a mini-cruise line with vessels that cruise the Caribbean, Central America, and North America.

- *Mayan Prince* makes twelve-day cruises from Nassau to Caicos, visiting Allans Cay, Highbourne Cay, Normans Cay, Sampson Cay, Little Major Spot, Staniel Cay, George Town, Long Island, Crooked Island, Acklins Island, Plana Cay, and Mayaguana (in December). There is also a twelve-day cruise from Panama City to Balboa (reverse itinerary also applies) that visits Colon, El Provenir, San Blas Islands, Coronado de Jesus, Isla Tigre, Portobelo, Panama Canal, Taboga, Isla del Rey, Contadora, La Esmeralda, Pt. Alegre, and Darien Jungle (January through April).

- *Niagara Prince* offers twelve-day, round-trip cruises from St. Thomas that stop in St. John, Tortola, Virgin Gorda, Prickly Pear, Great Camanoe, Anegada, Beef Island, Jost Van Dyke, Sandy Cay, and Norman Island (the Christmas cruise and during January). Another twelve-day cruise sails the beaches of Bonaire, Aruba, and Curacao in March.

THE SHIPS

Carnival Cruise Lines

Festivale: built in 1962; 38,175 gross tons; 1,406-passenger capacity

Purchased by Carnival in 1978, and later refurbished, the *Festivale* is not as glittery as the line's newest ships but what it lacks in glitz, it makes up for in cabin size (many are larger than average—a big

Kids of all ages can party on board. Photo courtesy Carnival Cruise Line.

> **TIP:** Remember, this is one of two Carnival ships
> (along with the *Tropicale*) that requires children to be
> at least four-years-old to participate in Camp Carni-
> val. Also, the fact that there is no in-cabin television
> is not necessarily a liability.

plus for families). The playroom and play deck are
located on the Promenade deck, aft.

There are twelve cabins on the Verandah deck that
sleep three (on a twin- or king- sized bed and single
convertible sofa). Triples and quads (which can accommodate a fifth passenger on a rollaway) are located on
all decks.

The sister ships *Fascination*, *Imagination*, *Inspiration*, and *Sensation* (numbers three, four, five, and six
in Carnival's series of new SuperLiners) are indeed
"cities at sea."

Fascination entered service in 1994, *Imagination* in
1995, *Inspiration* on April 28, 1996, and *Sensation*
in 1993.

Each ship is 70,367 gross tons with a 2,040-
passenger capacity. Although sister ships have the
same floor plans, the interior themes vary from ship
to ship. The following are among the standouts.

The *Fascination*'s distinctive interior evokes the
glamour of Hollywood past. The public areas feature
about twenty life-like mannequins, many of them the
spitting images of such Hollywood legends as Lauren
Bacall (draped over a piano), Elizabeth Taylor, and
Elvis Presley (who can be found in the Diamonds
Are Forever disco). It's all in good fun. Surprisingly,
designer Joe Farcus has made the decor more subtle

and less glitzy than some of his earlier creations for Carnival.

The *Imagination*'s theme runs to mythology, with winged Mercury and Medusa figures as part of the decor. Slightly less glitzy than her predecessors, this ship has a six-deck Grand Atrium like her sister ships, but the neon lights are less pronounced. Sure to be a hit by hungry children is the *Imagination*'s twenty-four-hour pizzeria.

None of the SuperLiners has a movie theater, but that hardly seems to matter because there's so much nonstop activity that you probably won't miss a night at the cinema. A similar Carnival liner, *Tropicale*, entered service in 1981 and has a 1,022-passenger capacity. For a complete description of this ship, see chapter eight.

The cabins are spacious (185 square feet). Staterooms with verandahs on the Verandah deck sleep three (a queen-sized and a single convertible bed). Triples and quads are located on every deck.

Celebrity Cruises

Horizon: entered service in 1990; 46,811 gross tons; 1,354-passenger capacity

New ships include the *Horizon*, a sister ship to the *Zenith*. The *Horizon*, which entered service in 1990, was the first ship built for Celebrity. With the 1996 summer season, the *Horizon* repositions to Alaska, marking Celebrity's entry into this market. Not glitzy, the ship tends toward the sleek and sophisticated. This ship sports a comfortable and spacious feel, largely due to the use of many windows for natural light. The Olympic Health Club offers scenic views, and is reasonably well equipped. The ship also features two outdoor swimming pools and a children's playroom and a teen room.

The cabins, at 185-square-feet, are comfortable and larger than those on many ships, and there's ample storage space. All cabins feature hair dryers and televisions. Cabins on the Bermuda deck have partially obstructed views, however. Four cabins are wheel-chair accessible. There are a range of three- and four-passenger cabins.

Century: slated to enter service in 1995; 70,000 gross tons; 1,750-passenger capacity
Galaxy: slated to enter service in November 1996; 72,000 gross tons; 1,840 passengers

Celebrity is hoping to take its passengers into the new century with two new ships, the *Century* and the *Galaxy*, both of which will cruise the Caribbean. The ships' grand foyers are dramatic—tiered open atria, spiral staircases, and domed ceilings with murals. A complete itinerary has not yet been announced for the *Galaxy*. These ships feature more spacious public lounges than the line's other ships. All cabins feature air-conditioning, larger bathrooms, hair dryers, televisions, direct-dial telephones, mini-bars, and safes. As part of the high-tech collaboration with Sony Electronics, Inc., cabins also feature an interactive guest services network. Other state-of-the-art audio and video systems are to be installed in the theater, the Sky Bar, and Images, a video bar.

The *Century*, constructed at a cost of $320 million, is touted to have 48 percent more space than her sister ships. As part of the new design, the sister ships *Century* and *Galaxy* both have more drawer and closet space in their cabins, as well as larger cabins. Standard cabins are 172 square feet, and eight cabins will be designed for the physically challenged.

For evening, the *Century* offers several interesting options. The Crystal Room, a show lounge, employs a motif of black and gold art-deco panels and etched glass to evoke the spirit of chic New York clubs of the thirties. The two-deck theater is specially designed with no obstructing views. The Hemisphere, an observation lounge by day, transforms into what Celebrity calls "a futuristic disco under the dome" at night. The AquaSpa, which has a Japanese garden and bathhouse theme, offers treatments such as a hydrotherapy bath, Aqua Mediation, and the Rasul, a treatment based on an Oriental ceremony that includes a seaweed-soap shower, a medicinal mud pack, an herbal steambath, and a massage.

The *Galaxy* will have many of the same features as the *Century*, including the increased space, larger cabins, and high-tech audio and video systems. In addition, the *Galaxy* plans include a retracting "Magrodome" over one of its two pool decks cupola, making this the ship's second atrium. Celebrity also plans to add a new multi-level observation lounge to afford passengers another area with panoramic sea views.

Costa Cruises

Costa Classica: entered service in 1991; 53,000 gross tons; 1,300-passenger capacity
Costa Romantica: entered service in 1993; 54,000 gross tons; 1,350-passenger capacity

The *Costa Classica* and the *Costa Romantica* are sister ships. Like the other Costa ships, these sport an Italian ambiance, created in part by the use of a good deal of Italian marble, ceramic tile, murals, and fountains. The ample use of mahogany and burled briarwood adds warmth.

A bronze sculpture by noted Italian artist Arnaldo Pomodoro highlights the main lobby of the *Costa Classica*. One of the main bars, the Piazza Navona Grand Bar (named for the Roman square), is especially large and welcoming, combining mahogany and Italian marble. A cafe, the Il Dolce Amore Patisserie, serves cappuccino, croissants, chocolates, and specialty teas.

On the *Romantica*, specialty coffees and teas are available at Juliet's Patisserie. The decor of the *Costa Romatica* was designed by the same architectural firm that designed the new Musée d'Orsay in Paris. The grand lobby is highlighted by "The Cloud," a suspended mobile sculpture created by Japanese sculptor Susumu Shingu. The Piazza Italia Grand Bar, a central gathering place, features soft green Venetian stucco walls accented by woven jacquard fabrics in green and blue patterns suggestive of English country style.

Each ship also has two pools. Like the *Costa Allegra*, the *Costa Classica* and the *Costa Romantica* feature the Caracalla Spa, a 6,500-square-foot spa that is well equipped with free weights, life cycles, and an aerobic floor. The spa also offers an array of pampering massages and treatments.

An open-air cafe serves pizza, focaccia, and other informal fare on the *Classica*. Children tend to congregate here and can order pizza any way they like it. On the *Romantica*, children like the pizza served at Romeo's Pizzeria. On both ships, dinner menus feature Italian cuisine as well as Continental, vegetarian, and heart-healthy dishes.

Both ships feature oversized staterooms. Inside cabins measure 175 square feet and outside cabins start at 200 square feet. Each cabin is equipped with a television, phone, air-conditioning, hair dryer, and safe deposit box. Three- and four-person cabins are available. Six cabins on each ship are wheelchair accessible.

Costa Allegra: entered service in 1992; 30,000 gross tons; 800-passenger capacity.

Because the *Costa Allegra* is smaller and more informal than the others in the Costa fleet, she attracts clientele who want a less formal cruise. The ship is easy to get around on because the public rooms are all located on one deck. The three-deck atrium is topped with a skylight that sends lots of light into the lobby. The spa is also smaller than those on other Costa ships. Children have their own designated play area on the Solarium deck as part of the Costa Kids program.

The cabins are a good size, and all have hair dryers and safes. Three- and four-person cabins are available, and eight cabins are wheelchair accessible.

Costa Victoria: entered service in June 1996; 75,000 gross tons; 1,950-passenger capacity

Beginning in June and throughout the summer, the *Costa Victoria* sails to the Greek Isles from Venice. In winter, this ship repositions to sail the Caribbean.

This ship and an unnamed one to follow in 1997 represent the next phase of Costa's expansion. Both ships have several dramatic features. The *Victoria* has two atria, a center hall spanning seven decks topped by a crystal dome, and an observation lounge that spans four decks and features a waterfall. As on the fleet's other ships, the observation area is reminiscent of an Italian piazza, a small village with shops and sitting areas.

The signature Caracalla Spa is even more elaborate on this ship than on the others. In addition to the weight, aerobic, steam room, sauna, and treatment areas, this spa also has an indoor pool and a 1,312-foot jogging track.

As on other Costa ships, the children's program is offered year-round. This ship sports a children's room and a designated teen room.

The cabins feature the typical Costa amenities. Three- and four-passenger cabins are available as are suites and wheelchair-accessible cabins.

Cunard

The *Cunard Countess* entered service in 1976 and was refurbished in 1992. It is 17,593 tons and has a 750-passenger capacity. The *Crown Destiny* entered service in 1993, is 22,000 tons, and can carry 800 passengers. For a complete description of these ships, see chapter eight.

Holland America Line

Westerdam: built in 1986; refurbished in 1989; 53,872 gross tons; 1,494-passenger capacity

Like other Holland America ships, the *Westerdam* has an understated elegance. The ship now features a two-deck show lounge that seats 800 passengers. The *Westerdam* sports a bronze cannon cast in Rotterdam in 1634 that was once on a Dutch admiral's warship.

Veendam: slated to enter service in May 1996; 55,000 gross tons; 1,266-passenger capacity

As a sister ship to the *Maasdam, Ryndam*, and *Statendam*, the *Veendam* has a similar cabin layout but a different interior decor. Like the *Maasdam*, the *Veendam* employs art and artifacts in the three-story atrium to evoke the era of eighteenth-century Dutch expeditions. The 600-seat Rubens Lounge, the showroom, is themed after the sixteenth-century Flemish painter Pieter Paul Rubens. Pen and ink drawings suggestive of a Rubens self-portrait adorn the glass doors.

Refer to chapter eight for specific descriptions of the *Nieuw Amsterdam, Statendam, Ryndam*, and *Noordam*.

Norwegian Cruise Line

Norway: entered service in 1960 as the *SS France*; rebuilt in 1990; 76,049 gross tons; 1,024-passenger capacity

"They don't build them like that anymore" is an apt way to describe the *Norway*, which, in its former incarnation as the French Line's *SS France*, transported the rich and famous across the Atlantic until the ship became part of the NCL fleet in 1980. While glitzy new megaships are winning over much of the mass market, the *Norway*—huge in her own right at 76,049 tons—adds to her girth touches of class such as sweeping staircases and crystal chandeliers. This ship offers a sense of cruising's bygone glory era, an ambiance that upstarts simply can't replicate. Many of *Norway*'s suites and cabins are larger than those on newer vessels and offer families much more space. Another advantage: if your children have problems with motion sickness, the *Norway* provides one of the smoothest cruises at sea thanks to her steam turbines. One disadvantage of the *Norway*, as on most big ships, is that it's easier for younger children to get lost. If you want to let your children roam free—a perk that is considered by many to be one of the major benefits of cruising with kids—you may prefer to chose a smaller ship. Also, because the *Norway* is so huge it must anchor offshore at all of its ports of call (many larger ships must do so at some ports). This means that passengers take a tender, a smaller boat, to and from port—an inconvenience with very young children.

Three youth coordinators staff the *Norway*'s Trolland, (the children's playroom) year-round, and seven work during the summer. The room includes the latest video games, the Sega Genesis system, books, and board games.

The cabins are roomy, with high ceilings and ample closet space. Cabins on the Olympic deck look out to the jogging track rather than the sea, and most cabins on the Fjord deck have an obstructed view. The *Norway* has two cabins and two suites that accommodate four and five people.

Seaward: entered service in 1988; 42,276 gross tons; 1,534-passenger capacity

The *Seaward*, moderately sized by today's standards, is a well-designed ship offering passengers a tastefully decorated interior with a stunning two-story entrance hall and the Crystal Court, which is complete with a cascading fountain and marble pool.

The Lido deck, the hub of activity, sports two back-to-back swimming pools. There's also an ice cream bar (though one passenger who sailed recently could never figure out exactly when this was open). The Big

Apple Cafe, also on the Lido deck, offers a convenient and casual alternative to breakfast or lunch in the dining room.

For a real adult treat, arrange for baby-sitting one evening so you can dine in the Palm Court, an upscale and intimate bistro tucked away on the top deck (reserve as soon as possible). Go ahead and splurge. Although pricey, the restaurant offers memorable dining in a romantic setting.

The children's program operates out of the Porthole, a smallish room stocked with video games. Some activities also meet in public areas. One youth coordinator is on board year-round, and there are four during holidays and in the summer.

The cabins, not the biggest or the smallest we've seen, sport plenty of drawer space and amenities, such as hair dryers in the bathroom. The *Seaward* has three- and four-person cabins plus four suites that accommodate five people. For a description of another NCL ship, the *Windward*, see chapter eight.

Princess Cruises

(Itineraries below are for fall/winter/spring seasons.)
Star Princess: entered service in 1989; 63,500 gross tons; 1,490-passenger capacity

The *Star* was the first Princess ship to be built after the parent company merged with the Italian Sitmar line. That line was noted for its fine service, a tradition that carried over to the Princess ships.

The *Star Princess* is a spacious vessel with traditional decor and artwork. The ship's centerpiece is the Plaza, a three-deck, dome-topped atrium with shops. Teens especially like the sports deck for basketball, volleyball, and paddle tennis. All ages gather for fun and sun on the Lido deck, which has three swimming pools and a waterfall. A special shallow-depth swimming pool for children enables counselors to supervise swimming, pool games, and snorkeling lessons. The children's room is cleverly designed with a separate area for toddlers, pre-schoolers, older children, and teens. Good news for those in-between meal munchers: the *Star Princess* has a pizzeria.

Standard cabins are spacious and have large modular bathrooms. Some staterooms on Baja, Aloha, Caribe, Dolphin, Emerald, and Plaza decks accommodate third or both third and fourth passengers. Ten cabins are wheelchair accessible.

Regal Princess: entered service in 1991; 70,000 gross tons; 1,590-passenger capacity
Crown Princess: entered service in 1990; 70,000 gross tons; 1,590-passenger capacity

The *Regal Princess* and the *Crown Princess* are sister ships with similar layouts. Their exteriors are designed to resemble the graceful lines of a dolphin, and the interiors are quietly elegant, featuring Burmese teak, Carrara marble, well-appointed public rooms, and a stunning $1 million art collection.

The three-deck atrium lobby serves as a popular central meeting place. These large ships were well thought out and, as a result, are extremely easy to get around. The theater, with two evening screenings, shows some movies suitable for school-age and older children. One organized teen activity on a recent sailing was a group showing of *Forrest Gump* complete with popcorn from the galley. In-cabin televisions show full-length films as well as occasional CNN reports, sitcoms, and other U.S. shows. The broadcasts depend on where the ship is located. If there is no television, however, you probably won't even miss it.

Although few of us imagine spending a vacation at sea doing laundry, both ships offer free laundry rooms complete with ironing boards and irons. Small, inexpensive packets of detergent can be purchased in the laundry room or at the duty-free shops. There is also a dry cleaning service with surprisingly reasonable prices. With active kids in tow, these can be helpful extras.

Neither of these ships has a designated area for the children's or teens' programs even though both have recently added a year-round program. (The children's program was previously limited to sailings with a minimum of fifteen kids.) However, the lack of a playroom doesn't hinder the activities. On one recent sailing aboard the *Regal*, the younger set was observed busily doing arts and crafts during the mid-afternoon in an empty corner of the spacious Lido cafe, while the teens were meeting for a swim.

TIP: Be sure to attend the kids' program orientation meeting the first evening at sea and have your teens attend, too. Kids and teens who sign up at this meeting receive an activity schedule in their cabin each morning. Surprisingly, on a recent non-holiday cruise aboard the *Regal,* a number of parents with 'tweens (ages eleven to thirteen) were overheard saying how bored their children were. It seems these parents and children were unaware of the activity program because they missed the orientation meeting. Check the purser's desk every day for activity schedules.

The service on board is very good. Waiters and cabin staff are friendly and particularly solicitous if you have children. While there is no special kids' menu, the staff goes out of their way to find something to please—and if your children like pasta, you're in heaven. The many Italian chefs cook up some great dishes. The pizzeria is open after lunch and dinner for excellent individual-sized pies. Sometimes, this is all the younger set wants to eat.

Standard cabins are quite large, with lots of closet and drawer space, plenty of hangers, and a television. Amenities include terry robes for adults. Some state-rooms on Caribe, Dolphin, Emerald, Playa and Baja decks accommodate a third or third and fourth passengers. Each ship has ten cabins that are wheelchair accessible.

Other Princess Ships

Sun Princess: entered service in late 1995; 77,000 gross tons; 1,950 passengers

Grand Princess: slated to enter service in May 1997; 104,000 gross tons; 2,600-passenger capacity

The *Sun Princess* and *Grand Princess* are the line's newest $300 million plus mega-liners. They represent the first phase of Princess' new expansion program. Following the *Sun Princess*' debut in late 1995, its sister ship the *Dawn Princess* takes to the seas in spring 1997. In the fall of that year, the largest cruise ship ever—the 104,000-ton *Grand Princess*—debuts in the Caribbean market.

These ships are part of the line's new Grand Class of ships, touted by Princess as "larger ships with small-ship intimacy, offering choices in dining, entertainment, and accommodations at affordable prices."

The *Sun Princess* rises fourteen stories high and measures 856 feet in length. Her main Promenade deck features two large showrooms at either end. There are two main 500-passenger dining rooms supplemented by kid-pleasing dining options that include a pizzeria, hamburger and hot dog grills, an ice cream bar, and a twenty-four-hour international food court with indoor and outdoor seating. The ship offers two age-specific youth areas, along with a full-time staff and comprehensive activity pro-grams. The "Fun Zone" children's center includes a splash pool (one of a total of six pools on board), a doll house, castle, children's theater, and ball-jump. Teens cavort in their very own Cyperspace center complete with a disco, refreshment bar, and video game collection.

Standard cabins measure approximately 180 square feet, larger than the cabins on many other lines. There are cabins that accommodate three and four passengers. Each ship has wheelchair-acces-sible cabins.

Royal Caribbean Cruise Line

Majesty of the Seas: entered service in 1992; 73,941 gross tons; 2,354-passenger capacity
Monarch of the Seas: entered service in 1988; 73,941 gross tons; 2,354-passenger capacity
Sovereign of the Seas: entered service in 1988; 73,192 gross tons; 2,276-passenger capacity

Majesty of the Seas, Monarch of the Seas, and *Sovereign of the Seas* all look identical, but the *Monarch* sports more cabins and has a somewhat better layout. Signature elements include a distinctive multi-story "centrum" (an atrium in the ship's center) and glass elevators. These floating resorts are, according to

RCCL, as tall as the Statue of Liberty and as long as three football fields. Depending on your idea of what a cruising experience should be, the enormity of these ships has its pluses and minuses.

One plus is that you'll find everything you could hope for on board these glamorous ships, from gracious dining rooms to wonderful public rooms, including movie theaters and lots of deck space. Moreover, these ships provide an extremely smooth sailing experience. But on the minus side, you may have to wait in long lines and the service can be impersonal. Also, huge ships can be somewhat confusing for younger passengers to navigate through.

All three ships offer programs year-round with designated children's playrooms; the *Monarch* and *Majesty* also have teen centers. The playrooms are especially pleasant—instead of being hidden away in a dark corner, these rooms are well placed and sport windows. A wooden ledge facing the windows, complete with mini-chairs, serves as a great surface for arts and crafts projects. A small area contains a slide and ball-jump, and there are shelves filled with toys and games. There's also a large-screen television for watching videos.

The staterooms on these three ships are generally small. Many have one or two upper berths in addition to the normal configuration, and there are a number of connecting staterooms on Mariner deck and above, except on the Promenade deck (where cabins look out onto a public area). The *Monarch* has a six-person suite, and the *Monarch* and *Majesty* each have four wheelchair-accessible cabins.

Grandeur of the Seas: entered service in 1996; 74,000 gross tons; 1,950-passenger capacity

Splendour of the Seas: entered service in 1996; 69,130 gross tons; 1,804-passenger capacity. This sister ship to *Legend of the Seas* cruises to Europe and the southern Caribbean.

Both the *Grandeur of the Seas* and the *Splendour of the Seas* are similar in design to *Legend of the Seas*, which is described in detail in chapter eight. These sleek ships feature Royal Caribbean's trademark multi-story atria, and the extensive use of glass affords great sea views. An "observatory," or deck area created for stargazing, gives passengers a place to enjoy this special evening activity. Each ship also features a solarium (an indoor/outdoor room covered by a removable glass canopy) to shield the swimming pools in inclement weather.

These ships devote lots of space to kids. For children (and adults) there is an eighteen-hole miniature golf course. The Club Ocean playroom is bright and well designed, and teens enjoy their own facility: the Optix Teen Center. Each of these ships offers a year-round comprehensive children's program for ages five through seventeen.

The cabins aboard these ships are larger than the ones on RCCL's older ships. Third and fourth passenger cabins, suites, and wheelchair-accessible cabins are available. There are complete ship descriptions of the *Nordic Empress* and *Song of Norway* in chapters six and eight, respectively.

American Canadian Caribbean Line

Mayan Prince: entered service in 1992; 92 gross tons; 92 passengers; 46 cabins; 175-foot length
Niagara Prince: entered service in 1994; 99 gross tons; 84 passengers; 42 cabins; 175-foot length

Caribbean Prince: entered service in 1984; 89.5 gross tons; 78 passengers; 39 cabins; 156-foot length

These vessels resemble smaller versions of traditional cruise ships (see chapter two for a description of the cruise line). Though smaller, these vessels have all the comforts of big cruise ships including a main dining room and deck and a pool. Both public rooms can accommodate all passengers in one seating. These ships do not feature casinos, so don't come aboard if you look forward to blackjack at night. All three vessels carry glass-bottom boats for viewing marine life in Caribbean waters, and Sunfish (small, easy-to-maneuver sailboats) are available on Caribbean itineraries. ACCL's ships are able to anchor near beaches, so there's no time wasted getting to the beach or returning for sandwiches.

The cabins are small, plain, bare-bones utilitarian spaces with little storage space, but all have private bathrooms. While the *Mayan Prince* and the *Caribbean Prince* don't have wheelchair-accessible cabins, the *Niagara Prince* has two. There are no third- or fourth-person cabins.

FAMILY-FRIENDLY CARIBBEAN ISLANDS

Sampling the pleasures of several Caribbean islands with your family—without having to pack and unpack—is one of the major joys of cruising.

All of the cruise lines offer shore excursions that can be booked on board through the tour desk. Generally, you will receive information on shore excursions in advance of your voyage, along with your ship's docu-

TIP: As a general rule, concentrate on doing *one* thing at each shore stop. Depending on the ship you're on, you may have somewhere between six to twelve hours on shore—not much time when you factor in eating and transportation.

ments. The important thing to decide before you go is what your family enjoys and what to do on each island. Keep in mind the length of the tour and the mode of transportation because many kids balk at having to get into a large motor coach for a long ride to a site that may be of marginal interest to them.

The following islands are visited by most major cruise lines and have been selected for their family-friendly qualities. We've outlined the best things to do with children of various ages on the most frequently visited islands. Please keep in mind that sometimes it is best not to over-program—just hit the beach and enjoy. To learn the island's highlights, attend (or watch on closed-circuit TV in your cabin) the cruise director's talks that are usually given the day before arriving in port. Remember that most ships dock directly at the pier in some ports, while in others it may be necessary to take a tender ashore. Rough seas occasionally make tender transportation unfeasible, so it's possible that

TIP: The telephone code for all the islands listed below is 809. Contact the tourism offices for a calendar of events. Visiting during a festival adds a special sense of island fun.

you may miss a port stop. Be sure to take your boarding passes with you when you disembark—and plenty of sunscreen. The Caribbean sun is hot, hot, hot all year-round.

ON SHORE: ARUBA

Small Aruba packs a lot for families into its just-under-twenty-mile length and six-mile width (at the broadest point). Among its attractions: friendly locals who welcome tourists, fabulous beaches, delightful trade winds (which account for the bent appearance of the famous divi divi trees), and a dramatic landscape that ranges from the splendid Caribbean shoreline to an inland full of cactus, aloe, and rock formations.

Quick Facts

Currency: U.S. dollars are accepted almost everywhere, so there's no need to change currency unless you're planning to take a bus or make a local phone call. The local currency is the Aruban florin (AFl).

Language: The native Aruban is a mixture of Dutch, Spanish, and Arawak Indian (*paiamento*). And though Dutch is the official language, Aruban children study English and Spanish from the age of ten, and most islanders speak these languages as well.

Emergency Numbers: Police: 100; Ambulance: 115.

Major Towns: Ships dock at Aruba Port Authority cruise terminal, a five-minute walk from downtown Oranjestad on the island's leeward (southwest) side.

Tourist Information: Contact Aruba Tourism Authority, 1000 Harbor Blvd., Weekhawken, NJ 07087, or call (800) TO-ARUBA. The Tourist Bureau has an information booth in the cruise ship terminal.

Transportation:

Buses: They run hourly between Oranjestad and the beach hotels. A convenient stop is located across the street from the ship terminal. Exact change ($1.80) is preferred.

Car Rental: Budget, Avis, and Hertz are all represented on the island.

Taxi: Taxis don't have meters, so confirm rates before getting in.

Best Bets

For ages two through seven:
Swimming at Baby Lagoon

For ages seven through eleven:
Palm Beach

For pre-teens and teens:
Snorkeling at Malmok Beach

For adults:
Golf at Tierra del Sol and the Alhambra Casino

Beaches

Beware: The water on the northern side of the island is too rough for swimming. **Palm Beach**, named one of the ten best beaches in the world, is the center of tourism and is fronted by a number of major hotels. Do expect crowds during peak season. For a truly delightful beach for toddlers, try **Baby Lagoon** on the island's southernmost tip. This small strip of beach with calm and shallow water entices young ones. Thatched shaded areas provide a retreat when the sun gets too strong.

At **Malmok Beach**, the best snorkeling beach located just north of the island's hotels, visibility can be up to ninety feet, and the shelling is great, too. Just off the beach is one of Aruba's most unusual sights and a popular dive destination—the wreck of the German freighter *Antilla*, scuttled here during World War II. Lessons, reef excursions, and other organized tours are available. Contact the Aruba Tourism Authorty, (800) TO-ARUBA, for their guide to dive sites. The guide, titled "Scuba in Aruba," includes a dive map highlighting wreck sites and major reefs.

The island's trade winds provide ideal conditions for windsurfing. Amateurs can start out in the shallow waters of Fisherman's Hut. **Machebo Beach** has a slalomboard area with small, choppy waves, and expert windsurfers ride the high waves of Boca Grandi. Every June, Aruba hosts the annual Hi-Winds Pro Am World Cup—fun for all to watch.

De Palm Tours provides equipment and instruction for scuba, snorkeling, and windsurfing, and offers hiking tours as well. The ubiquitous De Palm recently opened its own island with facilities for daytime scuba, snorkeling, windsurfing, and other activities. (297/ 8-24545).

Nature and the Environment

Take a ride on a submarine—a two-hour adventure starting with a catamaran cruise to your dive destination off Aruba. There you'll board the **Atlantis Sub-**

marine (see Barbados in the next section for details on the experience). Children four to sixteen are welcome and receive a free Atlantis pin after the tour. Ages four to ten also get a free Atlantis coloring book. Families of four or more receive a 10 percent discount. Call 297/8-36090. This tour is offered by most cruise ships. Remember to take your seasickness medicine ahead of time if needed.

Outdoor Sports

Aruba's first championship golf course, **Tierra del Sol**, opened recently on the island's northwest coast. The par 71, eighteen-hole Robert Trent Jones-designed course overlooks Aruba's crystal-clear waters. The course is managed by Hyatt Aruba NV and is located in a residential community with two swimming pools and lighted tennis courts. For more information, call (800) 233-1234.

Historical Sites and Museums

In charming downtown Oranjestad, stroll to **Fort Zoutman**, the island's oldest building (1796), which was once a major fortress in skirmishes between British and Curacao troops. There's also a museum in an eighteenth-century Aruban house that displays relics and artifacts (297/8-26099).

Other Attractions

Adults can place their bets at one of Aruba's casinos: The **Alhambra Bazaar**, across from the Divi-Divi

Hotel, is one of the most popular and also houses a showroom, a twenty-four-hour deli, and shops.

Best Eateries and Snacks

If your children crave American food, head to **Pirate's Nest**, a replica of a shipwrecked galleon with a terrace on the beachside of Bucuti Hotel. Burgers and club sandwiches highlight the lunch menu, and other typical American fare is available for dinner.

Your Aruba stop may be one of the few chances your children have to sample Dutch cuisine. In a casual, cozy surrounding, the **Coffee House De Dijssel** on Hospitalstraat in Oranjestad serves such Dutch staples as hearty pea soup, and the bakery next door sells homemade pastries and breads. Come for lunch from noon to 2 P.M.

Mi Cushina, in Cura Cabi on the main road about one mile from San Nicolas (telephone 48335), serves such Aruban delights as fried fish with funchi (cornmeal) and stewed lamb with pan bati (local pancakes). Children love the decor—the ceiling is made of coffee bags, the light fixtures are old wagon wheels, and there are family photos. A small museum demonstrates how aloe vera was processed on the island. Lunch is served from noon to 2 P.M.; dinner from 6 to 10 P.M.

Shopping

Dutch cheese (you're allowed to bring home up to one pound through U.S. Customs), chocolate, cameras, and binoculars are good buys. A number of designer stores, such as Ciro, Gucci, and La Pomme, are located in the Seaport Village Mall in downtown Oranjestad.

ON SHORE: BARBADOS

Barbados (twenty-one miles long by fourteen miles wide at its broadest point) is a charming place with lots of family appeal. **Bridgetown** is a popular stop on many Caribbean cruise itineraries.

With a standard of living among the highest in the Caribbean, this is not an island where visitors get coaxed and cajoled by overeager vendors. In fact, the government licenses vendors, who are not allowed to walk the beaches in search of buyers. Barbados incorporates many British traditions—the locals play cricket, the Bajan national sport, and relax with afternoon tea. Either of these would be fun for a family to sample.

A paradise for watersports enthusiasts, the island's powdery sandy beaches on the calm west coast are perfect for young children while athletic teens might enjoy windsurfing on the south coast shores.

Quick Facts

Currency: The Barbados dollar is tied to the U.S. dollar at a rate at press time of $1.98 Bds. to $1 U.S.
Emergency Numbers: Police: 112; Ambulance: 115.
Tourist Information: There are three Barbados Tourism Authority offices in the U.S.: 800 Second Ave., Second Floor, New York, NY 10017; phone (800) 221-9831 or (212) 986-9516; 2442 Hinge St., Troy, MI 48083; phone (810) 740-7835; and 3440 Wilshire Blvd., Suite 1215, Los Angeles, CA 90010; phone (213) 380-2198.

Cruise passengers may also obtain tourist information at Bridgetown's new port facilities, which offer nineteen duty-free shops, thirteen local retail stores, and a dozen vendors.

Language: English

Main Town: Bridgetown, the capital city, is the hub of island life.

Transportation:

Buses: Blue Transport Board buses and yellow, private minibuses cover the island's extensive paved-road network on regular schedules. While the system is good and buses are clearly marked with destinations, they can be crowded. Fares are $1.50 Bds. for any destination. For information on routes, call 436-6820.

Car Rentals: There are a dozen or so car rental sources including some, such as Sunny Isle Motors (809) 435-7979, that provide free pickup and delivery to the port. A visitor's driving license must be purchased from the rental company. Drivers must be over twenty-four and licensed for at least two years. Driving is on the left.

Cars with Drivers: VIP Tour Services, a small, family business, offers private, air-conditioned Mercedes Benzes with drivers who point out interesting sights as they drive. The typical charge for a car seating up to four persons is $30 U.S. per hour for a minimum of five hours (429-4617). Compare this with the individual shore tour fares and you may be surprised how much less expensive (and easier) it is to go on your own than with a busload of your boat comrades.

Taxis: Available everywhere, taxis have reasonable, set rates. There is a taxi stand at Bridgetown Harbour.

Mopeds and Bikes: These are also easily available, but stay away from the congestion of Bridgetown and its environs. Call Bike Barbados (422-2858) or Fun Seekers (435-8206).

Best Bets

For ages two through seven:
The hands-on Flower Forest; swimming at Mullins
Beach or other west coast beaches

For ages seven through eleven:
Folkestone Underwater Park with snorkeling,
aquarium, and museum

For pre-teens and teens:
Swimming on the west coast beaches; for expert
teens, windsurfing on the south coast

For teens and adults:
Golf at Sandy Lane

Beaches

All beaches in Barbados are public, with the calmest
waters found on the west coast. **Mullins Beach**, a
favorite, offers easy parking, food and beverages, and
clear, calm water plus lots of shade. Snorkeling equipment is also available for rent.

Best for windsurfers—or for watching them—are
the south coast beaches. The expansive **Casuarina
Beach**, where you'll find the Casuarina Beach Hotel
(food and beverages available at reasonable prices),
offers a good breeze and medium waves. The **Silver
Sands Beach**, close to the south point of the island,
presents a picturesque expanse of white sand beach
with superb windsurfing for more advanced enthusiasts. Boards are available for rent, and instructions
are given at Silver Rock Bar and Restaurant, or try
the Barbados Windsurfing Club Hotel in Maxwell
(428-9095).

> **TIP:** Be sure your kids are aware of passing boats
> when snorkeling. Also remind them to avoid touching
> or standing on sea urchins or coral (especially fire
> coral or fire worms), and not to put their hands into
> holes in the reef.

Beaches throughout the island offer snorkeling, but the west coast beaches are best-suited for families. **Folkestone Underwater Park** north of Holetown, and easily accessible by car or taxi from Bridgetown, features an underwater snorkeling trail around Dottin's Reef. A glass-bottom boat trip reveals the wonders of the sea to non-snorkelers. An aquarium and museum display coral, sponges, artifacts, and photographs of marine life. Other pluses: a playground, tennis courts, and restrooms on site.

Many cruise lines offer snorkeling shore excursions on the Tiami, a 60-foot catamaran with expansive deck space. The ship provides snorkeling equipment and vests. Prices usually range from $40 to $45 per person with lunch included. To arrange a sail, call 427-SAIL.

Nature and the Environment

At **Harrison's Cave** (438-6640/1/3/4/5), underground explorers find stalactites, stalagmites, waterfalls, and pools. Located in the central part of the island along Highway 2, the cave is a popular sightseeing stop. Formed by crystallized limestone and highlighted by special effects and lighting, the cave is viewed via guided tours from electric trams.

Many cruise lines combine a visit to the caves with a stop at historic **Gun Hill Signal Station** so visitors can enjoy its sweeping views. The tour may also visit the **Flower Forest** of Barbados, where fifty acres of flowers, plants, and nature trails delight people of all ages. Because the caves are so popular, there may be long waits. If your children have toured other caves, you may want to skip this one and head straight to the Flower Forest. Some nature trails may be too uneven for strollers. There are restaurant facilities on site. (Located on Highway 2 close to Harrison's Cave; open seven days; call 443-8152.)

Atlantis Submarine is another exciting—albeit expensive—way to see Barbados' marine life. The transfer boat, the *Yukon II*, takes passengers along the west coast to the dive site. The submersible vehicle, which descends to depths of 150 feet, seats twenty-eight and offers a number of viewing ports plus a narration by the copilot. Two divers appear on underwater scooters to answer guest's questions while feeding the numerous colorful fish that flock around them. Keep in mind that if your kids (or you) have a queasy stomach, there is sometimes considerable bobbing while entering and/or re-entering the sub. Also, people who tend to feel claustrophobic should avoid this trip. Most cruise

---

TIP: A family of four can save money by arranging a taxi to these points. Prices for a five-hour tour with a knowledgeable driver/tour guide run between $60 and $85 per taxi. Similar cruise line shore excursions combining several of the sights above usually cost $50 U.S. per person.

lines offer this ninety-minute dive as an excursion at about $69 per person, or book your own by calling 436-8929 in Barbados or (800) 253-0493 in the U.S. Children under twelve are half price; no children under three feet tall are allowed. (Some cruise lines set the minimum age allowed on Atlantis excursions at four years old).

Highland Outdoor Tours is a new tour operator specializing in adventure travel. Among the offerings are half- or full-day horseback treks, hiking expeditions, and tractor-drawn jitney rides. Best with younger kids: a two-hour plantation tour on a tractor-drawn open jitney through plantation lands. Travel through cattle fields, gullies, and historic paths with a stop for a fruit drink and beef kabob. Cost is $25 U.S. including transportation to and from the facility if you book yourself, or about $39 U.S. via your cruise ship. (Reservations required; call 438-8069/70.)

Finally, the **Barbados Wildlife Reserve**, north of Speightstown, is home to the famous Barbados green monkey as well as mongoose, otters, peacocks, tortoises, porcupines, and iguanas. Children delight at the site of free-roaming animals, including monkeys riding on the backs of tortoises. Other children, however, may find it frightening to be suddenly confronted by a scampering critter while strolling a nature trail. The only caged animal in the reserve is a giant python. An Information and Education Center includes a display of Arawak artifacts (422-8826).

Outdoor Sports

The eighteen-hole, par 72, 6,640-yard golf course at the **Sandy Lane Club** in St. James is open to the public and is considered the best on the island. Duffers find the views from the "signature" seventh hole to be sublime. Tee times may be easier to book through your cruise line (a little more than $100 doesn't include carts, rental clubs, caddies, or lunch) or call 452-4653.

Most of the larger hotels, including the Hilton, Marriott's Sam Lord's Castle, and Sandy Lane, offer tennis, but reservations are recommended.

Historic Attractions and Museums

About one mile south of Bridgetown on Highway 7, the **Barbados Museum** houses artifacts of military history and everyday nineteenth-century life in addition to wildlife and natural history exhibits. A Children's Gallery, along with a guidebook entitled "Yesterday's Children," helps bring to life these exhibits, many of which are hands-on. The gift shop has a good selection of adult and children's books on the West Indies, and there's a cafe for when the munchies hit (427-0201).

Other Attractions

Treat yourself and your kids to a different, very British experience—attend a cricket match. Cricket is played virtually year-round, with the domestic season running from May to December and the international matches held between January and April.

Best Eateries and Snacks

Sample Bajan-style lunch buffets where children can surely find something to please (perhaps Creole orange chicken or rice and beans?) at **Brown Sugar**, Aquatic Gap (426-7634), a popular multi-level restaurant behind the Island Inn just outside of Bridgetown. For fast, no-fuss, familiar food (including pizza, chicken nuggets, ice cream, etc.), find one of the six **Chefette Restaurants** throughout Barbados. The one at Rockley, across from Accra Beach, has a children's playground. Call 435-6709 for the locations of the other five.

Shopping

Go to Broad Street for shopping. Barbados offers tax-free shopping, which makes such purchases as jewelry and perfume good buys. For one-stop, tax-free shopping, try **Cave Shepherd** on Broad Street, with three floors of everything from fine china to perfume to leather goods to cameras to swimwear. Two restaurants are also on the premises. For local crafts—many made right before your eyes—head to **Pelican Village Handicrafts** Center on Princess Alice Highway near Cheapside Market, Bridgetown (426-1966).

ON SHORE: GRAND CAYMAN

Grand Cayman, the largest of the three Cayman Islands (the others are Cayman Brac and Little Cayman), is a popular cruise ship destination. The island offers one of the Caribbean's most vibrant living coral reef systems and is a snorkeler's and diver's delight. The famous **Seven-Mile Beach** is considered one of the Caribbean's best and is the main attraction of Grand Cayman's west coast.

The people of the Cayman Islands enjoy one of the highest standards of living in the Caribbean. At just seventy-six square miles with good highways and a flat terrain, this island is extremely do-able for cruise ship passengers. The condos, shops, and fast food restaurants around the island resemble the U.S. more than anywhere else in the Caribbean. As you drive though this small island you'll feel like you're in Florida.

Quick Facts

Currency: The Cayman Islands dollar (CI$) is on a fixed exchange rate: $1 CI is equal to $1.25 U.S. The U.S. dollar is accepted throughout the Cayman Islands.

Language: English is the official language, but it is often spoken with a distinctive brogue that harkens back to the islanders' Welsh, Scottish, and English ancestry. A number of Jamaicans are part of the workforce, so Jamaican patois are common.

Emergency Numbers: Police: 114; Ambulance: 115.

Major Towns: All ships call at George Town, the largest town on the islands.

Tourist Information: Cayman Islands Department of Tourism regional offices are located in Miami, (305) 266-2300; New York, (212) 682-5582; Houston, (713) 461-1317; Los Angeles, (213) 738-1968; Chicago, (708) 678-6446; and Toronto (416) 485-1550. Check the tourism information booths at the North Terminal dock in Grand Cayman.

Transportation: There is no cruise ship dock in the Cayman Islands, so ships anchor off shore, and passengers take tenders to the North or South Terminals in downtown George Town.

Buses: Local minibuses run along main routes in Grand Cayman.

Seven-Mile Beach on Grand Cayman. Photo courtesy of Norweigan Cruise Line.

Taxis: Taxi stands are located at both the North and South Terminals. For an island tour, taxi drivers charge $25 U.S. per hour for four people.

Car Rentals: There really isn't enough to see on the island to warrant renting a car. Driving is on the left and most rental jeeps and vans are right-hand drive, left-hand stick shift. Visitors can obtain temporary driver's licenses from the car rental agency—all the major international companies are represented—upon presenting a valid driver's license and payment of $5.

Best Bets

For ages two through seven:
The Turtle Farm; Seven-Mile Beach

For ages seven through eleven:
Turtle Farm; visit to Hell (a town on Grand Cayman)
For pre-teens and teens:
Visit to Hell; snorkeling at Sting Ray City; renting
"beach toys" from Red Sail Sports
For adults:
Stingray City

Beaches

Grand Cayman's pride, **Seven-Mile Beach** (actually 5.8 miles long), is located on the west coast, the island's most developed area, and is only three miles from the cruise passenger terminals. Taxi fare is about $4 per person each way to hotels that accommodate cruise passenger business, predominantly the **Beach Club Resort** (800-482-DIVE or 949-8100) located midway on Seven-Mile Beach. The water here is very calm.

Grand Cayman offers thirty-four dive operations, with a full range of professional dive services available, including equipment sales, rentals, and instruction for all levels. **Red Sail Sports**, located across from the Hyatt, offers a complete dive package and a full range of beach toy rentals including Waverunners, windsurfers, and sailboats. Waterskiing is also available (800-255-6425).

Stingray City, Cayman's most famous dive site, is located in the shallow depths of Grand Cayman's North Sound. More than thirty southern Atlantic stingrays swim freely with snorkelers and divers in depths of up to twelve feet. Another dive and snorkel site is Parrot's Landing, which is closest to the cruise ship terminal—just a few feet off the shore at George Town.

Nature and the Environment

The **Turtle Farm** on West Bay Road is the only one of its kind in the world. Home to thousands of turtles from tiny hatchlings to six-hundred-pound adults more than one hundred years old, the farm is dedicated to repopulating Cayman waters with the same species of green sea turtle that lived in abundance when Columbus dubbed these islands "Las Tortugas" (The Turtles). Children like this place, and guides may give them the opportunity to pet a turtle. A well-stocked gift shop offers turtle-themed souvenirs at reasonable prices (949-3893).

From here, it's just a short ride down the road to **Hell**—named for an unusual spiky rock formation that formed more than one and a half million years ago. Fences enclose this attraction. The real fun is to go to the small post office to mail postcards that are hand-canceled with the Hell postmark. Buy stamps here, but write your postcards in advance, particularly if you come on a shore excursion, because time is limited. Several souvenir shops offer T-shirts, bumper stickers, mugs, and other mementos bearing such phrases as "I've Been to Hell."

Most short excursions combine the visit to the Turtle Farm and the trip to Hell with what may seem like a disproportionately long stop at a small Tortuga rum outlet. Inside, adults sample rum punch and generous chunks of rum cake (all for sale, of course) while outside, children talk to the parakeets.

Outdoor Sports

Avid golfers enjoy the recently opened **Links at Safe-Haven**, the island's first eighteen-hole championship course, adjacent to Seven-Mile Beach. Tennis can be played at any of the hotel courts along West Bay Road. The newly refurbished Holiday Inn sports the largest number of courts.

Historic Attractions and Museums

The **Cayman Maritime and Treasure Museum**, in front of the Hyatt Hotel on West Bay Road, is quite interesting if you happen to be in this general area. School children are interested in the displays, which range from dioramas showing Caymanians from the past as well as fascinating artifacts from ship-wrecks (a professional treasure-salvaging firm owns the museum).

Other Attractions

Take a dive beneath Cayman waters aboard an **Atlantis Submarine** (949-7700). (See the Barbados listing above for a description of the experience.)

Best Eateries and Snacks

Eating in a restaurant in Grand Cayman is much like eating in a restaurant at home, and no wonder. Wherever you go, you'll see familiar names like Pizza Hut, KFC, Burger King, and Tony Roma's. Children who are a bit bored with cruise ship cuisine will be happy. For something a bit more West Indian, try the **Cook Rum** on North Church Street, George Town, where the meals come with a front porch view of the bay (949-8670). Salt beef and beans, anyone? Do try the coconut cream pie.

Shopping

The shops in George Town—all just a short walk from the passenger ship terminals—are filled with souvenirs, but a bit pricier than what you might expect, particularly if you stop in Jamaica first. Even finer items, though labeled duty-free, are not bargains. For something different, stop by the **Jewelry Factory** on Fort Street, famous for its shell, stone, and coral pieces.

ON SHORE: JAMAICA

Jamaica is a beautiful, lush country with its own special charm and much to offer. This said, Jamaica is one island that is probably better visited on a land-based vacation than a cruise. The reason? The country is so vast that a quick stop really doesn't do it justice. Moreover, many cruise passengers are startled by the aggressive vendors who pursue the cruisers as soon as they step on shore. Cruise passengers represent big dollars to Jamaicans, many of whom struggle to earn a living. Being hassled by street vendors annoys many cruise passengers, or worse yet, causes many to remain on deck while in port.

This is a pity because Jamaica is a jewel of an island. Once you get beyond the aggressive vendors, you will see that it is a country full of warm, friendly people and a wealth of wonderful things to do. To make the best of your stop here, plan to take an organized tour. If this includes shopping at stalls, be prepared for some heavy-duty sales pitches.

Quick Facts

Currency: The official rate of exchange fluctuates daily, with the rate at press time at approximately $1 U.S. equal to $30 JA. If you're going on a shore excursion, you needn't exchange money ($1 bills are happily accepted as tips and by vendors). There are currency exchanges at the docks at Montego Bay and Ocho Rios.

Emergency Numbers: Police: 119; Ambulance: 110.

Tourist Information: Jamaica Tourist Board offices are located in the following U.S. cities: Atlanta, Boston, Chicago, Dallas, Detroit, Los Angeles, Miami, New York, and Philadelphia. For the address of the one nearest you, call (800) 233-4582. The Jamaican Tourist Board maintains an office at the Ocean Village Shopping Center, less than a mile from the Ocho Rios cruise ship pier.

Language: English and patois (Jamaican Creole)

Main Towns: The capital is Kingston. Most ships dock at Ocho Rios, and, to a lesser degree, at Montego Bay sixty-seven miles away.

Transportation:

Car Rentals: Car rental agencies include internationally known companies, but it is rather time-consuming to rent a car, perhaps too much so for the short time you have here. You must be twenty-five to rent. Driving is on the left.

Taxis: Since neither Montego Bay nor Ocho Rios are within walking distance of town, it's advisable to hire a driver or tour guide if you're not taking a shore excursion. Some taxis are metered, but be sure you understand the price before you get in. Beware of taxi bargains and don't go with unregistered cabs. Chose a legitimate cab company and driver.

Buses: Buses take passengers from the cruise ship piers to shopping areas for about $6 per person round-trip.

Best Bets

For ages two through seven:
Swimming at Walter Fletcher beach

For ages seven to eleven:
Rafting on the Martha Brae; Doctor's Cave Beach

For pre-teens and teens:
Climbing Dunn's River Falls; riding at Chukka Cove

For adults:
Climbing Dunn's River Falls; golf at Runaway Bay and at Half Moon

Beaches

Montego Bay at Doctor's Cave Beach, a five-mile stretch with fine, sugary sand, is a favorite with tourists and locals alike. There will undoubtedly be crowds at this popular spot. For a small entry fee, you have access to changing rooms and bars.

Walter Fletcher Beach, on the bay near the center of town, is good for very young children because it has calm waters and offers protection from the surf when the wind is blowing. In Ocho Rios, the main beaches are **Mallard's Beach** and, the islanders' favorite, **Turtle Beach**.

Scuba, snorkeling, and windsurfing are offered through most hotels and by concessionaires on the beach near the Ramada Renaissance Jamaica Grande. The Jamaica Tourist Board can provide you with a list of licensed dive operators who are members of Jamaica Association of Dive Operators (JADO).

Nature and the Environment

Probably *the* most famous shore excursion from Ocho Rios is **Dunn's River Falls** (974-5015)—the "Niagara of the Caribbean." Here you'll find six hundred feet of mountain water that splashes over stone steps to the Caribbean. This is not for young children because climbing is involved. Most people don bathing suits and climb up the slippery steps, forming a chain of hands for the climb upward. Wear sneakers that can get wet rather than beach thongs or sandals. The Falls are less crowded in the afternoon.

For cruise lines docking in Montego Bay, the most popular excursion is rafting on the **Martha Brae River** on the island's north coast, less than an hour from port and just over an hour from Ocho Rios. Don't picture whitewater—this is a serene waterway, and the log rafts steered by standing guides generally have comfortable cushions for passengers to sit on. Rafts accommodate two adults or two adults and one small child. If you wear a bathing suit, take the plunge at the half-way point. The Rafters Village, capital of the parish of Trelawny, is one of the island's best-preserved old Georgian towns.

Outdoor Sports

Your best bet is to arrange golf through your ship's shore excursion director. In Ocho Rios, the best courses are at **Runaway Bay** and **Upton**, while Montego

Bay's best include **Half Moon**, **Rose Hall**, **Eden**, and **Tryall**. Tennis is available at most resort hotels, including **Sandals Ocho Rios**, **Ramada Renaissance**, and **Ciboney**.

Historic Attractions and Museums

A tour of a former plantation house provides a glimpse into the island's past. **Rose Hall** (953-2323) is just a short ride from Montego Bay, about seven miles east of the airport. This is a popular spot, but beware—the "history" is a lot of legend and faux facts. The famous owner of the Great House, Annie Potter, supposedly murdered three husbands and her lover on the premises. Johnny Cash (who owns a vacation home nearby) wrote a song about her, and there have been two novels on the subject. The sea view from the Great House is nice, but many children and adults are easily bored here. All in all, you might want to skip this tour.

Other Attractions

The **Chukka Cove Equestrian Center** (972-2506) offers several scenic horseback trails as well as polo and dressage lessons. This facility enjoys an excellent reputation throughout the Caribbean.

Best Eateries and Snacks

Do try Jamaica's savory jerk pork and jerk chicken, meats barbecued over coals and pimiento wood for hours. Served throughout the island, you can find the meats ready for lunch at about noon at the informal **Pork Pit** (952-1046), adjacent to the Fantasy Resort in Montego Bay. In Ocho Rios, try the Jamaican-Italian cuisine at **Evita's** where "Rasta Pasta" is the meal of choice. This eatery sits hillside above the cruise ship piers (974-2333).

Shopping

Wood carvings, Jamaican rum, and Blue Mountain coffee (not cheap, but cheaper than in the U.S.) are good gifts to tote home. Avoid the craft stalls if you can't stand high pressure—very high pressure—sales tactics. You're better off at **Ocho Rios' Island Plaza**, **Coconut Grove**, **Mo' Bay's St. James Place Shopping Center**, or **Overton Place**.

ON SHORE: PUERTO RICO

Surrounded by the Atlantic Ocean to the north and the Caribbean to the south, Puerto Rico, 110 by 35 miles in size, is the farthest east of the four major islands that form the Greater Antilles. Of all Caribbean cities, San Juan, a popular cruise destination, is the best-preserved Spanish colonial destination.

Just a short stroll away from the pier, **Old San Juan** offers seven blocks of restored sixteenth-century buildings, open air cafes, art galleries, bookstores, historic sites, and museums, all on cobblestone streets. Not too far away, the **Condado** and **Isla Verde** areas sport glamorous hotels, beaches, and plenty of watersports.

If your ship homeports in San Juan, you may find yourself with time to explore much of the city on your own (a number of cruise lines also offer post-cruise city tours).

Quick Facts

Currency: Puerto Rico is a Commonwealth of the United States, and the U.S. dollar is legal tender. Credit cards are widely accepted, postal rates are the same as in the U.S. and U.S. postal stamps are used.

Emergency Numbers: Police: 343-2020 or 911; Ambulance: 754-2222 (San Juan); 754-2550 (island).

Tourist Information: The government-sponsored Puerto Rico Tourism Company has maps and brochures, including "Que Pasa," an official guide to Puerto Rico. Write to: P.O. Box 4435, Old San Juan Station, San Juan, Puerto Rico 00902-4435; or call (809) 722-1093. In the U.S., the Puerto Rico Tourism Company has representatives in California, Colorado, Florida, Georgia, Illinois, Massachusetts, Michigan, Missouri, New York, Pennsylvania, Texas, Virginia, and Washington, D.C. Call (800) 223-6530 for more information. There are several Puerto Rico Tourism Company information centers located in San Juan, including one in Old San Juan, near Pier One, La Cassita; (722-1709).

Language: Spanish and English are both official languages, especially in San Juan. Many people speak English because it is taught from kindergarten to high school.

Main Towns: San Juan is the island's foremost cruise destination.

Telephone Tips: The San Juan metropolitan area commercial telephone directory has an English-language tourism section, identified by blue pages.

Transportation:

Buses: AMA (Metropolitan Bus Authority) buses have stops marked by magenta, orange, and white signs that read "Parada." Yellow and white lines run in special lanes against the traffic. Fares at press time were twenty-five cents. Visitors frequently use the terminals in Old San Juan, within the Covadonga Parking Lot, where the A7 and M7 buses leave for the Condado and Isla Verde hotel sectors. For more information, call 250-6064.

Trolleys: Free, open-air trolleys transport you and your family from the docks through the narrow streets of nearby Old San Juan. These free trolleys cover much the same ground as paid shore tours.

Car Rentals: All major U.S. rental agencies are represented on the island, and U.S. driver's licenses are valid. Be aware that many service stations don't take credit cards. Get a good map and note that distances are measured in kilometers while speed limits are posted in miles per hour. Driving is on the right side.

Public Cars: "Publicos" are blue-and-white or blue-and-red public cars that transport passengers island-wide for reasonable, fixed rates. Cars usually operate during the day and from the town plaza. While cheap, the cars are often crowded and uncomfortable.

Taxis: Taxis are metered ($1 initial charge, ten cents for each additional $\frac{1}{13}$ mile, and ten cents per each forty-five seconds' waiting time). Taxis may also be rented unmetered for a rate of about $20 per hour. Under the new Tourism Tax Program, tourism taxis that are painted white and bear the program logo charge set rates to tourism zones. Examples include: Zone 6, Piers to Condado, $10; Zone 7, Piers to Isla Verda, $16.

Best Bets

For ages two through seven:
Museo del Nino; Luquillo Beach

For ages seven to eleven:
The fort of El Morro and/or San Cristofal; El Yunque
National Forest; Condado Lagoon promenade

For teens and adults:
Horseback riding on the beach or in rain forest
foothills; resort golf and tennis

Beaches

Many good swimming beaches are scattered along the
coast. All of Puerto Rico's beaches are open to the public by law (except for the Caribe Hilton's artificial
beach). Government-run beaches, or *balnearios*, have
dressing rooms, lifeguards, parking, and sometimes
playgrounds. They're open Tuesday through Sunday,
or daily during the summer months, and are free
except for a nominal parking charge. Note that the
waters along the northwest coast are rougher than the
east, south, and west coast Caribbean. You might take
your teens to watch (just watch) the surfers who flock
to the unprotected beaches and large waves off the
island's northeast corner. Winter is the best season
for surfing.

To find miles of beaches, your best bet may be to take
a Zone 7 taxi or the A7 or M7 bus (see above) to the
Condado Plaza-Isla Verde hotel sector. The best overall choice for a swimming beach for families is **Isla
Verde**, a white sandy beach rimmed by several high-
rise resort hotels. There are picnic tables as well as
reasonably good snorkeling and equipment rentals
close by.

If you're going to **El Yunque** rain forest (see below)
northeast of San Juan, add a stop at the tranquil
Luquillo Beach where you'll find soft, white sand
shaded by groves of coconut palms alongside crystal-

blue, calm Caribbean waters. For lunch or a snack, bring some food from the ship or buy snacks from local vendors. For more information on Luquillo and other balnearios, call the Department of Recreation and Sports, 722-1551 or 724-2500, ext. 341.

Just about all of the resort hotels on the Condado and Isla Verde hotel strips rent windsurfers, paddleboats, and Sunfish and can make arrangements for scuba diving and sailing. The **Condado Lagoon** promenade, set between San Juan Bay and the Atlantic Ocean, is a popular site for watersports rentals as well as an attractively landscaped area that attracts walkers, joggers, and birdwatchers.

If you prefer the more gentle Caribbean waters, **Coral Head Divers**, (800) 635-4529 or 850-7208 locally, is one of a number of companies approved by the Puerto Rico Water Sport Federation, which sets standards and guidelines for companies specializing in scuba diving, snorkeling, sailing, deep-sea fishing, windsurfing, and other aquatic activities. Coral Head Divers offers scuba diving instruction for ages twelve and up as well as snorkeling and boat dives (child-size equipment can be rented). The company is located at the Palmas del Mar Resort in Humacao, about forty-five miles from San Juan on the eastern Caribbean coast.

TIP: Many ships offer excursions in which passengers are driven to a beach with changing rooms and— sometimes at an extra charge—given deck chairs. A buffet lunch may also be included. But with beach excursion prices ranging from $15 to $30 per person, you may want to consider venturing off on your own.

Sony Beach. Photo by Bob Krist for the Puerto Rico Tourism Company.

Nature and the Environment

El Yunque, thirty-five miles east of San Juan, (an easy forty-five-minute drive on Route 3 connecting with Route 191) is the only tropical rain forest in the United States National Park System. Teddy Roosevelt claimed it for the U.S. in 1903.

All cruise ships offer shore excursions here, but in spring 1995 the trips were temporarily suspended while the road to the national forest was being repaired.

One of Puerto Rico's most popular attractions is the twenty-eight-thousand-acre El Yunque—named by the Spanish for its anvil-shaped peak. El Yunque receives more than one hundred billion gallons of annual rainfall, resulting in a paradise of waterfalls, wild orchids, giant ferns, towering tabonuco trees, and sierra palms. Encompassing four distinct forest types, El Yunque is home to 240 species of tropical trees, flowers, and wildlife.

Children are fascinated by the sights and sounds of El Yunque. For example, more than twenty kinds of orchids share this diverse habitat with millions of tiny tree frogs whose distinctive cry of "coqui" has given them their name. Colorful tropical birds, including the Puerto Rican parrot that was once nearly extinct, dazzle all ages.

Dozens of walking and hiking trails traverse El Yunque, so you'll need to pick up information and maps at the Sierra Palm Visitor Center (Route 191, km 11.6). Trails are graded by difficulty. If time permits, combine this trip with an afternoon at Luquillo Beach (see above for description).

As this is being written, a new tropical forest center, El Portal del Yunque, is being built. Among other functions, this center will provide facilities for an interpretive visitor center. For more information on El Yunque, call (800) 223-6530.

Outdoor Sports

The island's palm-lined beaches are the perfect setting for horseback riding. Riding instruction and/or trail riding can be arranged through the **Palmas del Mar Equestrian Center** in Humacao, about forty-five miles east of San Juan (852-6000). Beach and rain forest foothill trail riding is available from Hacienda Carabali, Luquillo (889-5820 or 889-4954).

Advance reservations are necessary; inquire about age limits.

Tennis courts are available for rental to the general public at most major resort hotels including the **Hyatt Regency Cerromar Beach** and **Hyatt Dorado**, which together have twenty courts as well as four eighteen-hole golf courses that are open to the public. Greens fees and prices of equipment rentals vary with the season. Call Hyatt International at (800) 233-1234 for more information, or locally, call 796-1234 (Dorado) and 796-8915 (Cerromar).

Historic Attractions and Museums

If your children are "all beached out," or the weather isn't on your side, Puerto Rico sports a variety of interesting museums and historic sites with instant kid appeal. Your best bet is to walk directly from the pier to **Old San Juan**, where it's been said there are more museums per square foot than anywhere else on earth. The **Paseo de La Princesa**, a broad nineteenth-century palm-shaded esplanade, sweeps from the piers with a renewed beauty after a two-year, $2.8 million restoration.

The narrow, congested cobblestoned streets combined with Old San Juan's hilltop location can make walking, especially uphill, a chore for the very young and very old. However, feel free to climb on and off the free trolleys that traverse the old city's streets.

School-age children and older kids enjoy roaming **El Morro**, the four-hundred-year-old fort that rises high above the sea and once protected the strategic port from English, French, and Dutch attack. Located on a rocky promontory on the western tip of Old San Juan about a ten-minute walk from Plaza de Armas

*Folk dancers in Puerto Rico. Photo by Bob Krist for the
Puerto Rico Tourism Company.*

and the main shopping streets of the old city, the
fort features stunning vistas and a small museum.
Self-guided tour maps lead you through the tunnels,
dungeons, and turrets of the fort. (Be prepared to
climb stairs.)

Call 729-6960 for information and hours for El
Morro as well as for another fort that is more accessible to the cruise ship terminal. **San Cristobal** is a
seventeenth-century fortress that guarded the city
from land attacks. San Cristobal is a five-minute walk
north of the Covadonga Bus Station and parking lot.

San Cristobal towers at the top of the hill overlooking Plaza Colon, just west of the capitol building.
Inside one vault is a restored eighteenth-century

Spanish troop quarter. Pay special attention to the Devil's Sentry Box, an ancient, windswept watchtower from which several guards were said to have vanished into thin air. Admission is free to both forts and audio tours can also be rented for a small fee. Video presentations in English start every hour on the half hour.

From El Morro, it's only a short walk to **Casa Blanca**, the city's first fortress and the home of the family of Ponce de Leon, the great conquistador, colonizer, and first governor of Puerto Rico who, alas, never lived in his family's fortress home. In 1521, while Casa Blanca was being built, de Leon was in Florida where he was fatally felled by a poison-tipped arrow. (So much for his search for the fountain of youth.)

Casa Blanca, rebuilt in 1523 after a fire, is the oldest continuously occupied residence in the Western Hemisphere. The home sheltered San Juan citizens from Carib Indian attacks for several decades in the sixteenth century. While no longer a residence, the white house contains a museum whose artifacts offer a glimpse into sixteenth- and seventeenth-century family life. The **Taino Indian Ethno-Historic Museum** recreates the life and culture of Puerto Rico's first inhabitants. A highlight is the miniature model of an Indian village, or yucayeque. Open daily Wednesday through Sunday; (809) 724-4102.

Very young children often prefer another Old San Juan Museum: the **Museo del Niño**. If small enough, kids can enter by crawling through the legs of a large wooden figure of a child. Inside the museum, they'll find a village of playhouses and other exhibits. Open Tuesday to Thursday and on weekends (722-3791).

> **TIP:** Before you go on the tour of Old San Juan, get a
> walking tour map from the tourist information booth
> at Pier One (see above for details). Be sure to wear
> comfortable shoes.

Other Attractions

Chances are the performances will be in Spanish, but
your young ones might enjoy a Sunday visit to Old San
Juan's **Teatro La Princesa** on Paseo de la Princesa
from 4 to 5 P.M. when clowns, magicians, and pup-
peteers delight the island's youngsters. Also, **Family
Bicycling** organizes bike trips around the island; call
in advance, 751-4949.

Best Eateries and Snacks

If your kids are already experiencing fast food with-
drawal after a few days at sea, welcome to San Juan
where you'll find **Burger Kings** galore (including in
Old San Juan on San Francisco Street and several in
the Isla Verda-Condado hotel/beach areas). There's
also a sizable list of familiar chains, including **Pizzeria Uno**, in San Juan's Centro Europa and the **Hard
Rock Cafe** in Old San Juan (724-ROCK), which is
always fun with school-age and older kids, and the food
is good, too.

Sample a fritter—the favorite finger food of the
island—at a streetside stand. *Tostones* (fried green
plantains), the most famous fritter food, are also used
as a side dish with rice and beans. *Kioskos* all around

San Juan and the countryside also sell popular snacks, such as *empanadas* (flattened sandwiches) and *picadillas* (meat patties). For dessert, kids might like to try either the national dessert—flan—a condensed milk and vanilla custard concoction or *arroz con dulce*, a rice pudding cooked with condensed coconut milk, ginger, and raisins.

As you stroll along the Paseo de la Princesa, keep an eye out for a gazebo that serves light seafood dishes and salads. Outdoor tables with umbrellas and shade trees allow parents to mind the kids while they play at the nearby playground. Food carts with gaily colored awnings can also be found along the Paseo.

If you're at the beach in the Condado area, pop inside the lobby at the Condado Beach Hotel to the **Café del Arte**. Housed in a working artist's atelier, this facility has indoor and outdoor seating, and light snacks or full meal options (open twenty-four hours).

Shopping

Puerto Rico is not a free port, so the buys on big-ticket items may not equal those on other islands. Popular locally made souvenirs include carnival masks, hand-rolled cigars, handmade lace, *guayaberas* (casual men's shirts), and small, hand-carved figures of religious scenes or saints.

You'll find gift shops galore in Old San Juan, particularly on San Francisco, Cristo, and La Fortaleza streets. For more distinctive native crafts, try **Puerto Rican Arts and Crafts** at 204 Calle de la Fortaleza, Old San Juan (725-5596). Island craft markets take place on weekends at La Casita Information Center and along Paseo de la Princesa in Old San Juan.

Maria's, 204 Cristo Street, is known for a great selection of reasonably priced T-shirts, starting at size "one month." While you're there, treat the kids to a yummy frozen drink. A wide variety of choices range from chocolate frosts to mixed fruit frappes.

ON SHORE: ST. THOMAS

As the Caribbean's number one cruise ship destination, St. Thomas (thirty-three square miles in size) has much to offer families. Beautiful beaches with gentle, warm waters, sand perfect for building castles, and a reef system that offers good snorkeling are some of the reasons for the island's popularity. And don't forget the deals on shopping. That's why Charlotte Amalie, a main shopping area, is so crowded when cruise ships call. For many, the crowds in Charlotte Amalie are too reminiscent of home, especially during the pre-Christmas rush. If you'd rather avoid the crowds, forget downtown and head for the beaches or the less-populated neighboring island, St. John. (At press time St. Thomas and St. John were still recovering and rebuilding after being hit by hurricanes.)

Quick Facts

Currency: Because the Virgin Islands are part of the U.S., the currency is the U.S. dollar.
Emergency Numbers: Police: 915; Ambulance: 922.
Tourist Information: The United States Virgin Islands (U.S.V.I.) has tourism offices in Atlanta, (404) 688-0906; Chicago, (312) 670-8784; Los Angeles, (213) 739-0138; Miami, (305) 442-7200; New York,

(212) 332-2222; and Washington, D.C., (202) 293-3707. For more information, you can also call (800) USVI-INFO. The Cruise Ship Activities office located on the West Indian Company dock is an information center for cruise passengers.

Language: English is spoken with a local lilt referred to as "calypso."

Main Towns: Charlotte Amalie is the capital of St. Thomas and the number one Caribbean cruise ship destination.

Transportation: Cruise ships dock in Charlotte Amalie, either along Havensight—a good shopping mall—close to downtown or at the newer dock at the old sub base about ten minutes from town. If it's a busy cruise day, your ship may anchor off shore and you'll take a tender in.

Buses: There is bus service throughout Charlotte Amalie but, considering the traffic and congestion, you're better off on foot.

Car Rentals: No special license is required; driving is on the left. Keep in mind that getting out of town and back in again takes a good deal of time because of heavy traffic. Therefore, if here for only one day, renting a car isn't generally recommended.

Taxis: If you're not taking a shore excursion and want to see more than the island, hire a taxi at the cruise ship terminal. Standard rates are set based on destination, not mileage. Cars or vans that don't have "TP" on their license plates are not licensed taxi cabs. Example of taxi fares from Charlotte Amalie to Sapphire Beach: $8.50 first person plus $5.50 for every additional person.

Ferries: The lovely island of St. John is accessible by a forty-five-minute motor launch ride across Pilgrim Bay from Charlotte Amalie Harbor downtown. For those prone to seasickness, shorten the water ride by taking the ferry at Red Hook, St. Thomas, to Cruz Bay. This ferry ride is only about twenty minutes. When you reach Cruz Bay, a motorized surrey makes the short ride to Trunk Bay (see beaches below). Make sure you have made arrangements for the surrey to return to take you back to the ferry. Ferries are also available from Charlotte Amalie to Tortola, British Virgin Islands (forty-five minutes to the west end; ninety minutes to Road Town; both are about $35 round-trip).

Note: If you have signed up for a cruise ship shore excursion to St. John, you'll either be tendered into St. John before the ship docks in St. Thomas, or you'll take a bus ride to the St. John ferry.

Best Bets

For ages two through seven:
Magens Bay; Coral World

For ages seven through eleven:
Coral World; snorkeling at Trunk Bay or Cow and
  Calf Rocks; swimming at Magens Bay

For pre-teens and teens:
Snorkeling at Trunk Bay; lunch at Hard Rock Cafe;
  parasailing

For adults:
Golf at Mahogany Run

Beaches

All beaches in the U.S. Virgin Islands are public, although sometimes you have to gain access by walking through a resort.

St. Thomas' heart-shaped mile-long **Magens Bay** is considered by National Geographic as one of the three most beautiful beaches in the world. This splendid white sand beach has gradual water access, making it great for children. There are lifeguards, changing rooms, rest rooms, snorkeling equipment rentals, and eateries. Palm trees provide shade from the Caribbean sun. An entry fee is charged and you can rent paddle boats, windsurfers, and small sailboats.

On the north shore near Coral World, **Coki Beach** is a popular (and often crowded) spot for snorkeling thanks to the abundance of reef fish. Rentals and instruction are available. Coki Beach Dive Club specializes in beginning scuba diver instruction (775-422).

The beautiful **Sapphire Beach**, one of the island's best, is splendid for swimming and also for snorkeling, with a large reef teaming with colorful fish. Go to the far end of the beach that fronts Sapphire Beach Resort to take the plunge (the beach is open to the public, and you'll find equipment rentals at Dive In, 775-6100, ext. 2144). Watch out for rocks and shells in the sand when you're entering the water.

With its clear, warm waters, the U.S.V.I. sports some of the best snorkeling spots in the Caribbean and an incredible diversity of marine life. The island's best diving and snorkeling can be had at **Cow and Calf Rocks**, located off the southeast end about forty-five minutes by boat from Charlotte Amalie. A coral tunnel network boasts reefs, dramatic caves, archways, and cliff overhangs. Look for nurse sharks, horse-eye jacks, and glassy sweepers.

A number of cruise lines offer catamaran tours from Charlotte Amalie Harbor to St. John (you can also arrange one yourself at the pier or take a ferry). St. John's well-known **Trunk Bay** is still a good spot—despite the fact that fish numbers have decreased and some coral has been lost—especially for young snorkelers new to the sport. Underwater plaques identify coral species and a 225-yard marked snorkeling trail is easy to follow. Families will be glad to find lockers, changing rooms, and a snack bar. Bring your own equipment or rent snorkels, masks, and fins for a small fee. A credit card is needed to ensure a refundable deposit.

Another feature at Trunk Bay is Snuba, a shallow-water dive system requiring no certification and no heavy, restrictive gear or time-consuming training. Your air source is contained in a flotation raft that follows you while you explore underwater. A fifteen-minute beach orientation is followed by a forty-five-minute dive in fifteen to twenty feet of water directly off the beach. (Age and health restrictions may apply; call 693-8063 for more information if you're arranging this on your own.)

Not far from Trunk Bay is **Cinnamon Bay**, a lovely, small beach with changing rooms, showers, and a good outlying coral reef where a number of species can be observed by snorkelers.

Fat Boys Water Toys, with locations in St. Thomas and St. John, offers parasailing for all ages, Waverunners, electric floating lounges for two, and Big Banana speed boats (777-3055). Besides kayaking and windsurfing rentals, many watersports companies also offer windsurfing lessons. Most major hotels have watersports concessions where you can rent equipment by the hour. Ocean Fantasies (774-5223) offers basic and kids' windsurfing lessons and rentals.

Nature and the Environment

A trip to **Coral World** (775-1555) is a great way for a family to spend the day. Containing one of the largest underwater observatories in the world, Coral World offers a fascinating 360-degree view of sharks, eels, and other ocean coral life twenty feet under the sea. There's an eighty-thousand-gallon aquarium, the largest natural reef exhibit in the world, and also a marine garden aquarium, touch pools, a predator tank, and tropical birds. You'll find restaurants, shops, lockers, and showers for the adjacent Coki Beach. Be ready for crowds because Coral World is popular.

From Coral World, you can take the **Sea Explorer** semi-submarine to peruse the waters surrounding Turtle Rock. The vessel was developed in Australia for use on the Great Barrier Reef. Instead of submerging, you descend into the hull and sit five feet below the surface of the water to explore the sea life through large windows. This attraction is less expensive than the Atlantis Submarine (see below) at $29 for adults and $19 for ages two through twelve for a one-hour tour. You also get to watch divers feed hundreds of fish right in front of the vessel's windows.

For a dry view of the wonders beneath the sea, the **Atlantis Submarine** takes passengers on a one-hour voyage descending to depths of ninety feet. Guides

---

TIP: Coral World is included on all cruise ships' shore excursion lists for about $30 per person, which also includes a ride along Skyline Drive (with a view of Magens Bay). Investigate whether it's cheaper and easier to go on your own.

identify marine life, and divers swim with the fish. The tour leaves from Havensight Mall. (See Barbados listing above for more details about Atlantis tours.) Call (800) 253-0493 or, for local information, 776-5650.

Outdoor Sports

The eighteen-hole Fazio-designed golf course at **Mahogany Run** stretches 6,525 yards and plays to a par seventy, with the thirteenth and fourteenth greens along dramatic cliffs overlooking the Atlantic. Tee times can be arranged via your cruise ship tour director or by calling 253-7103.

Resorts that welcome cruise passengers for tennis include **Bolongo Bay**, **Frenchman's Reef**, **Sapphire Beach** (four courts each), and **Stouffer's Beach Resort** (six courts).

Historic Attractions and Museums

Many of the island's historical attractions are in town within walking distance of each other and the piers. **Fort Christian**, built in the 1660s, was the center of the first Danish settlement and is the oldest standing structure on St. Thomas. Amazingly, it withstood the fires and hurricanes that devastated much of the town in the eighteenth and nineteenth centuries. Until recently, the building housed the town jail, but now houses a museum. Call 776-4566 for information.

If you and your older children have the energy, walk up **Ninety-nine Steps** (actually, there are slightly more if you count them) leading from Government Hill to Lille Tarne Gade, for a great photo opportunity and view. When you reach the top, go right to **Blackbeard's Castle**, one of the oldest structures on the island. Pirates are said to have roamed in the area of this five-story watchtower that was built in 1679 and now houses a hotel and restaurant.

Other Attractions

If you visit St. Thomas in February, March, or April, when humpback whale cows and calves splash and spout about the islands, you'll be able to find a boat to take you out to spot them.

A $35 million project called **Carifest**, the first Caribbean cultural theme park, is scheduled to open in fall 1997 on more than nine acres of waterfront property within walking distance from the major cruise ship docks. The site will feature attractions, exhibits, and events that highlight the area's culture.

Best Eateries and Snacks

Picky eaters may resist some local favorites, although one stubborn young lady who refused such specialties as curried chicken and saltfish and fungi (cornmeal) found that she actually liked conch fritters and adored johnnycakes. For some of the best local delights, head to **Eunice's Terrace** at Smith Bay where fussy eaters enjoy peas and rice while mom and dad dig into the more exotic fare (777-3975). Pre-teens may want to skip this for lunch at the **Hard Rock Cafe** on the waterfront in Charlotte Amalie (777-5555). Downtown has a zillion choices for a quick, tasty lunch, including **Cafe Amici**, **Coconuts**, **Garden Restaurant**, and **Glady's Cafe**.

In St. John, try **Luscious Licks** across from the National Park Services for healthy vegetarian food, including soup, sandwiches, veggie burgers, and salads (693-8400).

Shopping

Shoppers will be in heaven in downtown Charlotte Amalie. You can take back $1,200 worth of merchandise to the U.S. duty-free. The main street and adjoining alleyways offer a plethora of shops where jewelry, watches, perfume, and liquor can be purchased. Noted shops include **Little Switzerland**, the leading Caribbean watch seller.

For the kids' sake, stop by **Land of Oz** in Royal Dane Mall where the selection includes Steiff, Brio, and nesting dolls (776-7888) or the **Mini Mouse House** at 3A Trompeter Gade, with animated animal, porcelain, and island dolls; kids' T-shirts; toys; and locally made gifts (776-4242). Beautiful resort and swimwear in colorful, all-cotton batik—from infant to adult sizes—can be found on the waterfront at **Java Wraps** (774-2280).

4

✺❊✺❊✺❊✺❊✺❊✺❊✺❊✺

Bermuda

Bermuda—pretty, safe, predictable, and very polite—feels like a designer version of a Caribbean island. The cottages are painted lilac, lemon, mauve, or lime, and the sands are pale pink. With clean streets, glorious beaches, no unemployment or hassling street merchants, Bermuda offers a nearby getaway (for those on the East Coast) with a touch of British panache.

Bermuda works hard at preserving this picture-book, pretty quality. Outdoor advertising, neon signs, and rental cars are banned. Lobster potting and net fishing are not allowed inside the reef that surrounds the island. In addition, no more than four cruise ships are allowed within Bermuda's harbors at any one time. April through October is Bermuda's high season and also the island's cruise season. The island weather is perfect for golf, scuba diving, snorkeling, and of course, swimming.

THE LINES

Several cruise lines sail to Bermuda in season, among them, Celebrity Cruises, Norwegian Cruise Line, Cunard, and Royal Caribbean Cruise Line.

Celebrity Cruises

- *Meridian*: seven-night cruise to St. George's from Ft. Lauderdale beginning April 1996, and from New York, June through September.
- *Zenith*: seven-night cruises to Hamilton and St. George's from New York; April through October.

Cunard Crown Cruise Lines

- *Queen Elizabeth II*: five-, eight-, and nine-day cruises departing directly from New York or with stops in either Ft. Lauderdale or Port Canaveral and Charleston; April, May, August, October, and November.
- *Sagafjord*: eleven-day cruises from Ft. Lauderdale with stops in Savannah, Charleston, St. George's, Hamilton, and Eleuthera; May.
- *Vistafjord*: fourteen-day cruises departing from Ft. Lauderdale with stops in San Juan, St. Thomas, St. Kitts, Pointe-a-Pitre, Hamilton, and St. George's; April.

Norwegian Cruise Lines

- *Dreamward*: seven-day cruises departing from New York with stops in St. George's and Hamilton; April to October.

Royal Caribbean Cruise Line

- *Song of America*: seven-day cruises departing from New York with stops in St. George's and Hamilton; April to October.

Best Bets

Best cruise ships for families with children under two:
During the day on the *QE II*, nannies take care of infants six weeks of age and older in the nursery.

Bermuda shorts are always in fashion. Photo courtesy of Bermuda Department of Tourism.

Best cruise ships for families with children two through six:

In summer (June through Labor Day), NCL's *Dream-ward* offers a program for ages three to five on the mornings of sea days. RCCL's *Song of America* has a year-round program that includes ages five and six.

Best cruise ships for families with children seven through eleven:

RCCL's *Song of America* and NCL's *Dreamward* offer extensive daylong programs for this age group.

Best cruise ships for families with pre-teens and teens:

RCCL's *Song of America* and Celebrity's *Meridian* and *Horizon* offer teen centers and teen programs.

THE SHIPS

Celebrity Cruises

Meridian: entered service in 1967; refurbished in 1990; 30,440 tons; 1,106-passenger capacity

Some experts call the *Meridian*'s layout the most child-friendly because most public rooms are near each other, making this the easiest of Celebrity's ships to negotiate. But because other ships aren't all that difficult to get around and they offer more modern conveniences, your family might prefer one of Celebrity's newer ships.

Age, however, has some bonuses. Experts rate this ship as exceptionally stable and sturdy and there is ample deck space, both covered and open to the sun. The *Meridian* started life in 1967 as the *Galileo* and underwent a $55 million renovation by Celebrity in 1990. This is the only one of Celebrity's ships that was not specifically built for the line. In addition to an outdoor pool, the *Meridian* also has a children's pool and a playroom, which is supervised form 9 A.M. to 5 P.M. A video game room draws pre-teens and teens. The health club is smaller than on other Celebrity ships.

The *Meridian* has three- and four-berth cabins, several connecting cabins, and two suites. Cabins do not have televisions. Two cabins are wheelchair accessible.

Zenith: entered service in 1992; 47,255 tons; 1,374-passenger capacity. (In late 1996, she will be taking *Horizon*'s 1995 Bermuda route.)

The *Zenith*, built two years after the *Horizon*, is the *Horizon*'s sister ship. Like the *Horizon*, this ship cuts a sleek profile, and the ample use of glass adds sunlight and a sense of spaciousness. The fitness center and some of the lounges on the *Zenith* are larger than those on the *Horizon*.

The *Zenith* also features a playroom that is supervised from 9 A.M. to 5 P.M. and a kiddie pool, plus two additional pools. Most seats in the showroom have good views. The wood-paneled library offers a comfortable place for reading.

On the *Zenith*, the cabins, at 185 square feet, are roomy and feature adequate storage space. Room service is available. The *Zenith* has three- and four-berth cabins, several connecting cabins, and several suites. All cabins have air-conditioning and television.

Norwegian Cruise Line

Dreamward: entered service in 1992; 41,000 tons; 1,242-passenger capacity

Like the *Windward*, the *Dreamward* was designed to present cruisers with an alternative to mega-liners— a midsize ship with modern comforts. To create a greater sense of intimacy than is possible on huge essels, the *Dreamward* employs four smaller dining rooms instead of one or two big ones. Passengers can sample the different dining rooms for breakfast and lunch because only dinner has assigned seating. Sports fans also appreciate the Sports Bar and Grill, an informal eatery with a wall of television monitors that are tuned to live ESPN broadcasts and baseball and football games.

The terraced decks and ample use of glass throughout the ship allow for natural light to give the ship a spacious feel. There is also a dedicated children's center.

On both the *Dreamward* and the *Windward*, 85 percent of the cabins are outside cabins, an unusually high rate. Cabin size is adequate at 160 square feet. For family groups, thirty-nine of the suites adjoin to create additional space. There are also a substantial number of four-berth cabins. Six cabins accommodate wheelchairs and twenty-eight accommodate the hearing impaired.

Cunard

Queen Elizabeth II: entered service in 1969; refurbished in 1994; 70,327 tons; 1,810-passenger capacity

The *Queen Elizabeth II* is the grande dame of transatlantic luxury cruise liners, providing a history of exemplary service and elegance. It is the only ship that continues to offer regular transatlantic service between New York and England. Among the public lounges added in the recent refurbishment was the Golden Lion, the *QE II*'s version of a traditional English pub. Amid burgundy leather and coats of arms, a variety of beers and other alcoholic beverages are served. For socializing, there's a karaoke system and a piano for sing-alongs (a bit hard to imagine). With its many lounges, the ship offers a variety of evening entertainment from the big show to cabaret fare, concerts, lectures, and dancing. There is also a large computer center.

Even infants are welcomed on board. Conveniently, the *QE II* offers a nursery for children up to age seven that is open 8 A.M. to 12:30 P.M., and 1:30 to 6 P.M. Arrangements need to be made with the nursery for child care after 6 P.M.

Club 2000 is a designated play area for ages seven and up. It includes a video game room, board games, and arts and crafts, and shows a Disney or Warner Brothers movie every afternoon. Club 2000 is open twenty-four hours a day, but is supervised only from 8 A.M. to noon and from 2 to 6 P.M. It might be a good idea to stay in the playroom with your child past 6 P.M.

A youth counselor in Club 2000 organizes activities intermittently throughout the day. These activities take place in and out of the playroom. Activities often run from 9:30 A.M. to noon, 2 to 4 P.M., and 8 P.M. to midnight. Some parents find the combination of organized activities and a well-stocked club room to be fine for their independent children as well as for those who'd rather stay with their families much of the time. Other parents prefer a few more counselors and more organized activities for children grouped closer together in age.

Another holdover of a bygone era: cruisers are assigned to a specific dining room based on the class of their cabin. In descending order, the dining rooms are: the Queen's Grill with its celebrated cuisine; the Princess Grill and Britannia, first-rate dining experiences; the Caronia, a good dining experience; and the Mauretania, the large dining room with two seatings.

Counselors also schedule an early supervised dinner with a kids' menu at 5:30 P.M.

Suites and cabins accommodate three and four passengers. Cabins were updated in 1994. Four cabins are wheelchair accessible.

Sagafjord: entered service in 1965; refurbished in 1983; 25,147 tons; 589-passenger capacity

Like Cunard's *QE II* and *Vistafjord*, the *Sagafjord* was rated by the World Ocean and Cruise Liner Society as an Ultra Deluxe cruise ship. For a ship description, refer to chapter eight.

Vistafjord: entered service in 1973; refurbished in 1994; 24,492 tons; 677-passenger capacity

The *Vistafjord* is the sister ship to the *Sagafjord*. The 1994 $15 million update added new public rooms, more suites, upgraded cabins, and a CD-ROM library research center. Other "techie" touches: an interactive scan map located near the purser's office, a self-operated business center, a beeper that enables you to call stewards from your cabin, and a 911 button for emergencies. Other updates include new lighting, stage, and seating for the theater, new carpeting for the ballroom, and a video library with more than four hundred titles.

Also new is the forty-seat Italian restaurant Tivoli. Located on the upper level of Club Viking, this restaurant offers an intimate, fine dining experience by reservation only. An ice cream parlor has been added for everyday treats.

Cabins are now equipped with telephones, safes, refrigerators, hair dryers, minibars, and VCRs. From their cabins, passengers can beep stewards and stewardesses, dial an automatic wake-up call, and press a 911 emergency button. The recent refurbishment also adds two duplex penthouses and eleven suites with balconies and ocean views. Private Jacuzzis and gyms are available in some accommodations. All staterooms are equipped with full baths, and many feature tubs. Third- and fourth-passenger cabins are available. There are no cabins accessible to conventional wheelchairs.

Royal Caribbean Cruise Line

Song of America: entered service 1982; refurbished 1991; 37,584 tons; 1,402-passenger capacity

Song of America has won the Ship of the Year award three times by World Ocean and Cruise Liner Society. Experienced cruisers especially like this ship, and families like it for its year-round children's programs.

Song of America sports RCCL's trademark Viking Crown Lounge, which is noted for panoramic views, but there are several additional spacious lounges and a casino as well. Passengers can work out in the fitness center or swim in the two pools. The Guys and Dolls lounge, a disco with special lighting and a background of video screens, attracts dancers, and the Madame Butterfly Dining Room has floor-to-ceiling windows to capture the views.

All cabins have telephones, radios, televisions, and air-conditioning. Three- and four-passenger cabins are available, as are suites. No staterooms are accessible to the physically challenged.

ON SHORE

Ships that cruise to Bermuda may dock in Hamilton, St. George's, or Dockyard. Often the ships anchor in two of these ports. It's easiest, therefore, to organize your on-shore tour by locale, exploring those areas nearest to your port. This saves both travel time and taxi fare.

As always, decide each day's priorities with your children. Bermuda offers a range of attractions from historic forts to glorious beaches and upscale shopping.

April to October is Bermuda's high season and also its cruise season. Even in summer the temperature rarely climbs above 85°F (29.5°C). The warmest months are July through September and the coolest are December through March. Frequent travelers to Bermuda like to say that this island has two seasons—never too hot and never too cold.

Quick Facts

Currency: One Bermuda dollar equals one U.S. dollar. U.S. currency and travelers checks are accepted at virtually all of Bermuda's restaurants and shops. Most chain stores and upscale shops accept credit cards.

Language: English

Major Cities: City of Hamilton and the town of St. George's

Tourist Information: The Bermuda Department Of Tourism has offices at: 310 Madison Ave., Suite 201, New York, NY 10017; and 150 N. Wacker Drive, Suite 1070, Chicago, IL 60606. There is also an office in Hamilton at the ferry terminal, in St. George's on King Square, and at the Royal Naval Dockyard.

Emergency Numbers: Medical: 236-2000 (Ambulance); Police: 295-0011.

Transportation: Because there are no rental cars on the island, getting around, while not difficult, takes planning. Taxis are available, but when relied on extensively they are expensive. Other alternatives: mopeds (scooters) and buses.

Mopeds: Some companies equip these with child seats and offer child-size helmets (call ahead to check and reserve if possible). A two-adult, two-child family would need to rent two mopeds, an expensive proposition for daily use. Drivers must be at least sixteen. Unless you are comfortable driving on the left and taking turns at an angle, don't give in to this temptation. It's safer and often less expensive, especially for a family with young children, to plan day trips using a combination of taxis, buses, and ferries. A one-day moped rental for one person is about $35, and the cost for a two-seater cycle is about $50 with a refundable deposit for keys, locks, and helmets. If you do rent a moped, remember that teens under sixteen may not drive and the island speed limit is 20 miles per hour. Don't forget to fuel up before 7 P.M. because most gas stations close at this time. Also read the rental agreement carefully.

There are many rental services. **Wheels Cycles**, with locations in St. George's (293-6437), Hamilton (295-0112), as well as other locales, offers courtesy pick-up service. Call 295-0112. Wheels Cycles also provides baskets, locks, and wheels for free.

Buses: The best option is to board the public buses, which are inexpensive and efficient. Ask your cruise director for information or stop by one of the tourist information centers in port to purchase booklets of discounted transportation passes. Three-day passes cost about $20. Seven-day passes are available as well, but you won't need these. Inquire at the **Central Terminal** near City Hall in Hamilton, the Visitor's Service Bureau in Hamilton, and at branch post offices.

Ferry: Public ferries, a pleasant and very Bermudian way to get about, depart from the Ferry Terminal on Front Street in Hamilton. Ferries run between Hamilton and the parishes of Paget, Warwick, and Sandys.

Taxis: With more than five hundred taxis on the island, it's easy to get one. Blue Flag taxi drivers are also licensed tour guides. Hail a taxi on the streets of

Hamilton, queue up at a taxi stand, or pick one up at a major hotel. The rate, the same for one to four people, is $4 for the first mile and $1.50 for each additional mile. The rate for private group sightseeing is $20 per hour for one to four people and $30 per hour for five to six persons for a minimum of three hours. After the buses stop running in the evening, taxis may be your only choice.

Carriages: Carriages offer a great way for little kids to get oriented. These can be arranged through hotels or picked up on Front Street in Hamilton. Rates are about $20 for the first thirty minutes for up to four passengers.

Best Bets

For families with children ages two through six:

Beach of Horseshoe Bay; Bermuda Aquarium and the adjacent Zoo; the Bermuda Botanical Gardens; horse-drawn surrey ride; Shelly Bay

For families with children ages seven through eleven:

The beaches of Horseshoe Bay and Elbow Beach; Royal Naval Dockyard; Enterprise Submarine ride

For families with pre-teens and teens:

Swimming at Horseshoe Bay; snorkeling at Church Bay on the South Shore; parasailing at Great Sound or Castle Harbour; Royal Naval Dockyard; renting a moped; horseback riding along the beach

For adults:

Golf at one of the island's many courses; Horseshoe Bay Beach

Church Bay. Photo courtesy of Bermuda Department of Tourism.

Beaches

Tobacco Bay near St. George's is a popular beach for cruisers because they can walk here from port. However, this small and often-crowded sandy spot is really nothing like Bermuda's grand beaches. Likewise, there's a public beach near Fort St. Catherine. Although less crowded, you can skip this one as well. Do yourself a favor and take a cab to some of Bermuda's legendary beaches.

Water enthusiasts who crave sun and sand should head for the beaches along the south shore, particularly the sweeping stretch between **Warwick Long Bay** and **Horseshoe Bay**. Not uncrowded, but never blanket-to-blanket with bodies, Horseshoe Bay has on-site lockers, lifeguard, snack shop, and umbrella rentals—items that assist in assuring that a family beach day, especially with young children, remains fun. With your spouse or older children, ride in rhythm to the pounding surf with **Spicelands Riding Centre**, (809) 238-8212, which offers early-morning horseback rides along these sands.

Families flock to **Elbow Beach**, a public beach in Paget Parish. Elbow Beach Hotel has day facilities for cruisers and day trippers, including lockers, towels, and changing rooms. In Devonshire Parish, east of Elbow Beach, families like **Devonshire Bay** because it also has facilities.

Shelly Bay Beach in Hamilton Parish, is the north shore's largest beach with facilities. Young kids are especially pleased with the playground, grassy area, and shallow slope that provides a safe place to wade in the water.

A trip to Bermuda wouldn't be complete without some time on the water. The least expensive way to enjoy the salt breeze is to take a ferry ride. The pleasant half-hour trip from Hamilton to Dockyard, a historic British fort, is inexpensive and provides you with a taste of this island's infatuation with the sea.

Nature and the Environment

Other not-to-be-missed day trips include a tour of the **Bermuda Botanical Gardens** in Paget Parish. Here you can see thirty-six acres of tropical blooms as well as Camden, the official residence of Bermuda's premier. Scented Garden, with a collection of scented and textured flowers and herbs, is meant for the visually impaired.

The **Bermuda Aquarium, Natural History Museum, and Zoo** are on North Shore Road in Hamilton Parish (809-293-2727). The aquarium offers more unexpected finds. Children especially love picking up portable "wands" that they use to listen to explanations about the tanks of rainbow-colored fish. Next door, the zoo features bird cages with macaws colored scarlet, green, and yellow; a host of pink flamingoes; and lizard cages with several long, slithery reptiles. All are open daily from 9 A.M. to 4:30 P.M.

The Bermuda Railway Trail consists of twenty-one miles of former railbeds that span the island from east to west. The trails are divided into seven sections, each with its own history, points of interest, and degree of difficulty. Some trails pass stunning seascapes and others include areas for public swimming. You will find brochures at the visitor's center.

Section 6, approximately 3.5 miles long and a three-hour walk, can be picked up from the Bermuda Aquarium, Natural History Museum, and Zoo. It passes along Shelly Bay, a good place to stop and swim.

Section 1, approximately 1.75 miles long, and about a 1½-hour walk, is suitable for bicycles and mopeds. Start this trail at the Somerset Bus Terminal and you'll pass through the typical Bermudian rural landscape of Springfield and Gilbert Nature Reserve. You wind by Fort Scaur, a very pleasant picnic stop and end up at Somerset Bridge—the world's smallest bridge. Conveniently, there's a ferry stop here.

Spittal Pond on South Road in Smith's Parish is the largest nature reserve on the island. This peaceful place has two mysteries: at Spanish Rock there is a bronze plaque with the etched inscription "TF 1543" (it is thought to have been left there by an early Portuguese traveler), and on a nearby rock ledge is an etched checkerboard pattern with no indication of who left it. Children enjoy finding these sites.

For travelers interested in spelunking, Bermuda has one of the largest number of limestone caves in the world. These caves, as well as inspiring the setting for Jim Henson's "Fraggle Rock" muppets, feature stalactites and stalagmites that date back to the Ice Age. Most popular are **Crystal Caves** (8 Crystal Caves Road, Bailey's Bay, 809-293-0640) and **Leamington Caves** on Harrington Sound Road (809-293-1188). Crystal Caves is open 9:30 A.M. to 4:30 P.M. daily, and Leamington Caves are open 10 A.M. to 4 P.M., Monday through Saturday.

Outdoor Sports

The seas surrounding Bermuda are most alluring, with visibility from seventy to one hundred feet and more than 350 shipwrecks. (Remember the legends of the Bermuda triangle?) Scuba enthusiasts and would-be divers can sign on with any of the island's five dive shops for lessons and guided deep water adventures that search out schools of rainbow-colored fish and the deep-sea gardens of orange and red coral reefs.

Some plunges to dive for include *L'Hermanie*, a French frigate sunk in 1838 off the island's west coast. In twenty to thirty feet of water, you can float by twenty-five canons as well as a host of sea critters who have come to call this craft home. Off **St. David's Island** on Bermuda's southern shore, the *Rita Zovetta*, a 360-foot Italian cargo ship, ran aground in 1924. Swim nearby the *Marie Celeste*, a paddle wheeler that sank in 1964, and marvel at the coral that has twisted around the fifteen-foot paddle wheel. **Blue Waters**

Divers, (809) 234-1034, offers wreck and reef diving as well as instruction for beginners.

Snorkelers like the waters of **Church Bay**, but be sure to bring your own gear because none is available for rent here. Several companies offer snorkeling and scuba cruises complete with lesson, mask, fins, and often a safety vest. **Fantasea Diving** (236-6339) offers snorkel and scuba cruises to several out islands (small islands off Bermuda's shores). A day trip with **Jesse James Cruises** (236-4804) takes you to three different snorkeling sites and plenty of time on and in the water. **Elusive Cruises** (234-8042) offers $3\frac{1}{2}$- to 4-hour snorkel cruises. Their morning cruise sails to Coral Reef on the north shore while their afternoon cruise goes to shipwrecks.

Make a splash at **Snorkel Park**, a facility located at the Dockyard area. While the snorkeling isn't the island's best, the shallow waters, available instruction, and conveniences such as showers and changing stalls make this a comfortable place, especially for younger kids. **Under Sea Adventures, LTD.** on Waterford Bridge Ferry Dock in Somerset (234-2861) offers helmet diving. In this kind of diving, a helmet with an air pump fits over your head. The dives off the boat *Rainbow Runner* take you down only eight feet. Non-swimmers and young kids too young to snorkel or dive get a thrill from walking on the sandy bottom among schools of tame angel, butterfly, and parrot fish. For deeper dives that are also great for non-swimmers, board the **Enterprise**, a submarine that shows you Bermuda's shipwrecks and coral reefs.

Fishing is a popular activity. Captain **Michael Baxter** offers half-day and full-day fishing trips on Bermuda's reef aboard the *Ellen B.*, a 32-foot cabin cruiser. Chances are you might catch grouper, chub, snapper, barracuda, or even shark (234-2963 or 234-9722). David Wayne Desilva's 38-foot glass-bottom *Princess* offers reef and deep-sea fishing and accommodates eight people (295-5813). His *Maranda*, a 47-foot craft fashioned from native Bermuda cedar, is equipped for reef and deep-sea fishing as well as cruising (295-2370).

Most hotels allow cruise passengers to pay for tennis court time. Ask your cruise director to assist you in booking this as well as golf, a Bermudian favorite. This tiny island offers more golf courses—eight of them—per square mile than any other country in the world. To get into the swing of things, practice first at the **Princess Golf Club**, an eighteen-hole, par 54, 2,684-yard course. Aficionados then head for the **Mid Ocean Club** with its eighteen holes at par 71 on 6,547 yards (accessible to visitors through their hotels). With spice and palm trees lining the fairways, and a signature fifth hole that takes a dogleg around a mangrove lake, Mid Ocean frequently lands in lists of the world's top fifty golf courses. Babe Ruth, the Sultan of Swat on another sport, came in as a runner-up in the Mid Ocean's 1937 Invitational.

More challenges await golf enthusiasts at **Castle Harbour Golf Club**, eighteen holes at par 71 on 6,440 yards, where some tees and elevated greens come with sweeping sea views. Other top tee-offs include **Port Royal Golf and Country Club**, an eighteen-hole, par 71 course on 6,565 yards, which has been rated by Jack Nicklaus as one of the best public courses, and **Riddell's Bay Golf and Country Club**, an eighteen-hole, par 69 course on 5,588 yards, which was built in 1922 and is Bermuda's first course (accessible via your hotel concierge).

Historic Attractions and Museums

The **Royal Naval Dockyard** is an interesting complex with a fort, maritime museum, and plenty of shops. Used by the British until 1951, the fort at Dockyard was built by slaves and convicts and completed in the 1820s. It is a peaceful place with old stone walls and wonderful views. Be sure to push through the old iron gate and climb the stairs to the ramparts. Here you not only glean some of the best island vistas but you can imagine the tall ships in an 1830s harbor. A guided nature walk leads visitors through two miles of woods, scenic views, parks, and wildlife sanctuaries on Sundays at 11:15 A.M. Later in the afternoon stop back for a tour and talk about the Royal Naval Dockyard.

The fort offers a fascinating, if eclectic, look at Bermuda's sea life through former magazines and also in storage rooms that house naval exhibits that now comprise the **Bermuda Maritime Museum** (809-234-1333). The artifacts range from sounding machines dated at 1878 to harpoons, fishing baskets, whale vertebrae, and sleek Bermuda skiffs. Open daily from 9:30 A.M. to 4:30 P.M. from May through November, and from 10 A.M. to 4:30 P.M. from December to April. Tickets are $7.50 for adults, $3 for kids age five to eighteen, and $6 for students and seniors.

Browse the reconstructed 1831 cooperage across the street, which features a variety of native crafts, and the nearby **Dockyard Clocktower Mall**, which has branches in many of Bermuda's downtown shops. (See Shopping.)

Just down the road from Dockyard is **Scaur Hill Fort Park** on Somerset Road in Sandys Parish. This area was garrisoned by the British troops through World War I. The low stone, polygonal walls were meant to be inconspicuous from the sea. The fort offers underground passageways to walk and great harbor views. Bring a picnic lunch and enjoy the peace of this free and uncrowded oasis.

Near the town of St. George's is **Fort St. Catherine**. Originally built in 1614, the current structure dates to the nineteenth century. This fort, complete with a resident ghost, overlooks the beach where Bermuda's first settlers landed. Another historic attraction in St. George's is the *Deliverance,* a full-size replica of the original ship built to carry the survivors of the *Sea Venture* to their final destination (the colony at James-

Gibb's Hill Lighthouse. Photo courtesy of Bemuda Department of Tourism.

town) after their ship was destroyed on Bermuda's reefs. Open daily from 10 A.M. to 4 P.M. Royal engineers built Fort Hamilton in the 1860s. It's a bit too far to walk from downtown Hamilton, but if your kids like dramatic views, moats, and eighteen-ton guns, take a taxi here.

Children like the view from **Gibb's Hill Lighthouse**, where the "Parish Lantern" has been warning ships since 1846. Climb the 185 steps to the viewing area 362 feet above sea level—the highest point on the island. Located on Lighthouse Road in Southampton, the lighthouse is open for tourists from 9 A.M. to 4:30 P.M. daily; tickets are $2 for adults and kids under five get in free (809-238-0524).

Best Eateries and Snacks

There are lots of places in Hamilton and St. George's for snacks and lunch. In St. George's the **White Horse Tavern** (Somer's Wharf, 14 Water St., 297-1515), has a pub-like atmosphere and food (anyone for steak and kidney pie?) plus kid-pleasing burgers. Go for a table on the covered outdoor patio.

Hamilton has **Kentucky Fried Chicken**, one on Queen Street and another on Burnaby Street, for those who need a reminder of home. Inside the **Windsor Place Mall**, Queen Street, the **Gourmet Store** offers an array of tuna, turkey, chicken, and other simple sandwiches as well as fresh-baked pies, all at inexpensive prices. **Pink's Deli**, Front Street, is another inexpensive eatery that serves hot dogs, macaroni and cheese, and salads. Relax with afternoon tea (or a light lunch) at the **Botanic Garden Tea Room**, Front Street, a part of Trimingham's Department Store. **La Trattoria** on Washington Lane in Hamilton, serves up good pizza and other Italian dishes. **Dock-yard Clocktower Mall** has several eateries. Children especially like the Haagen Dazs ice cream at Nannini.

Shopping

The **Dockyard Clocktower Mall** sports about twenty-five stalls, many of which are small branches of downtown shops. So if you don't feel like fighting the downtown traffic, you and the kids can buy T-shirts, cotton golf shirts, and, of course, Bermuda shorts from such island staples as **Davison's** of Bermuda, Calypso, and Island Fever. **Skywalker's** intrigues with an array of colorful wind socks, nautical flags, and kites.

In addition, for bargains on crystal and china, Dockyard Clocktower Mall has branches of **A.S. Cooper and Sons, Ltd.**, as well as **Trimingham's**, two good names that promise good buys. Goods are often as much as 25 percent less than stateside prices on such British items as English bone china and Waterford crystal. As always, know the U.S. prices before you go so you can comparison shop.

You can give the kids a breather from shopping at **Sparky's**. Located nearby the Clocktower Mall on 23 Freeport Road, this fun center has pinball and video machines as well as other games and a cafeteria.

The capital city of Hamilton, with its citified office buildings, malls, and specialty stores, offers many shopping opportunities. Both **A.S. Cooper and Sons, Ltd.** and **Trimingham's** have several locations. At the **Scottish Wool Shop** (7 Queen St.), good buys can be had on Scottish wool sweaters that are priced significantly lower than in the States. At the Windsor Place Mall, **Queen Street Glass** attracts attention with rows of rainbow-swirled plates, vases, and decorative ornaments, each hand blown by artisans from the **Bermuda Glassblowing Studio.**

For a bit of Bermuda to take home, many tourists buy watercolors of Bermudian scenes by local artist **Carole Holding.** Her works are available in shops in St. George's (above the White Horse Tavern in King's Square) and in the Clocktower Mall at Dockyard.

5

Mexico

A cruise offers families a wonderful way to sample some of Mexico's best resort towns, and in some cases, the real country beyond the resorts. Along with the family-friendly cruise ships listed below that specialize in Mexican itineraries, note that a number of the western Caribbean itineraries (listed in chapter three) also feature a stop at Playa del Carmen on the Yucatán mainland, where passengers who want to take shore excursions are tendered in before the ship proceeds to the island of Cozumel.

This chapter details the Mexican Riviera (or Gold Coast) resort cities of Acapulco, Mazatlán, and Puerto Vallarta, as well as Playa del Carmen/Cozumel in the Caribbean. Make note that in late 1995 some parts of Mexico suffered damage from a hurricane and some regions were hurt by an earthquake. Before heading ashore for an attraction or beach, always find out the current status of the site.

THE LINES

Carnival

- *Celebration*, as of May 5, 1996, offers seven-day cruises from New Orleans with port calls at Grand Cayman and Playa del Carmen/ Cozumel.

TIP: Many cruise ships sell bottled water to those debarking at Playa del Carmen before they head to the interior. Because the Mexican sun is extremely hot, it's important for you and your children to drink plenty of fluids, either bottled water or canned soda (to be on the safe side, skip the ice). Kids do like to be told to drink another Coke.

- *Holiday* offers three-day, round-trip cruises year-round from Los Angeles, calling at Ensenada, and four-day, round-trip cruises year-round from Los Angeles, calling at Catalina Island and Ensenada.
- *Jubilee* offers year-round, seven-day Mexican Riviera voyages from Los Angeles, with visits to Puerto Vallarta, Mazatlán, and Cabo San Lucas.

Norwegian Cruise Line

- *Leeward* follows a four-day summer itinerary round-trip from Miami, with ports in Playa del Carmen/Cozumel, and a four-day winter schedule round-trip from Miami that includes Key West, Cancún, and Cozumel.

Royal Caribbean Cruise Line

- *Song of America* offers seven nights on the Mexican Riviera round-trip from Los Angeles with calls at Cabo San Lucas, Mazatlán, and Puerto Vallarta; November to April.
- *Viking Serenade* offers three-night, year-round, round-trip cruises from Los Angeles to Baja Mexico with a call at Ensenada on weekends, and four-night, year-round, round-trip cruises from Los Angeles with calls at Catalina Island and Ensenada on weekdays.

Best Bets

Best cruise ships for families with children under two:

Although there's no children's program for tots under two, NCL's *Leeward* promises baby-sitting (for an extra fee) from noon to 2 A.M.

Best cruise ships for families with children ages two to four:

Carnival's organized children's programs on the *Celebration, Holiday*, and *Jubilee* start at age two.

Best cruise ships for families with children ages five to ten:

The sleek format of NCL's *Leeward* especially appeals to this age group. There are good programs on Carnival's *Holiday, Jubilee*, and *Celebration*. RCCL's *Viking Serenade* has a cheerful children's playroom.

Best cruise ships for families with pre-teens and teens:

This age group rallies around the $1 million entertainment complex, complete with virtual reality games, on Carnival's *Holiday*.

THE SHIPS

Carnival

Celebration: entered service in 1987; 47,262 gross tons; 1,486 passengers

Holiday: entered service in 1985; 46,052 gross tons; 1,452 passengers

Jubilee: entered service in 1986; 47, 262 gross tons; 1,486 passengers

We've already established that Carnival ships are not known for their understated elegance: expect bright colors, lots of neon, and lively, theme-decorated public areas as well as lively people who are obviously having a good time. These three sister ships are identical in most aspects, except for their themed decors. The *Celebration* sports a futuristic theme while the *Jubilee* focuses on nostalgia and *Holiday*'s theme is Broadway.

What sets the *Holiday* apart, however, is its one-of-a-kind $1 million entertainment complex that features the first virtual reality games on a cruise ship. Called the Blue Lagoon (formerly a show lounge located aft along the Broadway Promenade), the room also houses a teen disco and an ice cream parlor that serves snacks and refreshments.

Games range from high-tech thrillers, such as Virtual Racing Deluxe, Mortal Kombat, and Jurassic Park Driving, to more traditional favorites such as air hockey and pinball. Smart Toss, Killer T-Rex, and Feed Big Bertha might appeal to the younger set, while adults might like video basketball or video football. Two centerpiece attractions of Blue Lagoon: virtual reality and R360. The first consists of two machines with which players are immersed in a 3-D gunfight. This uses texture-mapped color and thirty-two channel digital sound. In R360, players strap themselves in for an aerial dogfight as the machine physically spins them 360 degrees and completely upside down (not for the queasy). The machines dispense tickets to winners that can be exchanged at the redemption center for a variety of prizes.

At the teen disco, a professional DJ presides over the dance floor at night. The ice cream parlor offers counter seating and serves sundaes, pretzels, popcorn, and pizza. Two outdoor pools are on the smallish side (each ship has a kid's wading pool). And there are playrooms (but no teen centers) aboard all three.

> **TIP:** The games have been programmed to accept
> guests' Sail & Sign cards directly, so watch out!
> These are credit cards that can be used to purchase
> items on the ship. Be sure to set a firm limit with
> your children.

These are nice-sized staterooms with an average of
185 square feet. The ten suites with verandahs on the
uppermost deck accommodate third and fourth passengers with twin/king beds and a double convertible
sofa. There are a good number of triples, with one upper. Quads, with two uppers, can accommodate a fifth
passenger on a rollaway. All cabins have televisions.
The *Celebration* has fourteen wheelchair-accessible
cabins, the *Holiday* has fifteen, and the *Jubilee* has
fourteen.

Norwegian Cruise Line

Leeward: entered service in 1992; refurbished in 1995;
25,000 tons; 950 passengers. Refer to chapter six for a
complete ship description.

Royal Caribbean Cruise Line

Song of America: entered service in 1982; refurbished
in 1991; 37,000 tons; 1,400 passengers. For a description of *Song of America*, refer to chapter six.
Viking Serenade: entered service in 1982; refurbished
in 1991; 40,000 tons; 1,500 passengers

Viking Serenade was built in France in 1982 as the
world's only cruise ship to carry cars and RVs (it was

owned by Admiral Cruises). In 1990, the ship was transformed by RCCL, which put millions of dollars into the project. While the ship may still look some-what barge-like, the renovation converted the car deck into cabins, renovated all existing cabins and public rooms, and added a three-story atrium. The bright, cheerful, modern interior includes a sunny children's playroom where kids have a ball-jump area plus toys, games, and videos.

The majority of cabins on the Pacific and Main decks accommodate third and fourth passengers. Don't book a cabin aft on Deck Nine—this is directly above the Bali Hai Lounge, which is open until 3 A.M., and directly below the Windjammer Cafe, which starts serving breakfast at 6 A.M. Cabins have televisions. Four cabins are wheelchair accessible.

ON SHORE: THE MEXICAN RIVERIA

Quick Facts

Currency: The Mexico new peso (N$) is the coun-try's currency, though in most ports U.S. dollars and credit cards are accepted in restaurants and many shops.

Language: Spanish is the official language, but many Mexicans involved in the tourism business also speak some English.

ON SHORE: ACAPULCO

Acapulco is the largest city on the Mexican Riviera. Built on hilly terrain and fronted by Acapulco Bay to the west and the tropical Sierra Madre Mountains to the east, the city is sprawling and bustling. The main boulevard, Costera Miguel Aleman (known simply as the Costera), is the hub of activity. This road leads to the municipal pier where cruise ships dock. If you haven't been to Acapulco in a number of years, you may be in for a surprise. This city of nearly two million residents has definitely cleaned up its act. It is a sparkling, fun-filled, and beautiful resort destination.

Quick Facts

Tourist Information: The State of Guerrero Department of Tourism (SEPOTUR) at Costera Miguel Aleman 187 (telephone 74/86-91-64) is open weekdays.
Emergency Numbers: Police: 74/85-68-62; Medical: Hospital Centro Medico at J. Arevalo 99 (telephone 74/82-46-92) is reliable, or call the U.S. Consulate (74/85-66-21) for a list of English-speaking physicians.
Transportation:
Buses: Cheap and convenient, but because taxis are also, you're better off going with a taxi.
Taxis: While you have to negotiate prices, it shouldn't cost more than $5 for a ride from the pier into the heart of town.
Other: Brightly decorated horse-drawn carriages (known as *calandrias*) traverse the Costera for about $15 per half hour.

Best Bets

For families with toddlers:
Strolling through Papagayo Park

For families with children ages two through seven:
Roqueta Island
For families with children ages seven through eleven:
CICI, the water theme park
For families with pre-teens and teens:
Parasailing and watersports
For adults:
The beach and golf

Beaches

While Acapulco is noted for its watersports and lovely beaches, swimming is not advised because of polluted water and, at many beaches, a dangerous undertow. All of the beaches in Acapulco are public.

All of the major hotels along the Costera resort zone in downtown Acapulco offer windsurfing, parasailing (said to have been invented here), and other watersports. **Caleta Beach**, on the peninsula in Old Acapulco, is a popular (crowded on weekends) family beach that also offers a swimming pool, two water slides, a restaurant, clean rest rooms, and rentals for inner tubes, Jet Skis, banana boats, and kayaks. From here, a launch leaves for a ten-minute ride to **Roqueta Island**, known for its small zoo that houses lions, an alligator, zebras, a leopard, a giraffe, an aviary, and a serpentarium. Palaos, the restaurant here, has a sandy cove, a pony, and a cage of lively monkeys.

If you want a quiet beach for fun and sun, your best bet is to take a taxi to the **Acapulco Princess** in the Puerto Marques zone. Children will be delighted

> **TIP:** Revocadero Beach is a good place for sunning, beachcombing, and sand play, but *not* swimming because of the undertow.

by the open-air lobby that leads to waterfalls, over footbridges, and past swimming pools to a lovely stretch of **Revocadero Beach**. A shopping arcade and several restaurant options—plus tennis and golf (see Outdoor Sports below)—make this a good place to spend the day.

Nature and the Environment

On the Costera, you'll find **Papagayo Park** set on fifty-two acres. As you stroll the tree-lined pathways, you can explore an aviary, see a model of a Spanish galleon, and have fun at the mini-racecar track, on bumper boats, and on other rides.

Outdoor Sports

Most hotels allow non-guests to play tennis for a fee. The **Acapulco Princess** has two indoor and nine outdoor courts. The two best golf courses in Acapulco are across from the **Acapulco Princess** and its adjoining sister property the **Pierre Marques**. Seldom crowded, the Pierre Marques course was designed by Robert Trent Jones Jr. Higher greens fees apply to non-guests. Both properties are located on the Carretera Escenica, Km 17; telephone 74/69-10-00.

Historic Attractions and Museums

Fort San Diego (El Fuerte de San Diego), perched on a hill overlooking the harbor, was originally built in 1616 and was rebuilt following a massive earthquake in 1776. The fort, which was the staging area for the loading and unloading of the Manila fleet, served to protect the lucrative trade link from Dutch and English pirates.

Surrounded by a moat, this classic, five-point fortress includes an interesting museum featuring exhibits that portray the city from its earliest days to 1821, when Mexico gained its independence from Spain. Closed Mondays; telephone 74/82-38-28.

Best Eateries and Snacks

If you're here for dinner with pre-teens or teens, you might want to head to **Carlos 'n Charlie's** (Costera Miguel Aleman 999, telephone 74/84-12-85), one of the most popular places in town. No reservations are taken, so expect a line outside before it opens at 6:30 P.M. Yes, it can be noisy, but good-natured fun abounds—there is a clever menu, witty waiters, and a decor that amuses the kids (the tool chest with gadgets hanging from the ceiling). American-style food includes ribs and shrimp.

Mimi's Chili Saloon (Costera Miguel Aleman 107, telephone 74/85-64-62) is an informal place with lots of good Tex-Mex food. No reservations are taken, so there will be a wait in the evening.

Your pre-teens and teens might opt for the **Hard Rock Cafe** (Costera Miguel Aleman 37, telephone 74/84-66-80) if given the choice, and why not? Along with the music and rock and roll memorabilia, the food is good, portions are large, and selections include chili, ribs, and fried chicken.

Shopping

The Mercada Municipal, several blocks west of the Costera, is a fun place to explore (though it may be too crowded for younger kids). The stalls, covered by awnings, are open from morning until early afternoon and sell everything from flowers to food to a plethora of souvenirs, which include puppets, toys, leather goods, and lots of kitsch.

If you're looking for small shops and boutiques selling such familiar names as Benetton and Fiorucci, head to the main shopping drag that stretches from the Acapulco Plaza to the El Presidente Hotel.

Shopping in the upscale arcade mall at the **Acapulco Princess** is a pleasant, air-conditioned experience. Shops include ACA Joe, which sells all-cotton sportswear, and La Joya, where you'll find a nice variety of inexpensive silver jewelry.

ON SHORE: CANCÚN, PLAYA DEL CARMEN/COZUMEL

The island of Cozumel has gorgeous beaches on the warm Caribbean Sea and superb coral reefs that attract divers, snorkelers, and nature lovers. Located twelve miles from the eastern coast of Mexico's Yucatán Peninsula, Cozumel is less developed than its nearby neighbor, Cancún, and certainly has a more Mexican feel.

Many cruise ships anchor off Cozumel for the day, stopping first offshore at Playa del Carmen, where passengers wishing to take shore excursions to the Mayan ruins of Tulúm or to Cancún can disembark and board tenders for the ride ashore. Ships that stay in the area for two days anchor off Cozumel for one day and off Playa del Carmen for the other.

Cozumel is about twenty-nine miles long and nine miles wide and has about forty-five thousand inhabitants. Most of the island is undeveloped, consisting of beaches, coves, jungles, palm groves, and lagoons.

Quick Facts

Main Town: San Miguel, where the ships dock, is the hub of activity on the island.

Tourist Information: A booth is located on the main pier in Cozumel next to the Playa del Sol on the second floor of the crafts mall at the east end of the plaza. Open weekdays; telephone 987/2-0972. Request emergency numbers from this office.

Transportation:

Buses: Cheap, but not that reliable, and they are not allowed in the north and south hotel zones because of a union agreement with taxis.

Car Rentals: Only a small percent of the island's roads are paved. Cars with four-wheel drive or open-air jeeps are popular ways to travel down the island's dirt roads that lead to a number of secluded beaches and coves. Budget has a rental desk at the cruise ship terminal; telephone 987/21732.

Taxis: Generally available at the pier. They are unmetered but have set rates for each destination. Confirm the fare with the driver before departing. (Your

ship may tender right in San Miguel's downtown and shopping area, or it may dock at the International Pier, which is about a $3 taxi ride into town.)
Ferry: Ferries and water jets make the crossing from Cozumel/Playa del Carmen up to ten times daily. Call 987/21824 for ferry information; 987/20827, for water jet service.

Best Bets

For families with toddlers and children ages two through seven:
Beach time at Playa del Sol
For families with children ages seven through eleven, pre-teens, and teens:
Chankanaab Nature Park
For teens and adults:
Day trip to Tulúm; snorkeling

Beaches

Playa San Francisco on the southwestern shore is considered by most to be the island's best beach. The three-mile stretch of beach offers full-service amenities (changing rooms, restaurant, and equipment rentals). A proposed resort development in this area has been suspended, at least for now, because of environmental concerns.

Playa del Sol, located south of town on the west (leeward) coast of the island where waters are calm, is another great beach that stretches along a pleasant cove. Once privately owned by a tour operator but now open to the public, the beach has a restaurant/bar, shops, and Jet Skis and snorkeling equipment.

> **TIP:** The eastern coast beaches have rough Pacific surf and are not recommended for swimming. Also, it's permissible to walk through the shallow lagoon, but be sure to wear rubber-soled shoes because the bottom is lined with rocks.

Chankanaab Nature Park at Caratera Sur (no telephone), about ten minutes south of San Miguel, is a beautiful salt water lagoon that has been turned into a wildlife sanctuary and botanical gardens by the government. The lagoon itself is a sinkhole filled from the nearby sea by underground tunnels. Around fifty species of fish can be viewed although snorkeling through the tunnels is prohibited. An army of snorkelers and divers are attracted to the offshore reefs at the nearby **Chankanaab Bay**, a full-service beach and a prime snorkeling spot. The jungle trail through the Botanical Gardens reveals three hundred different types of tropical plans and trees from twenty-two countries as well a museum depicting early Mayan life.

Outdoor Sports

Watersports are extremely popular in Cozumel, so you'll find rentals throughout the island. Cozumel is known for having the best diving and snorkeling in Mexico. With its extensive reef system, water visibility to two hundred feet, and more than two hundred species of tropical fish, it is truly a diver's dream.

More than forty dive shops on the island offer beginner instruction as well as advanced dives. The area's dive shops have formed a cooperative, so look for shops that display the CADO sticker because these are the most reputable. Dive shops also provide guides and transportation, among them Aqua Safari, Av. Rafael Melgar 39e; telephone 987/20101.

Most of Cozumel's best snorkeling spots are close to shore. The western side has a number of excellent sites. Equipment rentals are available throughout the island. Operators who specialize in snorkeling include Snorkozumel, Calle 5 S 11A, between Av. Rafael Melgar and Av. 5 (telephone 987/24166), which offers snorkeling excursions.

Historic Attractions and Museums

San Gervasio, located inland in the north central jungle, is a small Mayan archaeological site featuring Mayan and Toltec ruins. Once the island's capital, San Gervasio was occupied from 300 to 1500 A.D. A visit here is offered by many cruise lines, but don't expect too much—very few ruins remain.

If your children are older and you're not big on diving or snorkeling, you may want to skip Cozumel and take your ship's shore excursion to **Tulúm,** which leaves from Playa del Carmen, where tour buses wait to take you on the approximate one-hour ride south on Highway 307. The only Mayan port city ever discovered, it was one of the few to have been still occupied when the Spaniards arrived in the sixteenth century. This sprawling, white-walled city with small temples and buildings is in a spectacular setting overlooking the turquoise waters of the Caribbean.

Chichen Itza, the best known and best preserved Mayan ruins, is a three-hour drive from Cancún. If

Exploring ancient ruins in Mexico. Photo courtesy of Norweigan Cruise Line.

your ship docks in Cancún, Chichen Itza will be included on the shore excursion list. Keep in mind that this is about an eight-hour excursion and a very long haul for younger kids. Some ships that stop at Cozumel may offer an air tour to Chichen Itza.

If you can't make it to the ruins, the next best thing is a visit to the **Cozumel Archaeological Park** (Av. 65 S; telephone 987/20914), a five-minute taxi ride from the pier. Showcased here are three thousand years of pre-Hispanic Mexican culture and art, including more than sixty-five replicas of Mayan, Toltec, and other statues and stone carvings.

In San Miguel, the **Museo de la Isla de Cozumel** (Ave. Rafael Melgar between Calle 4 and 6N; telephone

987/21545) was once a luxury hotel that now houses exhibit halls filled with dioramas, sculptures, and explanations of the island's history. This is a nice place if you have some "down time" in port. The museum also serves as the island's cultural center, offering artisan demonstrations and live drama. There's a restaurant on the second-floor terrace that offers a wonderful view of the waterfront.

Best Eateries and Snacks

Fresh fish and shellfish are the specialties of Cozumel. Many typical Mexican dishes date back thousands of years One such dish is *pozole*, whole hominy and either pork or chicken in a spicy tomato broth.

Inexpensive and tasty chicken, seafood, and meat is on the menu at **El Moro**, on the eastern edge of San Miguel at Calle 75 N between Calles 2 and 4; telephone 987/23029.

Sports nuts have a ball at **Sports Page Video Bar and Restaurant** (Corner Av. 5a N and Calle 2 N; telephone 987/21199) where the big draw is the large-screen televisions that show simultaneous sports broadcasts. Mexican specialties along with burgers, fries, and steak are served. Open for breakfast, too.

Shopping

Downtown along the waterfront, Avenue Rafael Melgar, and in some side streets (or *calles*) around the plaza, you'll find a wide assortment of shops such as **Van Cleef and Arpels** (Ave. Rafael Melgar N 54) for gems and fine silver jewelry, and the huge **Lost Cinco**

Soles (Ave. Rafael Melgar N 27), which offers everything from papier-mâché fruit to T-shirts to reproduction Mayan art and other reasonably priced items to
take home as souvenirs or gifts. There is also a good
variety of fairly new shops dockside at the cruise ship
terminal, and prices are surprisingly reasonable.

ON SHORE: MAZATLÁN

Mexico's largest west coast port, Mazatlán is also one
of the country's most popular beach resorts. This city,
home of some half million residents and to Latin America's biggest fleet of commercial shrimp vessels, is not a
glitzy resort town like some of its counterparts.

Quick Facts

Tourist Information: The City Tourism Bureau is at
Paseo Olas Altas 1300 in the Bank of Mexico Building;
telephone 69/85-12-32; closed Sundays.
Emergency Numbers: The Public Tourism Ministry
is a division of the police department specifically for
tourists; call 69/14-32-22. To locate an English-speaking doctor, contact the U.S. Consulate (telephone
69/85-22-05).
Transportation:
Buses: Public buses run from the tourist area to downtown (*centro*), the Zona Dorada (the heart of the tourist
district), and Old Mazatlán.
Car Rentals: Hertz and National are among the major
chains located here.
Taxis: These are inexpensive and plentiful. Because
Mazatlán's main sightseeing spots are spread out, you

may want to arrange to hire a taxi for the day. An adventurous mode of transportation are the *pulmonias* (literally meaning "pneumonia"), which are five-person, open-air taxis that look like a cross between a carriage and a golf cart.

Best Bets

For families with toddlers and children ages two through seven:
The Acuario Mazatlán

For families with children ages seven through eleven:
Watching the cliff divers at High Divers Park

For families with pre-teens and teens:
Watersports at Playa Sabalo and/or Playa las Garlotas

For adults:
Strolling the Malecón

Beaches

Mazatlán's wide sandy beaches and rolling surf are quite like the beaches of Southern California. The city sports one of the longest stretches of uninterrupted beaches in Mexico, and much of it is protected from heavy surf by islands. **Playa Sabalo** and **Playa las Garlotas**, located along the Zona Dorada, are Mazatlán's most popular beaches. Expect to share the beach with an assortment of windsurfers, parasailers, boogie boarders, and also Jet Skis, Hobie Cats (rentals are available for all), a zillion vendors, and lots of locals and tourists alike. Don't expect really super diving or snorkeling.

Nature and the Environment

An aquarium, the **Acuario Mazatlán** (Avenue de los Deportes 111; telephone 69/81-78-15), pleases younger children with tanks bearing such marine denizens as sharks, eels, sea horses, and eye-pleasing, brightly colored tropical fish. A trained seal show and an auditorium showing films about sea life add to the fun. Next door is a large playground complete with slides and swings, a small zoo, and a botanical garden.

Outdoor Sports

Reserve one of the thirteen tennis courts in advance at **El Cid Resort**, (telephone 69/81-37-28). Unfortunately, El Cid's eighteen-hole golf course—the best around—is only open to guests of the resort and to those interested in buying a time-share. If you're determined to play, get a tee time at the nine-hole course at **Club Capestre Mazatlán** (telephone 69/80-15-70) on Route 15 on the outskirts of Mazatlán.

Historic Attractions and Museums

While Old Mazatlán is full of restored nineteenth-century buildings (including a splendid theater built in 1860), there's not much in this category to pique the interest of children.

Other Attractions

Strolling the **Malecón**, the palm-lined waterfront promenade that connects the Zona Dorada and Old Mazatlán, is a delightful morning or evening activity.

At **High Divers Park**, located along the Paseo
Claussen, young men climb up a platform and dive into
the sea. At night, they take the plunge carrying lit
torches—quite a spectacular vision.

Best Eateries and Snacks

Fresh seafood is the specialty of Mazatlán. Some of the
palapas (beach shacks) along the beach serve up deli-
cious smoked marlin and shrimp cocktail. One of the
nicest *palapas* is **Tres Islas** (north of the El Quixote
Hotel on Ave. Camaron Sabalo 69) though it gets fairly
crowded with families on Sundays.

Doney (Mariano Escobado at Calle Cinco de Mayo,
telephone 69/81-26-51) is large and homey, and serves
up tasty Mexican fare. There's always fried chicken if
your children are fussy eaters.

Shopping

While there is no particular regional handicraft, shops
are full of hand-crafted items from all over Mexico.
Mazatlán Arts and Crafts Center (Ave. Loaiza, telephone 69/13-50-22) contains shops and boutiques with
a good assortment of souvenirs such as straw som-
breros and leather jackets. The downtown **Mercado
Central** located between Calle Juarez and Serfan, is
packed with vendors selling everything from food
to handicrafts.

ON SHORE: PUERTO VALLARTA

This former sleepy fishing village was changed forever
after Elizabeth Taylor and Richard Burton filmed

The Night of the Iguana here. The ensuing publicity brought flocks of tourists. Even now, during the peak winter season, streets are chock-a-block with people and automobiles.

Yet, the area is not without its charms: while the hotel zone is a high-rise, condo heaven, downtown and the section south of the Rio Cuale still have a fishing-village ambiance. By city ordinance, stucco buildings are all white with flower-covered balconies and red-tiled roofs. Your kids might see a burro clip-clopping down the steep cobblestone streets. Though not heavy on notable sights, there are some nice beaches here.

Quick Facts

Tourist Information: Call the State Tourism Office in City Hall on Ave. Judrez (near the *zocalo*), telephone 329/2-0242 or 329/2-0243.

Emergency Numbers: Police: 329/2-0123.

Transportation: The cruise ship docks are almost three miles from downtown Puerto Vallarta.

Buses: Cheap, but their routes are too confusing to make them feasible, considering your limited time in port.

Car Rentals: Available, but traffic is congested and parking is hard to find. Take a taxi to avoid these hassles—after all, you are on vacation.

Taxis: Hire one at the pier and negotiate the rate in advance.

Best Bets

For families with toddlers and children ages two through seven:
The splashing pool at Vidafel Aqua Park

For families with children ages seven through eleven:
Water slides and tubing at Vidafel Aqua Park

For families with pre-teens and teens:
Watersports at Playa de los Muertos

For adults:
Playa Mismaloya—site of *Night of the Iguana* filming

Beaches

Nestled on the shores of Banderas Bay, Puerta Vallarta has three beach zones with almost forty different beaches. North of town, **Playa de Oro** and the marina are where most of the area's newest resort development has occurred. This wide, sandy beach is broken up by some jetties, making some areas a bit rocky, but the area is a great place for watersports and people-watching.

In town, on the south side of Rio Cuale, the popular (and crowded) **Playa de los Muertos** stretches along the city's palm-lined waterfront. All types of watersports equipment are offered for rent here. Vendors ply their wares and restaurants are nearby.

The best beaches are located south of town where the coast turns into a series of bays and coves that have a rugged, hilly, jungle landscape as a backdrop.

TIP: While the beaches here are lovely, they are hard to get to unless you have your own car or have rented a taxi for the day. (Otherwise, it's difficult to find a taxi to take you back.)

A trio of beaches found far south of town can only be reached by boat, all of which depart from either the marina north of town, the downtown pier at Playa de Los Muertos, or from **Playa Mismaloya**, which is eight miles south on Route 200 and the location where *Night of the Iguana* was filmed. Operators include: Princess Cruises (telephone 322/10415) and Bora Bora (telephone 322/43680).

Diving and snorkeling are generally not very good from most beaches in Puerto Vallarta. South of town, **Los Arcos** is a natural preserve with clear water. The best diving area is around the huge rock archway that gave this preserve its name. For information about dive trips and rentals, call Paradise Divers at 329/2-4064.

Outdoor Sports

Los Flamingos Country Club (telephone 329/2-0379), north of the airport in the neighboring state of Nayarit, is an older eighteen-hole course that is showing its age in places but is still challenging (it's in another time zone, so keep track of the time). Ask your shore excursion director to book this at least a day in advance. If you do it on your own, there are inexpensive shuttles from town that leave from the Sheraton Bugavilias and head north. Greens fees are a reasonable $25; cart or caddy optional.

Just north of town, **Marina Vallarta Country Club**, a par 71, eighteen-hole course that is part of the Marina Vallarta mega-resort, has lakes, ponds, lagoons, and lush tropical vegetation. Greens fees are $65 plus mandatory cart or caddy; call 322/1-0171.

Puerto Vallarta is considered one of the best Mexican resorts for tennis. Clay courts are common. There are dozens of courses at area resorts, and the town has two free tennis centers: the **John Newcombe Tennis Center** (telephone 329/4-6723) at the Continental Plaza Vallarta, and **Los Tules Tennis Center** (telephone 329/4-4560) near the Fiesta America Hotel.

Other Attractions

Vidafel Aqua Park, located in the marina area across from the Vidafel Resort, is spread out on two acres. The park features four water slides, a large swimming pool, a splashing pool with cartoon characters and animal figures for the younger set, and a winding canal for inner tube drifting. Lifeguards are stationed throughout. Open daily.

Take a stroll through downtown (also called Old Town), but remember that the cobblestone streets can be tough on little feet and baby strollers. The malecón promenade is a scenic walkway that stretches along the bay. Restaurants and cafes are conveniently located across the street.

Best Eateries and Snacks

Barbecued fish on a stick (*sarandeado*) is a local specialty and a popular beach-side treat. At Playa de los Muertos, it's sold at stands at the south end of the beach.

El Dorado, at Amapaz and Pulpita at Playa de los Muertes (telephone 329/2-1511) has a kid-pleasing menu that includes burgers and spaghetti. For adults, it's fresh fish.

Breakfast, lunch and dinner are served up at the **Pancake House** and the **Diner**, Basilo Badilo 39, telephone 329/2-6272—where you can choose from a selection of pancakes, waffles, and eggs, as well as basic, American-style food such as meat loaf and fried chicken.

Shopping

Bargaining is expected at such places as the **Mercado Municipal** (Avenida Miramar and Libertad) where vendors at stalls sell everything from piñatas to produce, and beach vendors sell a wonderful assortment of folk art that ranges from hand-dyed woven rugs to carved wood animals. **Querubines**, located at Juarez and Galeana, offers a fine selection of crafts, including jewelry and embroidered, hand-loomed clothing from all over the country.

Actually, it's hard to go anywhere in Puerto Vallarta without passing an inviting shop. Main shopping areas include the malecón; the outdoor flea market at the marina where the cruise ships dock, a good spot for T-shirts, folk art, and souvenirs; and downtown along Juarez and Morelos streets, where there is a wide variety of high-quality shops.

6

❋❋❋❋❋❋❋❋❋❋❋❋❋❋❋

The
Bahamas

The Bahamas, a nation of some seven hundred individual islands and cays, is blessed with powder white- and pink-sand beaches, aqua-blue waters, sunny days, and hospitable islanders. The island chain extends from fifty miles off the coast of Florida to sixty miles north of Cuba, making it a quick, easy vacation getaway for families.

Although the Bahamas consists of hundreds of islands and cays, only fourteen are inhabited. The major tourism areas center around Freeport/Lucaya on Grand Bahama Island, and Nassau on New Providence Island, which are also the ports of call for most Bahama-bound cruise ships. Both areas offer family-friendly fun. (Keep in mind that the itineraries listed below are subject to change.)

THE LINES

The Big Red Boat (Premier Cruises)

- *Star / Ships Atlantic* and *Oceanic* offer year-round three- or four-night cruises from Port Canaveral, Florida to Port Lucaya and Nassau. These can be combined with three or four days at an Orlando theme park: Walt Disney World (with accommodations either on- or off-site) or Universal Studios/ Sea World. In 1995 the Big Red Boat experimented with one seven-day sailing. In the future the line may be offering more of these.

Carnival

- *Ecstasy*: year-round, three-day, round-trip cruises from Miami to Nassau.

- *Fantasy*: year-round, three-day, round-trip cruises from Port Canaveral to Nassau, and four-day cruises to Freeport and Nassau. These may be combined with a Walt Disney World vacation or an Orlando/Central Florida package.

Norwegian Cruise Lines

- *Leeward*: year-round, three-day cruises round-trip from Miami with an alternating itinerary. One itinerary includes Nassau and Great Stirrup Cay, NCL's private island; the other visits Key West and Great Stirrup Cay.

Royal Caribbean Cruise Lines

- *Nordic Empress*: year-round, three- and four-day cruises departing from and returning to Miami. The three-day cruise stops in Coco Cay and Nassau; the four-day cruise also goes to Freeport.
- *Sovereign of the Seas*: three- and four-night, year-round cruises to the Bahamas from Miami (beginning December 1996). Ports had not yet been released at press time.

THE SHIPS

The Big Red Boat

Star/Ship Atlantic: built in 1982; refurbished in 1989; 35,148 gross tons; 1,550 passengers
Star/Ship Oceanic: built in 1965; refurbished in 1986; 40,000 gross tons; 1,800 passengers

Both of these former Home Lines vessels are pleasant, spacious ships with many public rooms, although the *Oceanic* is the more attractive of the two with its classic oceanliner exterior and tastefully decorated interior. In 1994, it was one of twenty-five ships reviewed by "Cruise Reports," a newsletter that reports on ships as reviewed through its travel agent survey system, and was named Best Cruise Ship for Families.

The hub of daytime activity on both ships is on the Promenade deck. Kids flock to the ice cream parlor near the two pools (one with a retractable plastic roof). On the *Atlantic*, ages two through four headquarter at the First Mates Clubhouse while ages five through seven meet in Pluto's Playhouse (where evening baby-sitting takes place). Ages eight through ten congregate in the Space Station. Activities for older children take place in various public areas, including the ice cream parlor and the Space Station.

On the *Oceanic*, ages two through four generally meet in the Astro Room, ages five through seven at Pluto's Playhouse, located on the Premier deck aft; ages eight through ten at Space Station, located on the Lounge deck forward, and Sunrise Terrace, located on the Pool deck; and older kids in the Space Station, as well as other public areas.

TIP: Ages eight and up are allowed to sign themselves in and out of the children's program, so you might get them their own cabin key to avoid lockouts. As we've recommended in other chapters, it's a good idea to keep a note pad handy for each family member to log his or her whereabouts.

The cabins are spacious with comfortable furnishings. The nine categories range from inside staterooms to apartment suites. There are outside staterooms that sleep five on a double bed, a convertible bed, and two upper berths. This option is an attractive plus for families with three children. Both ships have limited accessibility for the physically challenged. Single parents can sail in categories three to eight at 125 percent of the tariff rate.

Carnival

Ecstasy entered service in 1991; *Fantasy* entered service in 1990. These sister ships are each 70,367 gross tons and carry 2,044 passengers.

These two giant resorts-at-sea, numbers one and two in the Carnival fleet of SuperLiners, are identical except for their interior decor. While both feature spectacular six-story atria, the *Fantasy* is glitzier, with plenty of neon lighting that changes colors regularly. The ship's public areas have a Hollywood fantasy theme. For instance, Cleopatra's bar looks like an Egyptian tomb, and the Cats nightclub sports giant soup cans. Children invariably enjoy investigating these areas by day. Joe Farcus, the interior designer of the Carnival SuperLiners decorated the *Ecstasy* in a somewhat more toned-down manor with many of the public areas themed around cityscapes. Kids love the shiny silver diner with its quick snacks.

As on all of Carnival's ships, the action is nonstop. Each ship has two swimming pools, a wading pool and another with a slide for older kids.

The ships have surprisingly spacious cabins, starting at about 185 square feet, with in-cabin televisions (though viewing choices may be extremely limited.) Twenty-six verandah suites sleep four, in twins/king and double convertible sofa, and have VCRs and bathtubs with whirlpool jets, but some cabins on the Verandah deck have partially obstructed views. Triples and quads (two uppers) are available on all other decks. Twenty cabins on each ship are wheelchair accessible.

Norwegian Cruise Line

Leeward: built in 1992; refurbished in 1995; 25,000 gross tons; 950-passenger capacity

Introduced to the NCL fleet in October 1995 after an extensive renovation (it served as the *Viking Saga* when built in 1992), the *Leeward* is sleek and sophisticated. The ship has two dining rooms: the Four Seasons on the Promenade deck and Seven Seas on the International deck. For more informal fare, dinner is served on a "first-come" basis at Le Bistro on the Sun deck from 7 P.M. to midnight. Little appetites like such choices as a daily pasta dish selection made tableside, sandwiches, hot and cold appetizers, soup, and salad. The indoor/outdoor Sports Bar and Grill serves a breakfast/luncheon buffet as well as snacks. A wall of multiple televisions shows videotaped and live sports activities, making this a popular stop. This ship also has a sports bar, grill, health club, and spa.

The Broadway hit *The Pirates of Penzance*—good family fare—is performed at the ship's two-story theater.

NCL's fleetwide Dive-In shore excursions, a snorkeling program, includes all necessary equipment (mask, fins, snorkel, vest), full instruction, transportation, marine life tours, and fish identification card. At Great Stirrup Cay, NCL's private Bahamian "Pleasure

Island," the program operates all afternoon with snorkeling instruction available. Snorkeling here is good for beginners because you enter the shallow water from the beach; for those more experienced, there are deeper areas that reach approximately twenty feet. In addition, small and large floats, paddle boats, sailboats, kayaks, and view boards are available for rent.

The children's playroom, Trolland, is located on the Sports deck and is well stocked with toys and games. NCL Kid's Crew programs are announced on board through "Kid's Crew News" and "Teen Cruise News." Programs for ages six to eight (First Mates) are planned for mornings, afternoons, and early evening. Teen programs, exclusively for ages thirteen to seventeen, run intermittently throughout the day and evening. Kid's Club extends to include Junior Sailors (ages three to five) mornings only during summer months and major holidays.

The cabins are roomy and well furnished. All have televisions; none have bathtubs. In addition to third- and fourth-person staterooms on all decks except the Viking deck, there are seven family-sized staterooms with one double bed, one sofa bed and one upper bed (six of these rooms are located on Atlantic deck, the seventh on Biscayne deck). Six cabins are accessible to the physically challenged.

Royal Caribbean Cruise Line

Nordic Empress: entered service in 1990; 45,000 gross tons; 1,610-passenger capacity

Sleek and sophisticated, the *Nordic Empress* has a glorious nine-deck-high "centrum" (RCCL's term for atrium). Crystal and brass shine everywhere. Many of the ship's public rooms are adjacent to the centrum, making it easy for passengers to navigate the ship.

The Sun deck offers two swimming pools (one for children). The Windjammer Cafe serves buffet style, and is an option to the Carmen Dining Room, which features floor-to-ceiling windows and spans two levels. At night, the thirty-thousand-square-foot Sun deck is transformed into an outdoor entertainment area, with dancing under the stars to live music. While there's no cinema, a two-level showroom offers nightly entertainment.

The *Nordic Empress* visits RCCL's private island, CocoCay, for a day of fun in the sun. Opportunities include water sports (rentals are arranged in advance through the tour desk), shops with native crafts, and a sunken replica of Blackbeard's pirate ship to explore.

The children's program is offered year-round. The Kids' Konnection playroom on the Sun deck is bright and cheery, featuring a winding blue plastic slide and a variety of toys and games. There's no separate teen center, but a video room is on board.

RCCL's cabins are compact (read "small"), although there is a deck of deluxe-size cabins, with verandahs, that are quite roomy. Inside cabins are about 20 percent smaller. All decks have an ample number of triple and quad staterooms. Four cabins are wheelchair accessible.

Sovereign of the Seas: entered service in 1988; 73,192 gross tons; 2,276 passengers.

Sister ship to *Monarch of the Seas*, and *Majesty of the Seas*. Refer to chapter three for a ship description.

Best Bets

Best cruise ships for families with children under two:
NCL's *Leeward* offers baby-sitting for tots for a fee from noon to 2 A.M.

Best cruise ships for families with children ages two through four:
The Big Red Boat's *Star/Ship Atlantic* and *Star/Ship Oceanic* offer organized daylong programs that start at age two.

Carnival's *Ecstasy*'s and *Fantasy*'s organized programs start at age two.

Best cruise ships for families with children ages five through eleven:
All the choices are good ones. NCL's children's program has Circus at Sea; RCCL's *Sovereign of the Seas* also has a good children's program.

Best cruise ships for families with pre-teens and teens:
Carnival's *Ecstasy* and *Fantasy* delight this age. Pre-teens and teens have their own programs, and also find lots of regularly scheduled activities that interest them.

ON SHORE: THE BAHAMAS

Quick Facts

Currency: The Bahamian dollar and the U.S. dollar are used interchangeably throughout the islands and are always equivalent in value.
Language: English is spoken throughout the Bahamas.

Tourist Information: In the U.S., Bahamas Tourist offices can be found in most major cities, including: 150 E. 52 St., 28th Floor, New York, NY 10022, (212) 758-2777; 3450 Wilshire Blvd., Suite 208, Los Angeles, CA 90010, (213) 385-0033; 19495 Biscayne Blvd., Suite 809, Aventura, FL 33180, (305) 932-0051; and 8600 W. Bryn Mawr Ave., Suite 820, Chicago, IL 60631, (312) 693-1500.

In Nassau, the Ministry of Tourism Information Center is located in Rawson Square at the entrance to the docks. Free one-hour walking tours depart from here twice daily except on Thursdays and Sundays. In Freeport, there is a Ministry of Tourism office located at the port; depending on where your ship berths, it could be a short (or long) walk. The Ministry of Tourism's main office is located at the International Bazaar, which also houses a Grand Bahama Island Promotion Board office. Maps, brochures, and travel information are available here.

Emergency Numbers: Police and Fire: 919 in both Nassau and Freeport. Ambulance: 322-2221 in Nassau; 352-2689 in Freeport.

Main Towns: The two major Bahamian towns (and resort destinations) are Freeport (and neighboring Lucaya), located on Grand Bahama Island, and Nassau (and neighboring Cable Beach and Paradise Island), located on the northern end of New Providence Island.

Transportation: The cruise ship terminal is located right in downtown Nassau; in Freeport, it is located in a remote industrial center. The bustling, busy towns of Freeport and Lucaya are about four miles apart.

Buses: In Nassau, jitney buses run throughout the day from downtown Nassau, departing from the corner between Arby's and British Colonial Best Western on Bay Street in a westerly direction, and from Frederick Street in an easterly direction. Fare for adults is 75 cents; for children 50 cents. In Freeport, a number of privately owned buses run within the main Freeport/Lucaya area.

Car Rentals: Cars can be rented from major rental companies, including Avis, Hertz, National and Budget, in downtown Nassau and at a number of Freeport hotels. Driving is on the left throughout the Bahamas.

Ferry: A ferry travels between Nassau's dock area and Paradise Island. Another ferry goes to Coral Island.

Taxis: Metered taxis meet cruise ships in both Freeport and Nassau. Fares are fixed by the government at $2 for the first quarter mile and 30 cents for each additional quarter mile. (In Nassau, a bridge toll is added to the fare for transportation to Paradise Island.) Fares can be negotiated for longer trips; be sure to settle on a fee in advance.

Other Modes of Transportation: Air-conditioned limousines meet ships at the docks in Nassau. Generally, a two-hour tour can be negotiated for about $20 per couple. In Nassau's Rawson Square, across from the docks, horse and surreys are available for touring the old city; verify rates first. While a little bit hokey, children (especially little ones) enjoy this old-fashioned way to get around.

Best Bets

For families with children ages two through seven:

Marine life viewing area below sea level at Coral World

For families with children ages seven through eleven:
The Waterscape at the Atlantis Resort, Paradise Island; The Dolphin Experience, Lucaya
For families with pre-teens and teens:
Water sports at Xanadu Beach, Freeport
For adults:
Diving with UNEXSO in Lucaya; Atlantis Casino

Beaches

Nassau: Beautiful beaches abound throughout the island of New Providence. One of the most convenient

Diving into the underwater world of the Bahamas. Photo courtesy of the Bahamas Tourist Office.

for cruise ship passengers is the Western Esplanade that stretches west on Bay Street, across the street from shops and restaurants. There are rest rooms, changing facilities, and a snack bar, so it is particularly convenient for families with young children. Further west is a popular beach with locals, Saunders Beach. Even further west is Cable Beach, a strip of oceanfront hotels including the glitzy Carnival Crystal Palace.

Bahama Divers Ltd., 393-5644 or (800) 398-3483, offers a variety of scuba equipment for rent and a three-hour outing to wreck sites and coral reefs and gardens.

About a ten-minute taxi ride from downtown Nassau on Paradise Island, **Sea and Sky Ocean Sports** (363-3370) at the Sheraton Grand Hotel, a pleasant, quiet property next door to the new Atlantis Resort, offers waterskiing, windsurfing, parasailing, sailboat, and banana boat rentals. While the older children do their thing there's a nice, small patch of sandy beachfront (as well as a kiddie pool near a larger swimming pool) where younger siblings can playfully bide their time.

Atlantis (363-3000), a newly renovated resort, is a destination unto itself. Formerly a Merv Griffen resort, the sprawling property has been redone by Sol Kerzner, the South African hotel and casino developer. The centerpiece is the fourteen-acre Waterscape that includes what is billed as the "world's largest outdoor open water aquarium," an artificial "Lazy River" for rafters, water slides, a lagoon for watersports, a suspension bridge over a pool full of predators, and five swimming pools (choose from salt or fresh water). Inside the resort, adults play in the huge casino.

Freeport: Quiet, isolated beaches stretch for miles between Freeport/Lucaya and the eastern end of the island. About halfway between Freeport and Lucaya, **Xanadu Beach**, with its one-mile stretch of white sand, is popular. **Paradise Watersports** on Xanadu Beach, 352-2887, rents sailboards, water skis (with lessons available), Hobie Cats, and Sunfish (lessons also available). **Xanadu Dive Center**, 352-5856, also at the beach, offers a resort diving course.

Port Lucaya's **UNEXSO** (Underwater Explorers Society), 373-1244 or (800) 992-3483, is known throughout the world as a top-notch scuba diving facility that offers full equipment for rent, guides, underwater cameras (they will also videotape a dive for you), and dive sites that may include the nearby Treasure Reef, where a fortune in Spanish treasure was found in the 1960s. Minimum age is twelve. UNEXSO is located at 1 Royal Palm Way directly across from the Lucayan Beach Resort.

Nature and the Environment

Nassau: On the western end of New Providence, accessible by ferries and buses, **Coral Island** is a sixteen-acre marine attraction that presents twenty-four exhibits of brightly colored tropical fish, shark and turtle pools, a hands-on Marine Encounter pool and—the highlight—an observatory located twenty feet below sea level for spotting these delights. An observation tower that is more than one hundred feet high, offers two viewing decks and, of course, there's a gift shop.

Next door, the **Marine Park** bills its Reef Tank as home of the world's largest man-made living reef.

Visitors eye a panorama of sponges, coral, and other sea creatures. The facility has twenty-four aquariums, a shark tank, nature trails, waterfalls, tropical foliage, and a flamingo area. Check for feeding times—always a treat for kids to watch.

Close to Ft. Charlotte (see section on Historic Attractions and Museums), Ardastra Gardens on Chippingham Road is a gift to the eyes with tropical flowers, plants, and birds. Flamingoes perform daily; call 323-5806.

Freeport: **The Dolphin Experience**, the world's largest dolphin observation and training facility, is now located at **Sanctuary Bay**, about two miles east of Port Lucaya and accessible by ferry. Here you can get up close to blue bottle-nosed dolphins. If your older children are game (bring bathing suits), they can stand on a thirty-inch-tall wading platform and wait for a dolphin to swim past. It's wise to arrange this trip with your cruise ship. For example, the Big Red Boat offers this tour along with a souvenir T-shirt for $45; on your own it costs about $25, but the spots may all be taken by the cruise's shore tour company. You may make reservations several weeks in advance by calling the UNEXSO number listed above in the Beaches section.

Rand Nature Center (352-5438), a hundred-acre forest reserve in downtown Freeport, includes a half mile of winding trails. This walk affords a pleasant way to admire such local flora and fauna as wild orchids and birds such as the Bahamas woodstar (look carefully—they're smaller than hummingbirds) and other tropical delights. Perhaps you'll see a captive West Indian flamingo flock, curly tail lizards, fluttering butterflies, and harmless, native boa constrictors. Guided tours are offered twice daily; closed weekends.

Another super spot for interacting with nature is on the east end of the island. **Lucayan National Park** (same telephone number as Rand Nature Center) is a seaside preserve with trails, elevated walkways, and an observation platform. The natural forest is comprised of gumbo limbo and wild tamarind trees, sheltered pools teeming with marine life, and an extensive underwater cave system. Older children and teens might like to explore several caves, including Ben's Cave, where spiral steps lead to a pool of freshwater fish. The self-guided tour takes about thirty minutes. At the end, opt for a dip at Gold Rock, a quiet white-sand beach.

The Garden of the Groves, on the island's east end, intrigues horticulturists with eleven acres of rare varieties of flowers and trees landscaped among waterfalls and streams.

Outdoor Sports

Nassau: **The Cable Beach Golf Club,** owned by Radisson Cable Beach Casino and Golf Resort, is the oldest and the most highly respected on the island. Arrange a tee time through your cruise ship tour director or call 327-6000 or (800) 333-3333. Many major properties offer tennis at reasonable fees to nonguests. The Best Western British Colonial Beach Resort (322-3301) with three hard courts is a convenient location for cruise ship passengers.

The **Atlantis Submarine** tour (356-2837), which includes a cruise to the dive site and an island tour, descends the depths to see coral reefs and sea flora. The tour takes three hours; the actual sub time is fifty minutes. Children must be at least four years old. (If you book this through the Big Red Boat, you won't be paying much more than if you do it on your own.) Take precautions if you or your children are prone to seasickness because there's a good deal of bobbing and swaying before the sub actually submerges.

Freeport: Choose from two golf courses, both par 72, at **Bahamas Princess Resort & Casino**, 352-6721. **Lucaya Beach Resort and Casino** (373-7777) has four tennis courts.

Gallop along with the surf at **Pinetree Stables** (373-3600), which offers beach and trail rides Sunday through Tuesday. Group or private children's lessons are available.

Historic Attractions and Museums

Nassau: Named after the wife of British King George III and built in the 1700s, Ft. Charlotte (322-7500) is set high on a hilltop off West Bay Street at Chippingham Road. There is everything here that a kid could want from a fort: a moat, drawbridge, ramparts, and dungeons plus sweeping harbor views. At the foot of the hill, look for **Clifford Park**'s playing fields where you might catch a cricket or rugby game in progress.

If strolling downtown, stop in for a peek at the **Nassau Public Library and Museum** on Shirley Street (322-4907). Originally built in the late 1700s as a jail, the small prison cells now house books. There are also some historical documents here. This is a unique place that children might enjoy seeing.

If you happen to be in town at the right time—every other Saturday at 10 A.M. (check by calling 322-7500)—you'll be able to watch the colorful changing of the guard ceremony at **Government House** on George

Street, the official resident of the governor-general of the Bahamas.

Freeport: **The Grand Bahama Museum** (352-4045) adjoins the **Garden of the Groves**. The museum houses artifacts of the Lucayan Indians, a friendly tribe pursued relentlessly by the fierce Caribs. Remind your children that when Columbus arrived here in 1492, the island was already populated by natives.

Best Eateries and Snacks

Nassau: Many youngsters will be delighted to know that familiar fast food abounds in Nassau just a stone's throw from the cruise ship piers. But get them to try such local specialties as peas and rice and conch fritters. **Passin' Jacks**, on the top floor of the **Nassau Harbour Club** on Bay Street (394-3245), is a pleasant place for lunch or a light supper. Sit on the wrap-around porch with a harbor view and choose from fresh broiled grouper, cracked conch, or, for the more faint-of-heart younger set, nine types of burgers as well as salads and fajitas. Passin' Jacks has a children's menu as well. Also on Bay Street, next to the straw market, is **Skans**—a basic-looking cafeteria—which serves everything from barbecued chicken to steamed jackfish to cheeseburgers. (In other words, there's something for everyone.) Call 325-5536.

Freeport: Freeport's International Bazaar hosts a number of eateries. **Michel's Cafe** is a casual, comfortable spot for light snacks and simple meals. Eat outside under an umbrella-covered table or inside (there are only about a dozen tables). The choices include a nice mix of familiar American and basic Bahamian cuisine (352-2191).

Lucaya: **Billie Joe's**, next to the Grand Bahama Beach Hotel (formerly Radisson Lucaya Beach), is a little beach "hut" that serves up an amazing array of fresh conch in various forms from fritters to salad. If your kids won't bite, burgers are served, too.

Pusser's Co. Store and Pub, in the Port Lucaya Marketplace, is a restaurant/bar with a nautical decor. While casual, it's popular so you'll need reservations (373-8450), particularly for the outdoor terrace that overlooks Port Lucaya. The hearty English fare includes shepherd's pie and lamb chops. For more local cuisine, sample the Bahamian lobster tail.

Shopping

Nassau: The approximate fifty percent discount off what you'd pay in the U.S. makes duty-free shopping fun—and profitable—throughout the Bahamas. In Nassau, Bay Street is the main thoroughfare. The shops along the way (and the arcades that lead from the street) abound with a wide range of imported watches, crystal, china, cameras, perfume, and the like. As always, know the prices back home and factor in shipping charges, if any, before you count up your savings. Bargain at the **Strawmarket**, located in the middle of Bay Street. Eager and sometimes overeager vendors proffer hand-woven straw goods. If aggressive selling techniques bother you, skip this stop. While shopping, keep an eye out for the brightly colored batik clothing made on the Bahamian island of Andros. You'll find the fabrics in everything from tots' clothes to women's sarongs.

Bargain shopping in the Bahamas. Photo courtesy of the Bahamas Tourist Office.

TIP: If you're female, shortly after departing your cruise ship, a group of women will greet you in a large outdoor area asking if you'd like your hair braided. Your daughter may enjoy this—it's a cheap, fast, and a fun way to go native (the locals will add beads to the braids for a nominal charge). Be sure to apply sunscreen to your now-exposed scalp, which can sunburn, too.

Freeport: The best buys are at the **International Bazaar**, located on ten acres at the intersection of Mall Drive and West Side Highway. Dozens of shops sell fine, imported products at good discounts. Next door, a straw market has the usual array of souvenirs, and haggling is allowed. At Harborside in Port Lucaya, there are about seventy-five boutiques and restaurants housed in a dozen buildings. Browse, browse, browse.

7

Hawaii

The cruise line that sails to Hawaii most frequently is American Hawaii. Their two ships, the *Constitution* and the *Independence*, offer weeklong voyages to the islands year-round, whereas other cruise lines offer only occasional voyages to Hawaii. For a complete schedule of cruises, your best bet is to consult your travel agent.

THE LINES

American Hawaii

- *Constitution*: in dry dock for refurbishment until June 29, 1996.
- *Independence*: seven-day cruises round-trip from Honolulu (Oahu) to Kona and Hilo on the Big Island, visiting Lahaina (Maui) and Nawiliwili (Kauai). The *Constitution* departs Tuesdays, and the *Independence* departs Saturdays, year-round.

Cunard

- *Vistafjord* offers two Hawaii/Tahiti cruises in February.

Holland America Line

- *Rotterdam*: sixteen- or nineteen-day cruises leaving from Los Angeles and arriving in Vancouver with stops in Kona and Hilo on the Big Island, Port Allen (Kauai), Honolulu (Oahu), and Lahaina (Maui). One cruise in May and one in the fall.

Princess Cruises

- *Pacific Princess*: ten-, eleven-, and sixteen-day cruises from Los Angeles to Tahiti, Tahiti to Hawaii, Oahu to Tahiti, or Oahu to Mexico. Ports include the islands of Kauai, Oahu, Maui, Hawaii, Christmas Island, Bora Bora, Moorea, and Papeete; January and February.

Royal Caribbean Cruise Line

- *Legend of the Seas*: ten-night cruises, one from Vancouver to Honolulu stopping in Hilo and Kailua Kona on the Big Island, and Port Allen on the island of Kauai; the other cruise leaves from Honolulu and arrives in Ensenada, Mexico, with stops at Port Allen, Hilo, and Kailua Kona; spring and fall. Because these itineraries are relatively new for RCCL, they are subject to change.

Best Bets

Because American Hawaii is the only line offering year-round cruises, these ships are the best bet for families, especially in summer and on holidays when the children's programs are operating. At other times, check with RCCL's *Legend of the Seas*, which is supposed to operate children's programs for ages five through seventeen year-round. Try to find out how many children are booked for this cruise to see how extensive the program will be.

THE SHIPS

American Hawaii

Constitution: entered service in 1951; refurbished in 1996; 30,090 gross tons; 788-passenger capacity. (In dry dock for refurbishment until June 29, 1996.)

Independence: entered service in 1951; refurbished in 1994; 30,090 gross tons; 802-passenger capacity

American Hawaii Cruises is the only cruise line that has weeklong cruises through the Hawaiian islands all year. Each of these ships visits five ports on four islands in seven days. Not only do you sample the different islands (and they truly are different) but you arrive the easy way, without packing and unpacking, and without spending money and time on inter-island flights.

Among the changes made by the new parent company, the Delta Queen Steamboat Company, is a commitment to increase the presence of Hawaiian culture on board. The decor, entertainment, cuisine, and children's program all reflect the unique culture. The *Independence* also features hands-on exhibits on Hawaiian culture. In the Kama'aina Lounge, passengers peruse displays on the environment, legends, gods, early Polynesian voyages, the land, people, food, and the arts. A huge, colorful mural, painted by Hawaiian artists, depicting family village life adorns the room. Children and adults can create feather capes, participate in a game of Hawaiian-style checkers, touch lava rocks, and listen to recordings of oral histories at the Hoi Hoi Showplace. Hawaiian dancers and entertainers perform some evenings. Once

> **TIP:** Don't expect a casino with gambling (at least not until the laws change) because American Hawaii's ships keep to American waters.

refurbished, the *Constitution* should have a similar decor and emphasis on Hawaiian culture.

American Hawaii Cruise Line offers its *keiki* (Hawaiian for "child") program in summer and during Christmas for ages five to twelve and ages twelve to sixteen from 8 A.M. to 9 P.M. with breaks for meals. As part of the increased focus on Hawaiian culture, children participate in some hands-on fun Hawaiian style by pounding poi, creating a rubbing of a turtle petroglyph, making leis, and learning the hula (something one young traveler especially appreciated). All ages share a large children's room with big-screen television for watching movies and a Ping-Pong table. The room, below deck somewhere, can be difficult for some kids, especially youngsters, to find.

Along with Continental and American fare, the menu features Hawaiian-spiced dishes. Besides steak or chicken, entrees may include Maui mango Pasta with king prawns or mahi mahi. A children's menu with such staples as burgers and spaghetti is available. Of course, the coffee is Kona, one of

> **TIP:** For 1996, American Hawaii is running a promotion in which children under eighteen cruise free when sharing a cabin with two full-fare passengers except on the December 21 and 28 sailings.

the best varieties. There are *Pu'uwai* (heart-healthy) choices, too.

A limited room service menu is available, but the crew does aim to please. On one sailing, when we asked for an early dinner to be brought to our cabin so that our first-grader could eat before joining the evening children's program, our cabin steward gladly went out of her way to accommodate us even though bringing us plates of spaghetti and burgers did not conform to the "official" policy. We hope this helpful attitude hasn't changed.

The new decor in the *Independence* and the renovated *Constitution* displays the colors, textures, and traditional fabrics of Hawaii. Cabins are named for Hawaiian flowers, historical personalities, and items of Hawaiian culture. Want to relax in your cabin to ukulele music? ("Hang loose," as they say.) Just tune in to an in-cabin channel for authentic Hawaiian music. Cabins have phones but no televisions. Each ship has many cabins that accommodate three or four passengers. Some cabins are especially spacious with queen-sized beds.

Cunard

Vistafjord: (Refer to chapter four for a ship description.)

Holland America

Rotterdam: (Refer to chapter eight for a ship description.)

Princess Cruises

Pacific Princess: entered service in 1951; refurbished in 1992; 20,000 gross tons; 640-passenger capacity

Yes, the *Pacific Princess* is the one—the original ship
featured on the television show *The Love Boat*. Her
$40 million refurbishment added a two-story lobby and
lots of glass and mirrors to create a sense of space. The
ship has a casino, and one of the pools has a retractable dome ceiling, which is nice for inclement weather.

This Princess ship, older in some ways but more
sedate, offers a welcome alternative to the line's larger
glitzier vessels. But if you're accustomed to the choices
and bustle of larger ships, you might find the Pacific
Princess a bit stodgy.

Some cabins are workable at about 126 square feet,
but others are larger. All cabins have television and
terry cloth robes for adults, and some cabins have
refrigerators as well. Four cabins are wheelchair
accessible.

Royal Caribbean Cruise Lines

The Legend of the Seas: entered service in 1995; 70,000
gross tons; 1,808 passengers. (Refer to chapter eight
for a complete ship description.)

ON SHORE: HAWAII
(The Big Island)

No tour of Hawaii is complete without a visit to the
island of Hawaii, known also as the Big Island. The
nickname derives from the simple fact that this is the
largest of Hawaii's islands, with 4,038 square miles.
This is the Hawaii of legendary volcanoes and land-
scapes of lava-striped earth. Kilauea, one of the
island's volcanoes, is still active, sending hot lava

streaming across roadsides. Tours can take you to see the red lava flows. On this island, you'll also enjoy good snorkeling, lush gardens, and languid waterfalls.

Quick Facts

Main Towns: Hilo, Waimea, and Kona
Tourist Information:

Hawaii Visitors Bureaus: 250 Keawe St., Hilo, HI 96720, (808) 961-5797; 75-5719 West Alii Dr., Kailua Kona, Kona, HI 96740, (808) 329-7787.

Division of State Parks: (808) 933-4200.

National Park Service: 300 Ala Moana Blvd., Honolulu, HI 96850, (808) 546-7584.

Volcanic Activity Hotline: (808) 967-7977.

Emergency Numbers: Ambulance, fire, and police: 911.
Transportation:
Cars: If you want to do much sightseeing, rent a car. This can be done through the ship's tour office, but be sure to reserve as soon as possible after you board. Rental cars are in short supply in Hawaii. Rental car companies, available at the Hilo Airport, include:

Avis: (808) 329-1745 or (800) 331-1212;

Dollar: (808) 961-6059 or (800) 800-4000;

Hertz: (808) 935-2896 or (800) 654-3131; and

National Car Rental: (808) 329-1674 or (800) 227-7368.

The same companies are represented in Kona:

Avis: (808) 327-3000 or (800) 331-1212;

Dollar: (808) 329-2744 or (800) 800-4000;

Hertz: (808) 329-3566 or (800) 654-3131; and

National Car Rental: (808) 329-1675 or (800) 227-7368.

Buses: The Mass Transportation System (MTS) (25 Aupuni St. in Hilo, (808) 935-8241) operates the Hele-On Bus.

Taxis: Taxi service is available in Hilo through Hilo Harry's, (808) 935-7091, and Bob's Taxi, (808) 959-4800. In Kona, call Paradise Taxi, (808) 329-1234, or Marina Taxi, (808) 329-2481.

Best Bets

For all ages:
Hawaii Volcanoes National Park

For families with children six and younger:
Onekahakaha Beach Park, with lifeguards and a protected breakwater

For families with children ages seven through eleven:
Atlantis Submarine dives; Onizuka Space Center

For families with pre-teens and teens:
Hikes with Hawaii Forest and Trail

Beaches

If you swim only in designated areas, **Onekahakaha Beach Park** off Machida Lane, is a good bet. It features lifeguards and an area protected with breakwater. While not hard to get to, the directions sound complicated, so ask locals for the specifics. **Richardson's Ocean Park** (2349 Kalanianaole Ave., Keau-

Meet feathered friends in Hawaii. Photo courtesy of American Hawaii Cruises.

kaha, (808) 935-3830, offers good snorkeling and swimming.

A favorite beach for tourists in Kona is **Magic Sands Beach** (or Disappearing White Sands Beach), named for the winter storms that periodically wash away the sand and expose the rocky beach only to deposit more sand later. The beach is known for boogie boarding, but the surf is feisty, making it intimidating for small children and new swimmers.

Nature and the Environment

Don't miss **Hawaii Volcanoes National Park**, (808) 967-7311, about forty-five minutes southwest of Hilo.

The Visitor's center provides a brochure, "Road Guide to Hawaii Volcanoes National Park," and the self-guided tour is easy to follow with clear explanations and mile markers.

If you have the time, follow **Crater Rim Drive**, which makes an eleven-mile circuit around Kilauea caldera. Children are impressed with the steaming sulfur banks and **Kilauea Iki Crater**, a crusted lava lake three thousand feet wide. Get out of the car and walk through the **Thurston Lava Tube**, a 0.3-mile-long tunnel formed by cooled lava flow.

Akaka Falls State Park (Akaka Falls Road, Route 220, 808-933-4200, the general number for all state parks), is about 13.5 miles north of Hilo on Route 19, then five miles west on Akaka Falls Road. The park offers hikes to two waterfalls—Akaka Falls and Kahuna Falls. A circular forty-minute path through ferns, bamboo, and other greenery leads you to **Kahuna Falls**, which tumbles and crashes one hundred feet below, and to **Akaka Falls**, which plunges even farther to more than four hundred feet.

Outdoor Sports

Snorkeling enthusiasts can rent gear, including boogie boards and prescription snorkel masks (great if you need glasses), at **Snorkel Bob's** near the Kona Hilton, (808) 329-0770. **King Kamehameha Divers** in the King Kamehameha Hotel, (808) 329-5662, offers dives for beginners and for those who are certified, and it also rents snorkeling equipment.

Popular places to tee off in Kona are: **Makalei Hawaii Country Club**, 72-3890 Hawaii Belt Road (Mamalahoa Highway), (808) 325-6625 or (800)

606-9606, and the newly renovated **Mauna Kea Beach Hotel**, 1 Mauna Kea Beach Drive, (808) 882-7222 or (800) 882-6060, where one hole tests your skill by challenging you to hit over the Pacific Ocean (an inlet about 150 yards across).

Historic Attractions and Museums

While in Hilo, you'll want to visit the **Hawaii Tropical Botanical Gardens**, a nature preserve and sanctuary that features more than twenty acres of gardens. It is located at Onomea Bay, about seven miles north of Hilo on RR 143-A, Papaikou, HI 96781, (808) 964-5233.

And in Kona, you don't want to miss the **Onizuka Space Center**, (808) 329-3441, which is dedicated to Hawaii's first astronaut and houses many exhibits on loan from NASA. This museum has a moon rock, Apollo rocket model, NASA space suit, and such hands-on displays as a Manned Maneuvering Unit (truly a kid pleaser).

Pu'uhonua o Honaunau, formerly called the City of Refuge National Historical Park, off Route 160 about nineteen miles south of Kailua-Kon, was a sanctuary established in the fifteenth century as a refuge for those who broke religious taboos. Children like perusing the carved totem poles, seeing the koa wood canoes, and learning about ancient Hawaii.

The **Historic Parker Ranch** on Mamalahoa Highway is the site of the Parker family's 1800s ranch house and museum-like home. Here the exhibits are about Hawaiian-style cowboys.

The thirteen-hundred-acre **Kaloko-Honokohau National Historical Park**, (808) 329-6881, contains

> **TIP:** The Atlantis Submarine bobs for awhile until its descent. This may make some children (and adults) seasick. Take precautions.

more than two hundred historical artifacts, including Hawaiian grave sites, fishing shrines, and petroglyphs. The park is a short drive east of Kona.

Other Attractions

The **Atlantis Submarine** plunges into the ocean off Kona. Children should be at least thirty-six inches tall and unafraid of tight quarters, but the diver's-eye-view of coral and schools of fish is great. Reserve ahead at the Atlantis Submarine's desk at the King Kamehameha Kona Beach Hotel, Alii Drive, (808) 329-6626 or (800) 548-6262.

For an eco-adventure, call **Hawaii Forest and Trail** at (808) 329-1993, an outfitter that leads six- to eight-person hikes into private, remote lands. Trails vary from easy to difficult. Rob Pacheco's emphasis is the environment and local history. Tours also go to the Pu'U'O Ranch Rain Forest, the Hualalai Volcano, the Hakalau Forest National Wildlife Refuge and Hawaii Volcanoes National Park. Children under three go free.

Best Eateries and Snacks

There are lots of eateries in Hilo and Kona. Some picks: **Cafe Pesto**, (808) 969-6640, has good pizza. **Don's Family Deli**, 485 Hinano St., Hilo; (808) 935-9099, offers ribs, chicken, homemade chili, and fish for reasonable prices. In Kona, get a snack at the inexpensive **Lanai Coffee Shop** in the Kona Hilton Hotel, (808) 329-3111.

Downtown Kona and Hilo—and other places on the island—feature **Lappert's Ice Cream**. One location is Alii Drive, Kailua Kona, (808) 326-2290. Locals love the papaya and coconut macadamia nut fudge.

Shopping

Kona has several art galleries worth noting. **Holualoa Gallery** shows prints, sculpture, glasswork, ceramics, and paintings by local artists. Another popular shop is the **Kimura Lauhala Shop** in Holualoa, which features genuine Hawaiian crafts.

ON SHORE: KAUAI

Less developed than Maui and more lushly green, Kauai presents the languid and less-populated Hawaii of long ago. On the sands, fairways, and hiking trails, you're likely to savor some space.

Quick Facts

Main Towns: Waimea, Lihue, and Koloa
Tourist Information: The Chamber of Commerce is at 2970 Kele St., (808) 245-7363, and the Hawaii Visitors Bureau is at 3016 Umi St., (808) 245-3971.
Emergency Numbers:

Ambulance, fire, and police: 911.

Fire Department (non-emergency): 4223 Rice St., (808) 241-6500.

Police Headquarters (non-emergency): 3060 Umi
St., (808) 241-6711.

Transportation:
Car Rental: Companies include:

Budget: (800) 527-0700 or (808) 245-1901;

Dollar: (800) 800-4000 or (808) 245-3651;

National: (800) 227-7368 or (808) 245-5636; and

Hertz: (800) 654-3016 or (808) 245-3356.

Bikes: Pedal and Paddle, (808) 826-9069, rents mountain bikes, helmets, and locks so you and your teens
can enjoy a free-wheeling Kauai tour.

Best Bets

For all ages:
Waimea Canyon State Park

For families with children under age seven:
Poipu Beach

**For families with children ages seven through
eleven:**
Poipu Beach; Captain Zodiac raft trip

For families with pre-teens and teens:
Windsurfing at Anini Beach

For adults:
Golf in Princeville

Beaches

Kalalau State Park is a good bet. *Conde Naste Traveler* magazine has rated this as one of the best American beaches with the most beautiful surrounding
wilderness.

TIP: Rip tides and strong undertows claim many lives in Hawaii. Read the signs, observe the cautions, and, when in doubt, look but don't swim. Parts of Kauai have especially rough surf. (We are repeating ourselves, but this is important.)

The drive from Lihue to the popular **Poipu Beach** area is about fourteen miles, a thirty-minute drive. Bring along a picnic lunch because this beach has a wide grassy area with a few picnic tables.

Nature and the Environment

Snorkeling is a popular activity in Kauai due to its diverse coastal reef formations. Some great beaches for snorkeling are **Makua Beach**, or Tunnels Beach, on the north shore (also good for advanced windsurfing), and **Koloa Landing** and **Prince Kuhio Park** on the south shore. Again, check with the locals—some areas may be appropriate for strong swimmers only. Beginner and intermediate windsurfers enjoy the steady breezes and protected lagoon waters of **Anini Beach** on the north shore.

Hike part of the **Kalalau Trail**, the land route that stretches for eleven miles one way across the Na Pali cliffs, once home to ancient Hawaiian kings. The trails, part of the Na Pali Coast State Park can be adventurous (read "difficult"). The first half mile, scenic and uphill, is reasonably do-able.

If your family loves gardens, write ahead for tickets to the **National Tropical Botanical Garden**, P.O. Box 340, Lawaii, HI 96765, or call (808) 332-7361. A van takes you for a look-and-see tour of the 186 lush acres of the Limahuli Valley. You will stop to smell the orchids, admire ferns and flowers, and learn about plumeria, monkey pod trees, and banana plants.

If your time is limited, head straight to **Waimea Canyon State Park**, which is often called the Grand Canyon of the Pacific. The entrance is about thirty-six miles, one hour and fifteen minutes from Lihue. On your way to the **Waimea Canyon Lookout**, at thirty-four hundred feet, pick out some easy hikes. Brochures are available at the visitor center.

Outdoor Sports

Golf is a great draw to this island. Among the choices: **The Princeville Makai Golf Course** comes highly rated, (808) 826-3580, as do the **Prince Golf Course**, (808) 826-5000, and the **Lagoons Course at Kauai Lagoons**, (808) 241-6000.

A favorite eco-tour of Kauai is with **Captain Zodiac** (or Na Pali Zodiac, (808) 826-9371 or (800) 422-7824). On these Zodiac raft tours, which pass the majestic Na Pali Coast, you might see spinner dolphins and sea turtles and explore sea caves.

Fulfill a fantasy. Go horseback riding on the beach. Some stables that sport such trails are **CJM Stables** (1731 Kelaukia St., Koloa, HI 96796, 808-742-6096)

TIP: Some snorkeling outfitters that offer expertise with disabled travelers are **Aquatic Adventures**, (4-1380 Kuhio Highway, Kapaa, 800-204-4613 or 808-822-1431), **SeaFun** (P.O. Box 3002, Lihue 96746, 808-245-6400), and **Ocean Quest SeaSports Divers** (1672 Kuahale, Kapaa, 808-822-3589).

and **Garden Island Ranch** (9250 Kaumualii Highway, Waimea 96796, 808-338-0052).

Historic Attractions and Museums

Kauai is so lush, you're going to want to be outdoors. But for a change of pace or a rainy day activity, stop by the **Kauai Museum** at 4428 Rice St., Lihue, (808) 245-6931. This small museum has examples of such Hawaiian hand-crafted items as koa wood tables and calabashes, *ipu* (drums made from gourds), decorated *tapas* (cloth), and a bamboo *ohe hano ihui* (nose flute).

A popular tour is a helicopter flight over **Waimea Canyon** and along the **Na Pali Coast**. Fly by waterfalls, over ancient caves, and over cliffs. The adventure is both memorable and expensive. Make sure you go with a reputable company. It may be easier and more reliable to book this tour through your ship's tour desk.

Take a surfing lesson in the world-famous surf spot of **Hanalei Bay** on the south shore. A seven-time world champion surfer, Margo Oberg has her own surfing school outside of the Kiahuna Plantation Resort. Call **Margo Oberg Surfing School** (2253 Poipu Road, Koloa, HI 96756, 808-742-6411) for lessons or equipment rental.

Best Eateries and Snacks

Popular Kauai eateries include the **Koloa Broiler** on Koloa Road in Old Koloa Town not far from Poipu, (808) 742-9122. Here you broil your entree—mahi mahi, chicken, or steak—yourself. The **Kapaa Fish and Chowder House** at 4-1639 Kuhio Highway serves such island-inspired food as coconut shrimp, seafood fettuccine, and sautéed clams, (808) 822-7488.

Shopping

Old Koloa Town offers T-shirt shops and souvenirs. Browse **Crazy Shirts** and other shops. **Lappert's Ice Cream** is here as well as in other locations in town.

ON SHORE: LANAI

If you've been to the Hawaiian islands before and want to go someplace "new," take a day trip to Lanai. This island turned from a sheep and cattle ranch into the world's largest pineapple plantation when James Dole bought the island in 1922 for $1.1 million. Now the small island has traded in its pineapple plants for hotels and tourism. Because of the small size, some children and teens may be bored here.

To get here, take a forty-five-minute boat ride from Lahaina Harbor on Maui with **Expeditions**, (808) 661-3756. There are five round-trips daily. On the way, you might spot dolphins, whales, and flying fish.

Quick Facts

Main Towns: Lanai City is where nearly all of the island's residents live (not quite three thousand people), and all three roads on the island radiate out from the town.
Emergency Numbers: Fire, police, emergency: 911.
Transportation:
There are only three paved roads outside of town. A four-wheel-drive vehicle is necessary. The best way to

get information on jeep or bike rentals is to contact the
Manele Bay Hotel in Lanai City, (808) 565-7700, or the
Lodge at Koele in Lanai City, (808) 565-7300 or (800)
321-4666 for reservations.

Best Bets

For all ages:
Hulopo'e Beach

For families with pre-teens and teens:
Horseback riding

For teens and adults:
Golf

Beaches

One of the best beaches on Lanai's northeast coast
is **Kaiolohia**, also known as **Shipwreck Beach**.
Treacherous trade winds as well as strong currents
and shallow reefs have made this area a ships' graveyard. Follow the sign for "Federation Camp," onto Lapahiki Road to the beach. There is a liberty
ship here that was intentionally run aground from
1941 to 1942 by the Navy. Several other ships have
wrecked here and around Lanai, including a British
ship, the *Alderman Wood*, and American ships, the
London in the 1820s, *Charlotte C* in 1931, and the
Tradewind in 1834. Explore an abandoned lighthouse,
search for petroglyphs in the area (get a map from
the concierge at the Lodge at Koele), and look along
the beach for old bottles, shells, or artifacts that may
wash up.

Hulopo'e Beach is a marine reserve and the best
beach in Lanai for swimming. This beach is a good

place to wander, exploring the tidepools for marine life. Beach kiosks have brochures.

Nature and the Environment

Follow the **Munro Trail** from the summit of **Mount Lana'ihale**, which can be reached by four-wheel-drive vehicle only. Six islands can be seen from here on a clear day. If you're wondering about the abundance of pine trees on the island, they were brought here by a New Zealand ecologist, George Munro, in the early-1900s.

Outdoor Sports

Horseback riding is a popular activity on Lanai. The Lodge at Koele, (808) 565-7300, can make reservations for a two-hour Paniolo Trail ride through guava groves or a one-hour plantation ride.

Golf is exceptional on Lanai, which boasts two championship courses: the **Challenge of Manele**, designed by Jack Nicklaus, and **The Experience at Koele**, designed by Ted Robinson and Greg Norman.

Historic Attractions and Museums

Take a walking tour of this small city of old-fashioned cottages that date back to the 1920s. If your family is experienced in hiking, don't miss the **Luahiwa Petroglyphs**, a collection of ancient carved boulders, some of the best in the state.

Keomuku, a ghost town near Shipwreck Beach, was a prosperous sugar-producing town until 1901, when water at the mill became unexplainably unusable and unclean. The town was abandoned. Look for petroglyphs nearby on the large stones.

Best Eateries and Snacks

S & T's is a local fast food eatery, only open until 12:30 P.M., and next door is **Blue Ginger**, (808) 565-6363, the only bakery in town. The hotels (**Hotel Lanai**, the **Manele Bay Hotel**, and the **Lodge at Koele**) have good restaurants.

ON SHORE: MAUI

Your children will never be bored on Maui. Teens savor the snorkeling and the chance to bike ride down the side of a volcano. For adults, there's plenty of golf, spas, and scenic drives. Young ones love the beaches.

Quick Facts

Main Town: Lahaina

Tourist Information: The Maui Visitors Bureau can be reached by writing to P.O. Box 580, Wailuku, HI 96793, or call (800) 525-6284. For the County Department of Parks and Recreation in Wailuku, call (808) 243-7230; for permits, call (808) 243-7389; and for weather, call (808) 877-5111.

Emergency Numbers: Ambulance, fire, police: 911.

Transportation:

Car Rental: Companies include:

   Avis: (800) 331-1212 or (808) 871-7575;

   Budget: (800) 527-0700 or (808) 871-8811;

Hertz: (800) 654-3131 or (808) 877-5167;

National Car Rental: (800) 227-7368; and

CAR Rentals: (808) 877-2054 or (800) 367-6080.

Mopeds: A & B Moped Rental at 3481 Lower Honoapi-
ilani Highway, (808) 669-0027, rents mopeds to licensed drivers eighteen or older.

Best Bets

For all ages:
Haleakala National Park; snorkeling at Molokini;
    beach and golf at Wailea

For families with children under age seven:
Lahaina-Kaanapali & Pacific Railroad; beach at
    Wailea

**For families with children ages seven through
eleven:**
Haleakala National Park (driving and walking
    tours); snorkeling at Molikini; beach at Wailea

For families with pre-teens and teens:
Dig Me Beach, Kaanapali; Haleakala National Park
    (bike tour); snorkeling at Molokini

For adults:
Souvenir shopping in Lahaina; golf

Beaches

This is an island with miles and miles of beaches—a
mild surf that is great for swimming and watersports.
Favorite beaches for snorkeling include **Honolua
Bay**, a Marine Life Conservation District, and **Kapalua Bay**. Wailea has nice beaches along a strip of popular hotels and condominiums.

If you are traveling with a teen who is looking for some excitement, take the family to **Dig Me Beach** in Kaanapali where many young people gather. The windsurfing lessons are good here. **Mokuleia Beach** is a good place to watch expert surfing. (Don't even think about trying to put a board in the water here. The locals call this place "the slaughterhouse.")

Nature and the Environment

Spend at least one day exploring **Haleakala National Park** (Haleakala National Park Headquarters, Crater Road; 808-572-9306). This mountain is formidable at ten thousand feet. A favorite activity is to get to the peak in time to watch the sunrise. Your kids may not want to get up at 4 A.M. to begin the two-hour drive up; on the other hand, your teens may not have yet gone to bed yet. On the ascent, you pass farms and sugar fields, and craters at the top seem moon-like. Bring jackets. Even if it's seventy degrees at the bottom, it's much colder at the summit.

Stop at the **Visitors' Center** for books and brochures. Your children ages five to twelve can become Junior Rangers. Usually, they need to participate in (and complete) some activities. The program takes about two hours and is a fun way for children to learn about the delicate ecosystem of the mountain. The Junior Ranger patch makes a special Hawaiian souvenir.

Another popular and worthwhile hiking area is the **Iao Valley**, famous for a special rock formation called the Iao Needle. Along the drive up, there are some fun places to stop such as the **Bailey House Museum**, (808) 244-3326, in Wailuku where some artifacts from Hawaii's pre-colonial past are exhibited.

On the way to Iao Valley is the **Heritage Gardens at Kepaniwai Park**, a good place to stop for a picnic or for kids to run around. Throughout the park are replicas of dwellings and gardens of different cultural groups, such as Japanese, Chinese, Filipino, Portuguese and missionary. Admission to the park is free.

To obtain information on Iao State Park call the **Hawaii Nature Center**, (808) 244-6500. This educational center offers classes on a variety of subjects related to the park and Hawaiian history and guided hikes.

The road to **Hana** is fifty-two miles and takes about three hours one way. Resist the temptation to do this as a shore tour. Yes, the drive is spectacular—you pass cascading waterfalls, black sand beaches, and lush scenery. The trip however is bumpy and windy. Seven hours in a van (remember you have to come back, too) is far too much to do in one day. Instead, get outdoors and enjoy some other magical Maui moments that are nearer to you. Save Hana for when you can stay overnight.

Outdoor Sports

Molikini, a half-submerged volcanic crater about an hour's launch from **Maalaea Harbor** offers great snorkeling. Children will be wowed by the schools of rainbow-colored fish that are so tame they practically eat from your hand. This is a good trip to take through your ship's shore tour office.

Atlantis Submarines now offers combination tours, since teaming up with **Sunshine Helicopters**. The trips are dive and air tours of Hana or west Maui. You can still, however, just board the sub for an underwater view. For all 2 P.M. dives, the purchase of one full-fare ticket gets you one free admission ticket for a child twelve or under.

There are now enough biking trails on Maui to pedal from the east end of the island at the Wailea Resort to Kapalua on the west end. Much of the trail is along the shoreline. For bike rentals and tours, contact **Maui Mountain Cruisers** at 353 Hanamau, Kahului, Maui, HI 96732, (808) 572-0195.

Another popular bike trip: pedal all the way down Haleakala. The scenery is spectacular and the experience is memorable, but this tour can be dangerous because the road winds. This is recommended for agile teens and parents only. Some tour groups: **Maui Downhill**, 199 Dairy Road, Kahului, (808) 871-2155; and **Cruiser Bob's Downhill**, 99 Hana Highway, (808) 579-8444.

Try a kayaking and hiking tour. **South Pacific Kayaks and Outfitters**, (800) 77-OCEAN, offers a stream and waterfalls hike that lasts six to seven hours.

Some other companies that organize guided hikes with a range of skill: **Hike Maui**, (808) 876-0308; **Hawaii Nature Center**, (808) 244-6500; and **Nature Conservancy of Hawaii**, (808) 572-7849.

Historic Attractions and Museums

Take a guided tour through fields of local produce at the **Maui Tropical Plantation**, (808) 244-7643. Admission to the plantation is free, but for a fee you board a narrated Tropical Tram for a ride through sugar cane, pineapple, papaya, banana, coffee, macadamia nut, and tropical flower fields.

Young children especially like the **Lahaina-Kaanapali & Pacific Railroad** (or the Sugar Cane

Train), a replica of the 1890 Hawaiian railroad, (808) 661-0089. On this trip, a singing conductor intones information about the mountains and history of Maui's west shore.

For cultural entertainment, call the **Maui Arts & Cultural Center in Kahului** for a schedule of performing art shows and visual arts exhibits, (808) 244-SHOW.

Best Eateries and Snacks

There are too many eateries to mention in Lahaina, but not many on Haleakala's slopes. If you're going up to Haleakala, take a break at **Kula Lodge Restaurant** on Highway 377, (808) 878-2517. This informal eatery serves pasta, burgers, and fish. Your kids will welcome the time out of the car, not to mention the food.

Shopping

Lahaina is the place for souvenir shopping. The boutiques in town sell T-shirts, resort wear, jewelry (both fine and funky), and lots more. After browsing and buying, cool off with a cone from **Lappert's Aloha Ice Cream**, 808 Front St., (808) 661-3310, at the corner of Front and Marketplace.

ON SHORE: OAHU

Oahu is much busier than Waikiki, although there's many sites to see in Waikiki.

> **TIP:** Because American Hawaii cruises embark from
> Oahu, consider purchasing one of their reasonably
> priced add-on packages that allow for more days
> in Oahu.

Quick Facts

Main Towns: Honolulu, Waikiki, and Pearl City
Transportation:

Taxis: Cabs are readily available. Companies include
Aloha State Cab, (808) 847-3566, and Charley's, (808)
531-1333.

Buses: The Bus, (808) 848-5555, can get you around
most of the island, but cabs may be the easiest with
limited time.

Car Rentals: Rental companies include:

Avis: (808) 834-5536 or (800) 331-1212;

Budget: (808) 922-3600 or (800) 527-0700;

Dollar: (808) 831-2330 or (800) 800-4000;

Hertz: (808) 831-3500 or (800) 654-3131; and

National: (808) 831-3800 or (800) 227-7368.

Trolley: A great way to get around is the Waikiki Trolley, which stops every fifteen minutes from 8 A.M. to
about 1:30 A.M. at the following destinations: Royal
Hawaiian Shopping Center, Waikiki Aquarium, Hard
Rock Cafe, Maui Divers' Jewelry Design, Honolulu
Academy of Arts, Capitol/Iolani Palace, Hawaii Maritime Center, Dole Cannery Square, Hilo Harrie's,
Bishop Museum, Chinatown/Asia Mall/Maunakea
Street, Kamehameha Statue, Restaurant Row, Kewalo

Boat Harbor Fisherman's Wharf, Ward Warehouse, Ward Center, Ala Moana Center/Ala Moana Hotel, Ilikai Hotel, and the Hilton Hawaiian Village. Day passes and special rates for children age eleven and under are available. For tickets, call (808) 593-8073.

Best Bets

For families with children under age seven:
Swimming at Waikiki

For families with children ages seven through eleven:
Swimming at Waikiki; hiking at Diamond Head; Atlantis Submarine dive; Polynesian Cultural Center

For families with pre-teens and teens:
Snorkeling, riding, mountain biking at Kualoa Ranch

For adults:
Activities at Kualoa Ranch; hike with the Nature Conservancy

Beaches

The best beaches for families are on the south shore. But be careful because summer brings a strong, high surf. The south shore's beach park **Ala Moana** has the best public facilities as well as a reef to snorkel. Also on the south shore is Waikiki. Waikiki's sands are famous and very crowded, but the waves are relatively gentle. Arrive early if you want to pick your spot. Another popular spot, **Kailua Beach**, is located on Oahu's east coast. The waters here are good for experienced windsurfers. Also, **Fort DeRussy**, a large land area owned by the U.S. Army, is a rest and relaxation area for men and women of the military and their families. The beach is broad and the water pleasant for swimming.

Nature and the Environment

Diamond Head State Monument, off Diamond Head Road between Makapuu and 18th avenues, is probably Oahu's most noted landmark. Bring a flashlight and hike to the 760-foot summit. The round-trip takes about two hours; call (808) 587-0300.

The **Atlantis Submarine**, (808) 973-9811 or (800) 548-6262, also dives in Oahu and gives you a diver's-eye-view of the deep without the work. Passengers must be at least three feet tall.

The **Honouliuli Preserve**, on the summit of Oahu's Waianae Range, shelters many of Hawaii's disappearing flora and fauna. Outdoor-minded families with older children might like the rugged trails and lush scenery. Those under twelve are not allowed. The **Nature Conservancy Hike**, (808) 537-4508, also offers guided day hikes. Call for a schedule. These hikes allow you to see rare plants that grow nowhere else in the world as well as such critters as the Hawaiian owl. Another company that hosts hikes for adults and children is the **Hawaii Nature Center Hike** in upper Makiki Valley, (808) 955-0100.

At the **Waikiki Aquarium** (2777 Kalakaua Ave., 808-923-9741) rare monk seals sun and swim. The tanks of strangely striped, spotted, and rainbow-hued Hawaiian reef fish may delight young kids but tend to bore older ones.

About a twenty-minute drive from Waikiki, **Sea Life Park** at Makapuu Point in Waimanalo, (800) 767-8046, combines science and showmanship. Watch

the sea life in reef tanks. Learn about Humboldt penguins at the Hawaiian Ocean Theater; whales and
dolphins at the Whaler's Cove Show; endangered
birds, such as great frigates and boobies, at the bird
sanctuary; and green sea turtles at the turtle lagoon.

Outdoor Sports

Horseback riding is an ideal way to see the wonders
of Oahu's natural beauty. Just forty minutes from
Waikiki, the **Kualoa Ranch** is a 145-year-old, four-
thousand-acre ranch that is not only beautiful but
offers several outdoor activities, (808) 237-7321.
Guided horseback rides (walking only, no trotting)
follow paths that wind through lush green valleys.
Mountain biking/hiking tours lead to lookouts of
Kaneohe Bay, and swimming on Kualoa's private
island provides uncrowded beaches and great views of
the fluted Kualoa mountains.

Historic Attractions and Museums

Oahu has several museums dedicated to aerospace and
the military. Battery Randolph, a former beachfront
artillery defense installation that was once part of
Oahu's coastal defense forts, is now the **U.S. Army
Museum** at Fort DeRussy, (808) 438-2821. This museum documents Hawaii's military history in fifteen
exhibits, including several on World War II. Admission is free. The American Legion organizes narrated
walking tours of the **National Memorial Cemetery
of the Pacific**, a 116-acre graveyard at Punchbowl
Crater, the final resting place of more than thirty-

seven thousand American soldiers who lost their lives during three wars in the Pacific, (808) 946-6383. Tours are scheduled three times a day, Monday through Friday and include the graveyard's map galleries, the chapel, and the Courts of the Missing, which contain lists of almost thirty thousand missing servicemen or those buried at sea during the three wars.

The **U.S.S. Arizona Memorial and Visitor Center**, is dedicated to the attack of Pearl Harbor, (808) 422-0561. The guided tour includes a twenty-minute film and a ride to the memorial that floats above the midsection of the sunken battleship on which 1,177 Navy men lost their lives. Pick up free tickets to the memorial early in the morning because they go fast. Next to the Arizona Memorial Visitor Center, is the **Submarine Memorial Park** where the **U.S.S. Bowfin**, a World War II submarine, is docked, (808) 423-1341.

Another local tour option is **Top Gun Tours**, (808) 396-8112, which operates the only historic tour of Oahu's military bases. The Home of the Brave van tour stops at the Pearl Harbor Memorial, Hickham Air Force Base, Wheeler Army Air Base, and Schofield Barracks, all four of which look as they did during World War II. The tour also includes a drive through the National Memorial Cemetery of the Pacific at Punchbowl Crater. The tour does not operate on weekends.

The Bishop Museum at 1525 Bernice St., (808) 847-3511, offers extensive exhibits on the islands' natural history and cultural heritage. Children especially like learning about Hawaiian royalty and legends.

The Royal Hawaiian Mint's brand-new facility opened in 1995 in Honolulu, (800) 808-6468 or

(808) 949-6468. Children might like the exhibits of rare Hawaiian coins.

Best Eateries and Snacks

There are scores of eateries and good restaurants in Waikiki. **Restaurant Row** has more than ten restaurants, including Burger King and Sunset Grill (500 Ala Moana Blvd., 808-538-1411). The recently opened **Planet Hollywood**, (808) 924-7877, on Kalakaua Avenue is the twenty-third restaurant in the chain, which is famous for movie and television memorabilia. This is a good choice, especially if your pre-teens and teens want to add another Planet Hollywood T-shirt to their collection.

A restaurant with an all-natural, vegetarian menu is **Down to Earth Deli**, 2525 South King St., Honolulu, (808) 947-7678.

Shopping

You won't lack for stores. There's lots of shopping and much of it is expensive. **DFS Hawaii** at 330 Royal Hawaiian Ave. in Waikiki, (808) 931-2655, has duty-free goods for foreign shoppers.

With its outdoor bazaar atmosphere, the **Aloha Tower Marketplace**, at piers eight and ten in Honolulu, is a fun place to look for souvenirs. Honolulu has a two-hundred-year-old **Chinatown**, another interesting place to wander and visit such unique places as herb shops, noodle factories, and lei stands. The **Ala Moana Shopping Center** at 1450 Ala Moana Blvd. in Oahu, (808) 946-2811, is the largest open-air mall in the world with offerings from surf shops and boutiques to standards such as Sears and JC Penney. **Treasures of Polynesia** has unique items such as Samoan war clubs, handmade decorated bark cloth from Fiji, dolls dressed in traditional Maori attire, shell letter openers, and hand-painted trays from Tonga, (800) 367-7060, (808) 293-3333, or (808) 923-1861.

Clair De Lune (1050 Ala Moana Blvd., Honolulu, 808-596-0808) features Hawaiian collectibles and antiques such as restored koa works and 1940s fabrics.

8

✹❀✹❀✹❀✹❀✹❀✹❀✹❀✹❀✹❀✹❀✹❀✹

Alaska

Alaska's natural wonders make even the most blasé kid say, "awesome." A cruise here treats you to glacial ice fields, pristine lakes, and panoramas of snow-capped mountains. Alaska presents some of America's last great wildlands. Whether you hop aboard a float plane for a bird's-eye view of Misty Fjords National Monument, a thirty-six-hundred-acre wilderness of granite cliffs, spruce tree forests, and glacier-carved fjords, or take a raft through narrow inlets and coastal waterways in search of eagles, moose, and brown bear, Alaska's expansive landscape impresses.

This fascinating destination, however, comes with a few "bewares." Forget really warm summer weather. Sitka is no St. Thomas. On warm days, the temperature reaches the mid-seventies. Your children will not be frolicking in off-shore waters. So for relaxing down time, if your kids like to swim, choose a cruise ship with a covered or heated pool.

Another caution: to see the Alaska of your imagination, you must get away from the cruise dock. Doing so requires money. Nature-oriented shore tours, while worth it, are costly. Plan to spend a few hundred dollars per person (yes, per person) on float planes, helicopters, trains, Zodiac rafts, kayaks, and other conveyances that take you away from town and into the backcountry. It would be a shame to cruise to Alaska and see only city sites and museums. Come prepared to treat yourself and your children to at least a few of the outdoor thrills. (See the On Shore section.)

TIP: Wear layers and bring rain gear to combat the frequently wet weather.

THE LINES

Carnival

- *Tropicale*: seven-day cruises sailing northbound from Vancouver or southbound from Seward and Anchorage. All cruises visit College Fjord, Columbia Glacier, Lynn Canal, Skagway, Juneau, and Ketchikan. Southbound cruises also call at Valdez and cruise Yakutat Bay and Hubbard Glacier. Northbound cruises also visit Sitka and cruise Endicott or Tracy Arm. May through September.

Celebrity

- *Horizon*: seven-night cruises round-trip from Vancouver with stops at Juneau, Ketchikan, Tracy Arm, Skagway, Haines, and Misty Fjord; May, June, and September. Seven-night cruises from Vancouver to Seward with stops at Ketchikan, Juneau, Skagway, Hubbard Glacier, Valdez, and College Fjord; June, July, and August. Seven-night cruises from Seward to Vancouver with stops at Hubbard Glacier, Sitka, Juneau, Tracy Arm, Skagway, and Ketchikan; June, July, and August.

Cunard Cruise Lines

- *Crown Dynasty*: seven-day cruises leave from Vancouver to Seward, cruising the Inside Passage with stops at Skagway, Juneau, Wrangell, Ketchikan, Sitka, Hubbard Glacier, Misty Fjord, and Tracy Arm Fjord. May through September.
- *Sagafjord*: ten- and eleven-day cruises travel between Vancouver and Anchorage, visiting Ket-

chikan, Tracy Arm Fjord, Juneau, Skagway, Glacier Bay, Sitka, Hubbard Glacier, College Fjord, Valdez, Seward, Kenai Fjords National Park, and Cook Inlet. June through September.

Holland America Line

- *Nieuw Amsterdam*, *Statendam*, and *Westerdam*: ten-, twelve-, thirteen-day cruises, leaving from Vancouver or Seattle and cruising the Inside Passage, with stops in Ketchikan, Juneau, Mendenhall Glacier, Lynn Canal, Skagway, Valdez, and Sitka. May through September.

- *Noordam*, *Rotterdam*, and *Ryndam*: eleven-, twelve-, thirteen-, and fourteen-day cruises from Anchorage, Seattle, and Vancouver, touring Denali National Park, Fairbanks, Anchorage, Seward, Valdez, Harriman Fjord, College Fjord, Hubbard Glacier, Sitka, Juneau, and Ketchikan. May through September.

Norwegian Cruise Line

- *Windward*: seven-day cruises round-trip from Vancouver, sailing the Inside Passage with stops at Sawyer Glacier, Skagway, Haines, Juneau, Ketchikan, Misty Fjords, and Glacier Bay. May through September.

Princess Cruises

- *Golden Princess*: seven-day cruises round-trip from San Francisco, stopping at Victoria and Vancouver, cruising the Inside Passage, stopping at

Juneau, Skagway, Hubbard Glacier, Sitka, and Ketchikan. May through September.

- *Crown Princess, Regal Princess, Star Princess,* and *Sky Princess*: seven-day cruises of the Gulf of Alaska, departing from Vancouver and cruising the Inside Passage, stopping at Ketchikan, Juneau, Skagway, Glacier Bay, Hubbard Glacier, College Fjord, and arriving in Anchorage. May through September.

- *Sun Princess*: seven-day cruises of the Inside Passage, round-trip from Vancouver, stopping at Juneau, Skagway, Glacier Bay, and Sitka. May through September.

Royal Caribbean Cruise Line

- *Legend of the Seas*: seven-night cruises round-trip from Vancouver, cruising the Inside Passage with stops at Hubbard Glacier, Skagway, Haines, Juneau, Ketchikan, and Misty Fjords. May through September.

- *Song of Norway*: ten- and eleven-night Inside Passage cruises round-trip from Vancouver, stopping at Sitka, Skagway Haines, Juneau, Tracy Arm Fjord, Ketchikan, and Wrangell. May through mid-September.

SMALL SHIP VOYAGES: THE BIG CRUISE SHIP ALTERNATIVE

For Alaskan sailings, two alternatives to big cruise ships standout: World Explorer Cruises and Alaska Sightseeing/CruiseWest. Both emphasize educating

*Spirit of Alaska. Photo courtesy of Alaska Sightseeing /
Cruise West*

passengers about Alaska's wildlife and environment.
World Explorer's only ship, the *Universe*, is relatively
small (550 passengers), and Alaska Sightseeing/Cruise
West's vessels are even smaller (58 to 101 passengers).
Passengers on both lines tend to be older couples
and sometimes families with pre-teens, teens, or adult
children.

Alaska Sightseeing/CruiseWest

- *Spirit of Alaska*: eight-, thirteen-, and fifteen-
  day cruises with stops in Juneau, Ketchikan,
  Sitka, Petersburg, Misty Fjords, Anchorage, and

Fairbanks. April through September. Passenger capacity: 82.

- *Spirit of Discovery*: eight-, thirteen-, and fifteen-day cruises offering the same itinerary as the *Spirit of Alaska*. May through September. Passenger capacity: 84.

- *Spirit of Glacier Bay*: eleven-day cruises departing from Seattle with stops in Misty Fjords, Ketchikan, Wrangell, Petersburg, Tracy Arm, Sitka, Skagway, and Juneau. April through September. Passenger capacity: 58.

- *Spirit of '98*: eight-, thirteen-, and fifteen-day cruises of the Inside Passage from Seattle to Alaska. The cruises visit Ketchikan, Sitka, Haines, Skagway, Misty Fjords, Tracy Arm, and Lynn Canal. April through September. Passenger capacity: 101.

World Explorer Cruises

- *Enchanted Seas* (leased from Commodore Cruise Line): fourteen-day cruises departing from Vancouver with stops at Wrangell, Juneau, Skagway, Anchorage, Sitka, Ketchikan, and Victoria. May through August. Passenger capacity: 739.

Best Bets

Best cruise ships for families with children under two
Norwegian Cruise Line: *Windward*

Best cruise ships for families with children ages two through four:
Princess Cruises: *Star Princess*

Celebrity Cruises: *Horizon* for ages three through four

Best cruise ships for families with children ages five and six:
Royal Caribbean Cruise Line: *Legend of the Seas*
Carnival Cruise Line: *Tropicale*

Best cruise ships for families with kids seven through eleven:
Royal Caribbean Cruise Line: *Legend of the Seas*
Norwegian Cruise Line: *Windward*

Best cruise ships for families with pre-teens and teens:
Royal Caribbean Cruise Line: *Legend of the Seas*
Celebrity Cruises: *Horizon*

Children's Programs

Although Norwegian Cruise Lines' *Windward* does not offer a supervised children's program for those under two-years-old, guaranteed baby-sitting is available from noon to 2 A.M. Another plus: as on all NCL ships, passengers under two-years-old stay free when accompanied by two or more passengers in the same cabin. Even though Celebrity Cruises allows tots under two to cruise for free, no guaranteed baby-sitting or children's program is offered.

Princess' *Star Princess* offers a supervised program for ages two and older. The ship's toddler and preschool area is both child-friendly and secure. Celebrity starts their program at age three. Both RCCL's *Legend of the Seas* and Carnival's *Tropicale* have well-thought-out programs for ages five and older. NCL's Circus At Sea keeps kids clowning around, and RCCL's activities and supportive counselors combine to create a memorable program.

NCL's *Windward* sports a teen activity center, and RCCL's *Legend of the Seas* features Optix, an intriguing clubroom for teens. Celebrity scores high for tempting teens with a full range of activities all geared to engage this hard-to-please group. Some favorites: a reggae Jacuzzi party, Dating Game "show," and a midnight film festival.

THE SHIPS

Alaska Sightseeing/CruiseWest

Because of their small size, the ships of Alaska Sightseeing/CruiseWest can sail closer to shore and between islands; they can also navigate the many narrow straits, including Wrangell Narrows and Peril Strait, that larger ships cannot approach. Another plus: these ships spend an entire day within the borders of Glacier Bay National Park. For many cruisers, this allows access to the ideal Alaska, a glacier-strewn blue ribbon of waterways far removed from big cruise vessels.

Note: This cruise line caters to adults, so consider this choice only if you are traveling with adult children.

Passengers on these small ships often say they see more wildlife because they can travel the less accessible inlets. These ships also have the option of altering their itinerary to linger if a pod of whales shows up. The line advertises itself as a way to experience Alaska "up close in a casual, intimate, uncrowded way—without missing a thing." Well, you do miss some things—

all the trappings of glamour, entertainment, and non-stop food as well as the organized children's programs that come with big ship voyages. But if these items are not on your must-have list, then a cruise on one of this line's four ships may be ideal.

Dress on board these ships is always casual and there's ample, if sometimes average, food. Nighttime entertainment is what you make of it. If the Northern Lights are bright and showy, a kind crew member knocks on your door so you won't sleep through the dazzling display. None of the ships feature organized children's programs.

The four ships have similar layouts. Each has an indoor lounge, a dining room, and open deck areas for viewing. The *Spirit of '98* has some triple cabins, including the owner's suite. The *Spirit of Alaska* features a few triples, as does the *Spirit of Glacier Bay*. The *Spirit of Discovery* does not have any triples (only singles and doubles), and none of the ships has quad cabins. The line also offers day cruises along Prince William Sound between Valdez and Whittier.

Carnival Cruise Lines

Tropicale: entered service in 1982; 36,674 gross tons; 1,022 passengers

The *Tropicale*, a serviceable ship, was the model for many succeeding Carnival "Fun Ships." The *Tropicale* features open decks, a glitzy disco with colored lights, a swimming pool with slide, and a children's playroom.

Even on this ship, one of Carnival's first, the cabins are larger than is typical (180 square feet), comfortably furnished, and equipped with televisions. Twelve cabins have verandahs and eleven are wheelchair accessible.

Celebrity Cruises

Horizon: entered service in 1990; 46,811 gross tons; 1,354 passengers

The *Horizon* was the first of Celebrity's fleet. With the 1996 summer season, the *Horizon* repositions to Alaska, marking Celebrity's entry into this market. This ship sports a comfortable and spacious feel that is largely due to the use of glass and natural light. The Olympic Health Club offers scenic views and is reasonably well equipped. The ship also has two outdoor swimming pools plus a children's playroom and teen center.

The cabins, at 185 square feet, are comfortable and larger than those on many ships. There's ample storage space, and all cabins feature hair dryers and televisions. Cabins on the Bermuda deck have partially obstructed views. Four cabins are wheelchair accessible. There are a range of three- and four-passenger cabins.

Cunard Cruise Lines

Crown Dynasty: entered service in 1993; 20,000 gross tons; 800-passenger capacity

This ship feels bright and spacious, employing lots of glass to achieve that effect. The five-story atrium has glass walls as does the dining room. Because there is tiered seating, most diners get a good view to enjoy with their meals. Besides a spa with a sauna, steam room, and fitness center, the ship has a wading pool (good for kids) and another pool. The Rainbow Room Youth Center has a variety of kid-friendly games and toys.

The *Crown Dynasty* has four hundred staterooms, most of which are standard size and located toward the outside of the ship. The average cabin size is 146 square feet. Cabins have picture windows, televisions, safes, card key access, and bigger-than-usual bathrooms (for a ship). Twenty-four-hour room service is offered but only for continental breakfast and sandwiches. Four-berth cabins are available and four of the cabins are wheelchair accessible.

Sagafjord: entered service in 1965; refurbished in 1993; 25,147 gross tons; 589-passenger capacity

Like Cunard's *QE II* and *Vistafjord*, *Sagafjord* was rated by the World Ocean and Cruise Liner Society as Ultra Deluxe. The ship was designed to create intimacy for the passengers while maximizing space. The *Sagafjord* is known for its excellent service. Dining is an experience—from your entrance via a grand staircase to the noteworthy cuisine. Expect a dressed-for-dinner look. Casual nights, especially popular with children, don't exist. But there are outdoor and indoor pools (a plus for adults and children).

On summer cruises to Alaska, *Sagafjord* features the Passage International program in which a team of Cousteau divers and naturalists serve as underwater guides and lecturers. Connected to passengers via an audio system and video screens, the team explores the deep waters off Alaska, providing passengers with a fascinating firsthand view.

Cabins are relatively spacious with good storage areas. Some of the amenities you find in a first-class hotel are offered as well: hair dryers, terry cloth robes, sofas, and refrigerators. Some of the cabins on the Sun and Officers' decks have obstructed views. Three- and four-berth cabins are available. Cabins feature radio, telephone, and air-conditioning, and 90 percent have both a bathtub and a shower. Connecting rooms are available. Cabins are not accessible for full-size wheelchairs.

Holland America Line

Holland America is known as an upscale cruise line. In its commitment to make its Alaskan cruises the nature and wildlife experience that families (and other cruisers) can share, Holland America offers a variety of excursions that take passengers into Alaska's natural and scenic regions.

Nieuw Amsterdam: entered service in 1983; 33,930 gross tons; 1,214-passenger capacity
Noordam: entered service in 1984; 33,930 gross tons; 1,214-passenger capacity
These sister ships, like many in Holland America's fleet, tend to attract repeat passengers, many of whom are older. The ships feature similar layouts and decor. The wide corridors and ample public rooms create a sense of spaciousness. Teakwood decks, rosewood paneling, and more than $2 million in art and antiques on each ship create an upscale ambiance. Many of these pieces and nautical memorabilia serve to evoke the seventeenth and eighteenth centuries, the golden era of Dutch exploration. After all, Henry Hudson sailed to what became Manhattan and claimed the island for the Dutch long before the Pilgrims landed in Plymouth, Massachusetts. In addition to several lounges and bars, guests have the use of a health center, library, video game room, and computer room.

The cabins, with neo-art-deco decor, are relatively large and comfortable. Cabins in the top three categories also have bathtubs. All cabins have telephones and televisions. Views from most cabins on the Boat and Navigation decks are partially obstructed. Four cabins are wheelchair accessible.

Rotterdam: entered service in 1959; refurbished in 1989; 38,645 tons; 1,075-passenger capacity

As the fleet's flagship, and one of Holland America's older ships, the *Rotterdam* looks and feels like a "grande dame," especially after her $15 million renovation in 1989. Special features include rare wood paneling and Delft ceramics, including a porcelain mosaic in the theater foyer and two in the dining room. Noteworthy are the grand staircases, large movie theater with balcony, and Ritz Carlton ballroom. Some passengers compliment the food, and others complain that the meals aren't memorable.

The well-equipped cabins have telephones and televisions. A number of cabins are designed for singles. Some cabins on the Sun and Boat decks have partially obscured views. Three- and four-passenger cabins are available. Cabins are not wheelchair accessible.

Ryndam: entered service in 1995; 55,451 gross tons; 1,266-passenger capacity
Statendam: entered service in 1993; 55,451 gross tons; 1,266-passenger capacity

These sister ships look sleek and modern but they also retain some of Holland America's touches, including a grand staircase in the dining room. Like their two sister ships, the *Maasdam* and the *Veendam*, instead of being carbon copies of each other, these ships sport differences in decor that are carried out largely through art and accents. On the *Statendam*, for example, the Vincent Van Gogh Show Lounge centers

around the artist's paintings *The Starry Night* and
Irises. On the *Ryndam*, the Vermeer Show Lounge has
a tulip motif inspired by Jan Vermeer, the seventeenth-century Dutch painter. The *Statendam* and the
Ryndam both feature three-story central atria and dining rooms with lots of windows for expansive sea
views. A noted improvement on both ships—terraced
seats in the showroom.

Staterooms are good sized. Even standard cabins
have a small sitting area. All cabins have a television
and a telephone. Six passenger cabins are wheelchair
accessible.

Westerdam: Refer to chapter three for a specific description of this ship.

Norwegian Cruise Line

Windward: entered service in 1993; 41,000 tons; 1,246-
passenger capacity

Windward was designed to mimic its sister ship, the
Dreamward. Both ships present an alternative to the
industry's mega-liners—the *Dreamward* and *Windward* are midsize ships with modern amenities. With
these designs, NCL adds some intimacy to the big-ship
experience. Instead of employing one huge dining
room, each ship features four dining rooms that range
in capacity from 76 to 282 passengers. Although dinner
is assigned seating, breakfast and lunch are open
meals so that passengers can sample the other restaurants. Another bonus: there is less noise because more
insulation is used throughout the ship, including between staterooms. Terraced decks and lots of windows
create great sea views. Each ship features a dedicated
children's playroom.

Sports fans appreciate the Sports Bar and Grill, an informal eatery with a wall of television monitors tuned to live broadcasts of ESPN and professional basketball and football games. Sports devotees can have their lazy sea days and enjoy their favorite ballgames, too.

On both ships, 85 percent of the cabins are outside cabins, an unusually high rate. Cabins are good sized at more than 160 square feet. For family groups, thirty-nine of the suites adjoin to create additional space if needed. There are also a substantial number of four-berth cabins. Six cabins accommodate wheelchairs, and twenty-eight accommodate the hearing impaired. Some cabins on the Norway deck have obstructed views.

Princess Cruises

For a description of the *Sun Princess* and the *Star Princess*, refer to chapter three.

Sky Princess: built in 1984; refurbished in 1992; 46,000 tons; 1,200-passenger capacity

The *Sky Princess* exudes a sophisticated yet casual style, with modern colors, carpeting, and details. This ship also has one of the largest showrooms afloat, an intimate Melody Bar, and three swimming pools (including a separate children's pool). The *Sky Princess* has a youth center with separate rooms for teens and younger kids. The children's program is offered for ages eighteen months and up from 9 A.M. to midnight. See chapter two for precise details.

All staterooms have phones, televisions, and a private bath with shower. Six are wheelchair accessible.

Regal Princess: Refer to chapter three.

Golden Princess: entered service in 1973; refurbished in 1993; 28,000 tons; 830-passenger capacity
This ex-Royal Viking ship features much open deck space plus roomy public areas. Fitness enthusiasts are offered a well-equipped health center and two outdoor pools.
All staterooms have private bath with shower, television, phone, and terry cloth robes. State rooms average about 168 square feet. Three- and four-berth cabins are available. Suites come with verandahs. Ramps aid in accessibility. There is limited accessibility for the physically challenged.

Crown Princess: Refer to chapter three.

Royal Caribbean Cruise Line

The Legend of the Seas: debuted May 1995; 69,130 tons; 1,804 passengers
This is a spiffy and exciting ship with RCCL's signature multi-storied atrium and lots of windows. Glass elevators zip up through the centrum, the open-tiered lobby, to the Viking Crown Lounge, where more windows let you enjoy panoramic sea views. Walls of glass add great sea views to Romeo and Juliet, the two-level dining room.
Legend, the first of six new Royal Caribbean ships slated to debut between 1995 and 1998, incorporates lots of sybaritic pleasures, including a spa with sauna, and an outdoor pool with a solarium, an indoor/outdoor public room that incorporates another pool that is protected by a glass roof (the crystal canopy) in inclement weather. This is especially important for kids—as well

as adults—because a nice day in Alaska may only reach temperatures in the mid-seventies.

Along with the usual jogging track and fitness center, *Legend* adds a new on-board pastime: the first eighteen-hole miniature golf course at sea. Legends of the Links comes complete with sand traps and water hazards. You can putt at night, too, because the course is lighted for after-dark play. In addition, *Legend*'s Club Ocean, the children's center, seats forty children and is well equipped. There's also a video room and a separate teen scene meeting room, Optix, that wins over this age group with its juice bar and trendy techno music.

Legend's cabins are good sized and attractive, with a decor that blends pastels with brass accents. The cabins are larger than those on RCCL's older ships. One out of every four cabins has a private verandah, and all cabins have sitting areas. Seventeen cabins, more than on many ships, are designed to accommodate the physically challenged.

Legend of the Seas also has two family suites that each sleep seven. Children are allowed to be in an adjoining cabin when sailing with their parents, but there is no special rate for families in multiple cabins. For the most on-board space, the ship's Royal Suite (which costs a princely sum) is one of the largest on the seas, boasting a grand piano and a private whirlpool.

Song of Norway: entered service 1970 and stretched in 1978; 23,000 tons; 1,004 passengers

The *Song of Norway* was RCCL's first ship. In 1978 it was one of the first cruise ships to be "stretched," a practice that adds a new midsection with additional public areas and cabins. As an older ship it has its pluses—a relatively large pool—and its minuses—a somewhat dated look. This ship was built before RCCL began using the tiered, open centrum (atrium lobby).

As an older RCCL ship, this one suffers from the line's early fondness for small cabins. The typical cabin is only about 120 square feet, a tight squeeze. Cabins do not have televisions. Three- and four-berth cabins are available. There is limited accessibility for the physically challenged.

World Explorer Cruises

Enchanted Seas: entered service in 1957; refurbished in 1990 and 1995; 23,000 tons; 739 passengers

World Explorer Cruises offers an alternative, or compromise, for some passengers to the small ships of Alaska Sightseeing/Cruise West and the mega-liners of the traditional cruise companies. This ship visits more Alaskan ports than many larger cruise ships, and this one also spends a full day in Glacier Bay. While the emphasis on the *Enchanted Seas* is squarely on the Alaskan environment, the size of the ship offers a few more cruise amenities and services than are possible on a 50-passenger vessel.

Commodore Cruise Line's *Enchanted Seas*, which begins summer service with World Explorer Cruises in 1996, replacing the line's 550-passenger *SS Universe*, adds even more creature comforts to this experience. The *Enchanted Seas* features more public rooms, larger cabins, and more outdoor deck space than the *Universe*. There are also two outdoor pools.

The on-board library features twelve thousand volumes, many on the Alaskan experience; passengers also enjoy the herbarium exhibits as well as the lectures and slide shows presented by university professors. The *Universe*, however, also has movies, aero-

bics, afternoon tea, a midnight snack, and evening
activities. Along with such cruise entertainment staples as "wooden horse racing" and talent shows,
evenings consist of classical performances by violin-
ists, singers, pianists, and string quartets. Two nights,
dinners require men to wear sports jackets, but on
other nights the attire can be as informal as jeans.

Many of the passengers are seniors, and some take
their grandchildren along. The ship has a dedicated
youth room and a children's program operates on every
summer cruise. The cruise line stresses, though, that
this program "does not attempt to account for the daily
whereabouts of the child." Rather than a comprehensive program in which children are supervised for
large blocks of time, this is a drop-in program that
offers intermittent activities. The program is best
suited to older elementary-aged children. Some events,
such as workshops with on-board artists and visits
from Glacier Bay park rangers, complement Alaska's
attractions. Others, such as Ping-Pong tournaments,
scavenger hunts, and bingo, offer traditional fun.

As the *Enchanted Seas* was originally built for first-
class passage, the cabins are generally large with ample closet space, but not as spiffy as you might expect.

Note: Generally, this ship offers a series of fourteen-
day cruises, but because of private charters in the
summer of 1996, the ship will offer seven- and fourteen-day cruises.

ON SHORE: ALASKA

There's an area of land and water beginning from the
U.S.–Canada border (near Seattle) that winds north
past Vancouver, Victoria, Ketchikan, and Sitka, and

around Admiralty Island to Juneau and the longer inlets of Glacier Bay, Haines, and Skagway. These finger-like fjords, islands, glaciers, and coves make up what is known as the Inside Passage. Visitors have long delighted in the passage's unique cities, native villages, and historic Alaskan sites, but of special wonder is the abundance of natural beauty and wildlife.

Here are some quick picks for ports along the Inside Passage as well as for other cruise stops in Alaska.

Quick Facts

Tourist Information: Write or call the Southeast Alaska Tourism Council, Department 802, P.O. Box 20710, Juneau, AK 99802, or call (800) 423-0568, for a free guide to the Inside Passage. Haines Visitor's Bureau can be reached at P.O. Box 530, Haines, AK 99827; call (907) 766-2234 or (800) 458-3579. And the Alaska Division of Tourism, Department 401, P.O. Box 110801, Juneau, AK 99811-0801, (907) 465-2010, offers the Official State Vacation Planner.
Emergency Number: Ambulance, fire, and police: 911.
Main Towns: Anchorage, Haines, Juneau, Ketchikan, Sitka, Skagway, and Wrangell

ON SHORE: ANCHORAGE

While all cruises don't call in Anchorage, some do stop at Alaska's largest city, which houses half the state's population. The average age of its citizens is twenty-six, and the average income is $28,000. People living outside of the city claim that "Anchorage is not

Alaska" because it hardly represents the Alaskan wilderness.

Weather in Anchorage is uncommonly mild for Alaska due to the warm Japanese Current. In summer, temperatures generally hover between 60 and 70 degrees through nineteen-hour-long days. Mention of the Anchorage Bowl refers to the orientation of the city: the Chugash Mountains curve around the city on the east, and the northwest and southwest are bounded by the Cook Inlet. Mount McKinley is usually in sight.

Quick Facts

Tourist Information: For information about the city, get in touch with the Anchorage Convention and Visitors Bureau at 1600 A St., Suite 200, Anchorage, AK 99501. For outdoor activity information, write or call the Alaska Division of Parks and Recreation, 3601 C St., Suite 206, (P.O. Box 7001), Anchorage, AK 99501; (907) 271-2737.

Transportation:

Buses: The People Mover Mass Transit System runs twenty-two bus lines to all parts of the city from 5:30 A.M. to 11:05 P.M. weekdays, and Saturdays from 7:30 A.M. Some buses operate on Sunday. Fares must be paid with exact change; P.O. Box 6-650; (907) 343-6543.

Taxi: Companies include:

Alaska Cab: (907) 563-5353;

Checker Cab: (907) 276-1234;

Eagle Cab: (907) 694-5555; and

Yellow Cab: (907) 272-2422.

Car Rental: Rental companies include:

National: (907) 274-3695;

Budget: (907) 243-0150 or (800) 527-0700;

Hertz: (907) 654-8200; and

Thrifty: (907) 276-2855 or (800) FOR-CARS.

Best Bets

For families with children ages two through seven:
Chugash State Park

For families with children ages seven through eleven:
Big Game Alaska

For families with pre-teens and teens:
Hike with Outland Expeditions; Hike at Bicentennial Park

For adults:
Golf and family hikes

Nature and the Environment

If you want guaranteed wildlife sighting, head for the **Alaska Zoo**, 4731 O'Malley Road; (907) 346-2133. All the animals are indigenous except for the African and Indian elephants, but what would a zoo be without elephants? Open 9 A.M. to 6 P.M. daily from May to September. There's more wildlife at **Big Game Alaska**, (907) 783-2025, the state's only drive-through wildlife park, where you observe buffalo, elk, and moose from the safety of your car.

Chugash State Park, (907) 694-2108, is thirteen miles north of Anchorage and offers nature programs on most weekends. At the Eagle River Visitor Center, explore a homestead log house, touch a caribou antler, and feel the pelts of native animals. Bird lovers should head to **Potter Point State Game Refuge**, which is just a short drive south of town. From the boardwalk, watchers can observe 130 different types of waterfowl. **Bicentennial Park**, south of Tudor Road, offers five thousand acres that cut through eighteen miles of hiking trails.

Just twenty-eight miles northeast of Anchorage is **Eklutna Village Historical Park** (16515 Centerfield Drive, Suite 100, Eagle River, 99577, 907-688-6026). This is the 350-year-old home to the Dena'ina (or Tanaina) Athabascan native people. Several families still lead a traditional lifestyle here. On the half-hour tours, a guide describes the tribe's traditional hunting, fishing, and craft-making. The tour ends at the Eklutna Cemetery, where more than eighty colorfully decorated little "spirit houses" stand over graves of the natives.

Outland Expeditions can design a custom excursion to fit your family's needs. Adventures include kayaking, photographic safaris, and trekking. Call or write ahead, P.O. Box 92401, Anchorage, AK 99509; (907) 522-1670.

Outdoor Sports

Golf in Alaska? Of course. Alaska is ideal: its nineteen hours of sunlight in the summer provide the longest playing time on Earth. The **Eagle Glen Golf Course**, an eighteen-hole golf course just outside the city on Elmendorf Air Force Base, is open to the public. A stream teeming with salmon runs through the course.

Moose Run Golf Course, built for those stationed at Fort Richardson Army Base, is also open to visitors and is an easier course than Eagle Glen. Moose Run has a view of the Anchorage skyline. The **Anchorage Public Golf Course**, called O'Malley's by the locals, is hilly and tree-lined with a view of the surrounding mountains.

Historical Attractions and Museums

The best way to see downtown is by foot. Stop by the **Log Cabin Visitor Information Center**, (907) 274-3531, for a map to follow the self-guided walking tour. Many buildings in Anchorage date back to the early 1900s, and various markers detail the city's native Alaskan heritage.

Anchorage Museum of History & Art, 121 West Seventh Ave., (907) 343-5174, displays Anchorage's unique blend of Russian, Native American, and gold rush history. In the summer, there are daily performances by Alaskan natives.

Relive gold rush euphoria with your children at **Crow Creek Mine**, (907) 278-8060. You get to pan for the mother lode in this authentic gold mine. Eight of the original buildings have been restored. Children who just want to walk through are admitted free.

Let your children discover science mysteries at downtown Anchorage's science center, the **Imaginarium**, 725 West Fifth Ave., (907) 2766-3179. Some of the more exciting hands-on exhibits are Bubbles, Planetarium, and the Marine Animal Touching Pool. Open until 8 P.M., Tuesday through Saturday, and noon to 6 P.M. Sundays in the summer.

Best Eateries and Snacks

Simon and Seafort's Saloon and Grill, 420 L St., (907) 274-3502, is a real kid pleaser with its gold rush-era atmosphere, marble and brass trim, and view of Cook Inlet.

ON SHORE: HAINES

Along the Inside Passage on the northern end of the Lynn Canal, Haines is located on a narrow peninsula between the Chilkoot and Chilkat inlets. John Muir first visited Haines in 1879, and in 1903 the U.S. Army selected Haines for its first outpost in the Alaskan Territory. The city is known for its scenic setting and for its gathering of bald eagles in the fall. In spring and summer, you can watch the eagles courting. They dive, lock their talons, and then somersault through the air. A highlight of the first two weeks of May: the migration of sea lions, which may be accompanied by humpback whales and orca (killer) whales.

Quick Facts

Tourist Information: For brochures and information, write to the Haines Visitor's Bureau, Second Ave. and Willard St., P.O. Box 530, Haines, AK 99827; (907) 766-2234 or (800) 458-3579.
Emergency Number: Ambulance, fire, and police: 911.
Transportation:
Ferry: The Haines Ferry Terminal, (907) 766-2111, is four miles out of town. Haines Shuttle and Towers,

(907) 766-2819, provides shuttle service to the ferry terminal.

Bikes: Sockeye Cycles, (907) 766-2869, rents bikes and arranges tours in the high season.

Car Rentals: Companies include:

Affordable Cars: Captain's Choice Hotel, P.O. Box 392, Haines, AK 99827; (907) 766-3111;

Avis: Halsingland Hotel, P.O. Box 1589, Haines, AK 99827; (907) 766-2733;

Hertz: Thunderbird Motel, P.O. Box 589, Haines, AK 99827; (907) 766-2131; and

Independent Car Rental: Eagle's Nest Motel, P.O. Box 250, Haines, AK 99827; (907) 766-2891.

Walking: Be sure to stop by the Haines Visitor's Bureau, Second Avenue and Willard Street, (907) 766-2234. Pick up a walking tour of town and information about the eagle preserve, lodgings, and restaurants.

Best Bets

For all ages:
Float trip with Chilkat Guides

TIP: Haines-Skagway Water Taxi and Scenic Cruise operates mid-May to mid-September, connecting these two cities which are only fifteen miles apart by water, but 360 miles by road. Take an early water taxi shuttle and you can probably tour both towns in one port stop. Write or call P.O. Box 246, Haines, AK 99827; (907) 766-3395.

**For families with children ages five through
seven:**
Dalton City; Chilkat Guides float trip

Nature and the Environment

There are several opportunities to enjoy the outdoors. During the summer, the **Alaska Chilkat Bald
Eagle Preserve** at 400 Willoughby in Juneau, has
about two hundred resident eagles. For a nice view
of the Lynn Canal, take a short hike on the 2.4-mile
Battery Point Trail, which begins at the end of
Beach Road on the south side of Haines. Contact
Chilkat Guides, Ltd. to arrange for a daylong boat
trip through the Chilkat Bald Eagle Preserve,
Dept. SATC5, P.O. Box 170, Haines, AK 99827; (907)
766-2491.

Historic Attractions and Museums

Sheldon Museum & Cultural Center presents the
history of the Tlingit Indians and the pioneers who
inhabited the upper Lynn Canal, P.O. Box 269, Haines,
AK 99827; (907) 766-2366.

Dalton City, (907) 766-2476, is where the movie
WildFang was filmed. It is a re-creation of the 1890s
gold rush town. In summer, the area offers gold pan-
ning demonstrations. The town features shops and
restaurants as well.

Fort William H. Seward is located on the west side
of town at the south end of Haines Highway. Take a
self-guided tour through the fort, which was decom-
missioned after World War II and named after the

Nosing up to a waterfall in Alaska. Photo courtesy of Alaksa Sightseeing / CruiseWest.

U.S. Secretary of State who arranged the purchase of Alaska from Russia.

A replica of the **Chilkat Tribal House** is adjacent to the **Chilkat Center for the Arts**. Local artists gather here to make jewelry and carve totem poles. The Chilkat Indian Dancers perform in summer. Call (907) 766-2160 for their schedule.

Best Eateries and Snacks

Chilkat Restaurant and Bakery on Fifth Avenue, (907) 766-2040, offers an American menu as well as freshly baked breads and pastries. **Howsers Deli** on Main Street adjacent to Howsers Supermarket,

(907) 766-2040, is great for lunch on the go: salads, breads, pastries, and the usual deli sandwiches. **Porcupine Pete's** has sandwiches, sourdough pizza, and homemade soup, Main Street and Second Ave.; (907) 766-9999.

ON SHORE: JUNEAU

Quick Facts

Transportation:
Buses: City Bus, (907) 789-6901. The Mendenhall Glacier Transport Ltd. (MGT), (907) 789-5460, is a tour van that stops at the town's highlights.
Car Rentals: Rental companies include:

Allstar/Practical Rent-A-Car: (800) 722-0741 or (907) 790-2414;

Hertz: (800) 654-8200 or (907) 789-9894; and

Rent-A-Wreck: (907) 789-4111.

Best Bets

For all ages:
Mendenhall Glacier
For ages eight to adult:
Taku Glacier Lodge Salmon Bake

Nature and the Environment

From Juneau, it is about a twenty-minute drive to the **Mendenhall Glacier**, thirteen miles outside of town. This twelve-mile-long "river" of white-blue ice is impressive. The **Taku Glacier** is another must-see. Wings of Alaska, (907) 586-8258, offers a "flightseeing" trip to the **Taku Glacier Lodge Salmon Bake**. If your ship offers this tour, sign up. You'll enjoy the meals, the lodge, and the views. To get there, however, you must fly in small planes. If this makes you uncomfortable, don't book the tour.

Bird's Eye Charters, (907) 586-3311, offers full-day cruises through Tracy Arm Fjord where you pass waterfalls, glaciers, and wildlife. **Tracy Arm Fjord Glacier Bay Tours & Cruises**, (800) 451-5952 or (907) 463-5510, features half-day flights and cruises or full-day cruises into this wilderness fjord. On this tour, if you're lucky, you can spot whales.

Outdoor Sports

Juneau's waters, known as the best in Alaska for fishing, are filled with king and silver salmon. Inquire with your ship's activities director about arranging boat charters and guided fishing trips.

Historic Attractions and Museums

The **Juneau-Douglas City Museum** at Fourth and Main streets, (907) 586-3572, exhibits mining memorabilia and artifacts from the gold rush days. The **Alaska State Museum** on Whittier Street, (907) 465-2901, has an impressive collection of Native American and Aleut artifacts.

There's a forty-five-foot totem pole on Main Street outside the city museum on the corner of Fourth and Main streets. **St. Nicholas Russian Orthodox Church**, Fifth and Gold streets, is interesting as well. Constructed in 1894 by Russians, the church features an onion-shaped golden dome and beautiful eighteenth-century icons.

Best Eateries and Snacks

Thane Ore House Halibut Salmon Bake has an on-site mining museum as well as good salmon, 4400 Thane Road; (907) 586-3442. At the **Heritage Coffee Company** relax with a cappuccino or a quick soup and sandwich snack, 174 South Franklin; (907) 586-1752.

ON SHORE: KETCHIKAN

This long, narrow city is known for both its rain and its heritage. Ketchikan is the hub of three different Alaskan tribes: Tlingit, Haida, and Tsimshian. Ketchikan is also the closest city to Misty Fjords National Monument, Prince Wales Island, and the Tsimshian town of Metlakatla on Annette Island, the only reservation in Alaska.

Quick Facts

Tourist Information: Visit (or write) the Ketchikan Visitors Bureau located near the cruise dock at 131 Front Street, Ketchikan, AK 99901; (907) 225-6166; fax: (907) 225-4250. For information about hiking or boating, contact the U.S. Forest Service Information Center: (907) 225-3101.
Emergency Number: Ambulance, fire, and police: 911.

Transportation:
Buses: The town maintains a city bus service that runs every half hour between the ferry and the city center from 6:45 A.M. until 6:45 P.M. The fare is $1.
Taxis: If you want a cab, call Alaska Cab, (907) 225-2133; Yellow Taxi, (907) 225-5555; or Sourdough Cab, (907) 225-6651.
Car Rentals: All Star Rent-A-Car has a downtown office at 2842 Tongass Ave., Ketchikan, AK 99901; (907) 225-5123.
Motor Scooters: Scooters can be rented at the dock from S.E.A. Skooters.

Best Bets

For families with children ages two through seven:
Totem Bright State Historical Park; Saxman Totem Park

For families with children ages seven through eleven:
Ketchikan Mountain Lake Canoe Adventure

For pre-teens, teens, and adults:
Flightseeing Tour of Misty Fjords National Monument

Nature and the Environment

Misty Fjords National Monument Cruises, P.O. Box 7814, Ketchikan, AK 99901, (907) 225-6044, lets you get close to the cliffs, waterfalls, and wildlife of the region. The 65-foot yacht takes you places that a big cruise ship could never go. An hour-long flightseeing tour of **Misty Fjords National Monument**, which costs about $150, is spectacular. On this bird's-eye tour

> **TIP:** These flights offer great views that give you a
> true sense of the vastness of Alaska's wilderness. But
> beware—to enjoy the views you must feel comfortable
> flying in small planes.

of the thirty-six-hundred-acre wilderness, you fly over
granite cliffs, spruce tree forests, glacier-carved fjords,
and snow-capped mountains. Several companies offer
tours, and most are easily arranged by booking them
through your cruise ship's shore activities center.

Outdoor Sports

With **Ketchikan Mountain Lake Canoe Adventure**, 9085 Glacier Highway, Suite 204, Juneau, AK
99801, guides lead visitors around Tongass National
Forest, one of the region's highlights with more than
seventeen million acres. You may also want to check
with your cruise director for fishing trips.

If you know how to paddle, rent a canoe from
the City Parks and Recreation Department, (907)
225-3881, and take your own personal tour of the
Ketchikan coastline and inlets.

Historical Attractions and Museums

From 1902 until 1954, Ketchikan had "the Line," a red-
light district, which is now the **Creek Street Historic
District**. During Prohibition, boats from Canada
smuggled liquor into the brothels by hoisting the cases
through trap doors. Today, the row of frame structures
houses shops and a museum. **Dolly's House** at
24 Creek St., (907) 225-6329, tells the story of this era

by detailing the life and work of Dolly Copeland Arthur, the area's preeminent Madam. The museum sounds more interesting than it actually is.

The **Tongass Historical Museum** details the history and traditions of native cultures. There are old photos, baskets, boxes, totem poles, and other items; 629 Dock St., (907) 225-5600. Combine a visit here with a stop at the adjacent **Totem Heritage Center**, 601 Deermount Ave., (907) 225-5900, which houses thirty-three authentic totem poles and house posts from the abandoned Tlingit and Haida villages in the area.

The largest collection of authentic totem poles is in the **Saxman Totem Park**, three miles south of Ketchikan in the Tlingit village of **Saxman**. Native guides tell the history of the totem poles and the stories they represent. The village hosts the Cape Fox Dancers and the Naa Kagikdi Theater and has a craft museum and eateries where visitors sample native food, (907) 225-9038.

Best Eateries and Snacks

Rose's Caboose is a great place to take the younger kids for milkshakes and burgers; 35 North Tongass Ave., (907) 225-8377. **Roller Bay Cafe** is known for its Alaskan halibut; 1287 Tongass Ave., (907) 225-0696. The **Diaz Cafe** has pizza and Mexican food; 335 Stedman St., (907) 225-2257.

ON SHORE: SITKA

Sitka combines remnants of the native Tlingit Indian culture and the ambiance of the Alaskan frontier with traces of a Russian heritage. In 1799, Russian fur trader Alexander Baranov arrived here. In 1804, Baranov and others established a settlement called New Archangel. This became the thriving capital of Russian America with a population of about 3,000 in the mid-1800s. In 1867, ownership of Alaska transferred from Russia to the United States.

Sitka is an easy town to visit on your own. Pick up a map at the Centennial Building Visitors Bureau near the dock, and walk to all the attractions.

Quick Facts

Tourist Information: Write or call the Sitka Convention and Visitors Bureau, 330 Harbor Drive, Sitka, AK 99835, (907) 747-5940; Greater Sitka Chamber of Commerce, P.O. Box 638, Sitka, AK 99835, (907) 747-8604.
Emergency Number: Ambulance, fire, and police: 911.
Transportation:
Ferries and Buses: Sitka Ferry Terminal buses (Prewitt Enterprises) meet the ferries in season and transport passengers seven miles into town; P.O. Box 1001, Sitka, AK 99835, (907) 747-8443.
Taxis: Arrowhead Taxi (907-747-8888) and Sitka Taxi (907-747-8228).
Cars: A car is not really necessary when visiting Sitka because the downtown area is reasonably compact, but if you do require one, try Avis at 600 Airport Drive, Sitka, AK 99835; (907) 966-2404.

Best Bets

For families with children ages two through seven:
Alaska Raptor Rehabilitation Center

For families with children ages seven through eleven:
Sitka National Historical Park

For pre-teens, teens, and adults:
Sitka Sea Kayaking Adventure

Nature and the Environment

The **Alaska Raptor Rehabilitation Center**, P.O. Box 2984, Sitka, AK 99835, (907) 747-8662, rehabilitates wounded or ill birds of prey and then releases them back into the wild. This facility gives youngsters a chance to get up close to eagles, hawks, and other majestic raptors. The summer hours are extended to follow cruise ship schedules.

The 107-acre **Sitka National Historical Park**, P.O. Box 738, Sitka, AK 99835, (907) 747-6281, begins a half mile from town. A guided nature trail leads to the sight of the Tlingit fort, burned by the Russians in 1804. At times, crafts people demonstrate. Children especially like the Tlingit arts program, the Native Indian carvers, and the Indian and Russian artifacts.

Outdoor Sports

Fishing is a popular sport in Sitka. Try it just for the halibut—as well as for the king and silver salmon. Contact **C-Jo Charters** at 204 Cascade Creek Road, Sitka, AK 99835, (907) 747-8862, to go aboard their 43-foot boat for fishing tours. **Alaska Adventures Unlimited**, P.O. Box 6244, Sitka, AK 99835, (907) 747-5576, offers sportfishing as well as natural history and photography tours. **Alaska Dream Charters** also offers sportfishing from April to September,

713 Katlian St., Sitka, AK 99835, (907) 747-8612 or, in the U.S., (800) 354-6017.

Historic Attractions and Museums

Ask at the visitor's bureau for the schedule of performances of the **New Archangel Russian Dancers**, a dance troupe that performs in Russian costumes. You can't miss **St. Michael's Russian Cathedral** on Lincoln Street, (907) 747-8120. The onion-shaped domes harken back to Sitka's Russian heritage. Originally built 1844 to 1848, the church was burned in 1966 and rebuilt, but many of the original icons were saved.

The **Sheldon Jackson Museum**, 104 College Drive at Sheldon Jackson College, features Eskimo and Indian sleds, kayaks, masks, and other artifacts.

Best Eateries

El Dorado features good Mexican cuisine, 714 Katlian St.; (907) 747-5070. **Bayview Restaurant** has traditional hamburgers and sandwiches, 407 Lincoln St.; (907) 747-5440.

ON SHORE: SKAGWAY

Skagway, which in native Tlingit means "home of the north wind," is located at the northern end of the Inside Passage. Skagway's boom days were from 1897 to 1898 when gold drew the adventuresome.

Quick Facts

Tourist Information: The **Skagway Convention and Visitors Bureau**, between Second and Third avenues and Broadway in the AB Hall, (907) 983-2854, offers a variety of pamphlets and walking tour brochures.

Emergency Number: Ambulance, fire, and police: 911.

Transportation: The downtown area of Skagway, only about six blocks long, is easily toured by walking. Rent a car only if you want to enjoy a scenic drive. Rental companies are Avis, (907) 983-2550, and Sourdough Shuttle Car and Van Rental, (800) 478-2529 or (907) 983-2523.

Best Bets

For all ages:
The White Pass and Yukon Railroad

Nature and the Environment

In Skagway, the best way to sample the outdoors is by enjoying a scenic drive, cruise, or train ride.

Scenic drive: If a walking tour of the town or a narrated bus trip makes you yawn, rent a car and drive fifteen miles on the **Klondike Highway** from Skagway to the Canadian border at White Pass. This road passes scenic waterfalls and huge chasms and crosses an impressive cantilever bridge.

Scenic cruise: Aboard the **Haines-Skagway Water Taxi and Scenic Cruise**, (907) 766-3395, you are treated to shore views of the area and the chance to tour both towns.

Scenic train ride: This is a great shore tour. Follow the arduous path of the Klondike fortune seekers in comfort with a day trip on the **White Pass and Yukon Railroad**. This narrow-gauge train takes you along one of America's great history trails, climbing almost three thousand feet in twenty miles. You pass canyons, gorges, waterfalls, rushing streams, and such spots as Dead Horse Gulch, named for the three thousand animals that died in the struggle to cross this pass. The three-hour tour costs about $75. The easiest way to book this is through your ship's shore tour activities desk.

The **Klondike Gold Rush National Historical Park** occupies six blocks of downtown Skagway. Some of the wooden facades, created to make the buildings appear Victorian, house collections of interesting photographs, including the Corrington Museum of Alaskan History. Most of the buildings, however, have shops or eateries catering to cruise passengers.

Best Eateries and Snacks

Prospector's Sourdough Restaurant, (907) 983-2865, is a favorite among locals, who swear that the inexpensive salmon dishes are the best in town. **Northern Lights Cafe**, (907) 983-2225, serves burgers and sandwiches. **Dee's Salmon Bake**, Second Avenue and Broadway, features salmon, halibut, steak, and burgers.

ON SHORE: WRANGELL

This tiny town is the only one in Alaska to have been owned by four different nations: Tlingit, Russia,

Britain, and the United States. Wrangell has weathered three gold rush booms and busts, and still retains a frontier-town feel, the type that once defined all of Alaska. Wrangell now is a center for forestry and fishing.

Quick Facts

Emergency Number: Fire, police, and ambulance: 911.

Transportation: Because everything is located within an easy distance of downtown, the best way to tour is on foot.

Car Rental: The one car rental agency is Practical Rent-A-Car, (907) 874-3975, fax: (907) 874-3911.

Taxis: Star Cab, (907) 874-3622 or (907) 874-3511, and Porky's Cab Co. & Island Tours, (907) 874-3603.

Best Bets

For families with children ages two through seven:
Petroglyph Beach

For families with children ages seven through eleven:
Mount Dewey Trail

For pre-teens, teens, and adults:
Stikine Wilderness Adventure

Nature and the Environment

Take the twenty-minute walk from town to **Petroglyph Beach** to explore the ancient rocks carved more than eight thousand years ago. It is best to visit at low tide because most of these special rocks are just above the tide line. Come prepared with rice paper from local shops if you're interested in making rubbings (this works better than crayons and charcoal).

Five miles away, **Garnet Ledge**, which is owned by the Boy Scouts, is a natural garnet deposit. Adults are forbidden to sell these wine-colored semiprecious gems, but you may get a permit for digging the ledge with hand tools. Your children might like the prospect.

For an easy historic hike, follow John Muir's steps on the **Mount Dewey Trail**. The path starts on Third Street near the high school. At the top, enjoy the view and keep an eye out for bald eagles.

Take an eco-tour of the **Stikine River** or the **Le Conte Glacier** wilderness areas. On these forays enjoy views of glaciers, icebergs, forests, and hot springs as well as eagles, seals, sea lions, and, sometimes, black bears. **Stikine Wilderness Adventures** offers jetboat excursions of the wilderness areas in the Wrangell area. There are also flightseeing trips to the Stikine River and Le Conte Glacier, Box 934-SATC, Wrangell, AK 99929; (907) 874-3613 or (800) 874-3613.

Historic Attractions and Museums

Chief Shakes Island is a tiny restored Tlingit settlement, accessible via the Shakes Street footbridge. The Tribal House of the Bear is a replica of the Chief's sleeping and living area, complete with a firepit and sleeping platforms. There are also several totem poles. On Sundays in the summer, native dancers perform between 1 and 3 P.M. Nearby, the grave of Chief Shakes V is marked by two killer-whale totem poles.

Near the ferry dock, the **Wrangell Museum** at Second and Beaver streets, (907) 874-3770, tells the story of the town's history. Located in a little schoolhouse built in 1906, this museum houses photographs, artifacts, and tape recordings teaching Wrangell's native and pioneer history.

Best Eateries and Snacks

The **Dock Side Restaurant** located in the Stikine Inn (107 Front St.) has a coffee shop and a dining room. The **Diamond C Cafe** at 215 Front St., (907) 874-3677, is a favorite for homemade desserts. **Maggie's and Son**, located in the Yamasaki Mall on Lynch Street, (907) 874-3205, offers deli sandwiches, salads, pizzas, and ice cream.

ON SHORE: VANCOUVER, CANADA

Almost all cruises headed for Alaska begin or end in Vancouver, Canada, a truly beautiful city.

Quick Facts

Emergency Number: Ambulance, fire, and police: 911.
Tourist Information: The Vancouver Travel Information Center (Plaza Level of Waterfront Center, 200 Burrard St., 604-683-2000) provides tourist information and literature.
Transportation: B.C. Transit, (604) 261-5100, runs city buses.

Best Bets

For families with children ages two through seven:
Stanley Park Zoo; Second Beach

For families with children ages seven through eleven:
Vancouver Public Aquarium

For families with pre-teens and teens:
B.C. Sports Hall of Fame; Science World British Columbia; walking through Stanley Park

For adults:
Walking through Stanely Park; Dr. Sun Yet-Sen Classical Chinese Garden; Vandusen Botanical Garden

Beaches

Second Beach, located in Stanley Park, may be the only swimming beach on the entire Alaskan cruise. There's a large saltwater pool watched by lifeguards.

Nature and the Environment

In the heart of the city is **Stanley Park**, a one-thousand-acre park where families can picnic, swim, lawn bowl, or play miniature golf. Located on a peninsula with a 5.5-mile seawall, this park is ideal for strolling or biking. Near the entrance is the free **Stanley Park Zoo**, where species include seals, penguins, monkeys, and polar bears. Children love the **Vancouver Public Aquarium**, (604) 682-1118, with its beluga and killer whales, sea otters, and reef sharks. Be sure to catch the educational demonstrations in which animals show off behaviors such as jumping and diving.

For a look at a traditional Asian garden, head to Chinatown to **Dr. Sun Yet-Sen Classical Chinese Garden** at 578 Carroll St., (604) 662-3207. This is said to be the first classical garden ever planted outside of China. Another garden to check out is the **Vandusen Botanical Garden** with its impressive variety of flowers, plants, sculptures, and water displays; 5251 Oak St., (604) 257-8670. Queen Elizabeth Park, 33rd Avenue and Cambie, is the location of the **Bloedel Floral Conservatory**, (604) 872-5513, where a glass dome houses more than five hundred varieties of tropical and subtropical plants as well as tropical birds and Japanese koi.

To learn more about the effects of logging in this region, tour the **Seymour Demonstration Forest**, (604) 432-6286 or (604) 987-1273, which opened to visitors in 1987. The idea of this forest is to show that there are methods of logging that are more environmentally sound than clear-cutting. While there, you can hike, bike, or Rollerblade (bring your own) on thirty-one miles of paved and gravel logging roads and hike on the 13.7-mile (round-trip) path to Seymour Dam, an impressive concrete dam.

Historical Attractions and Museums

If you or your children are sports fans, don't miss the **B.C. Sports Hall of Fame and Museum**, B.C. Place Stadium, 777 Pacific Blvd. South; (604) 687-5520. Besides lots of sports memorabilia, the interactive Participation Gallery lets you sprint, row, climb, and throw. The museum is open from 10 A.M. to 5 P.M. Wednesday through Sunday.

If the weather's especially nippy or nasty, young children appreciate **Science World British Columbia**, 1455 Quebec St.; (604) 443-7440. The interactive fun here includes a chance to walk through a camera, play with giant bubbles, or compose music on an electric piano. Kids can also see demonstrations of real tornadoes, explore a beaver's lodge, walk through a hollow tree, and watch big-screen OMNIMAX movies; call 875-OMNI for a schedule.

North Vancouver is full of things to do, so plan to spend at least half the day here. The area's main attraction has enticed Marilyn Monroe, Walter Cronkite, Katherine Hepburn, the Rolling Stones, and Margaret Thatcher (she did it twice). Take the thirteen-minute SeaBus ride to Lonsdale Quay to experience the adventure yourself: walk across the dizzyingly high, gently swaying **Capilano Suspension Bridge**, 3735 Capilano Road, North Vancouver; (604) 985-7474. This is the longest and highest suspension bridge in the world; it spans 450 feet and is 230 feet above the Capilano River. Nearby, at the **Capilano Salmon Hatchery**, (604) 987-1400, salmon make their way up fish ladders to lay eggs and spawn a new generation (July to August).

Best Eateries and Snacks

Pick up the Vancouver City Guide for a comprehensive listing of restaurants. The local seafood not to miss includes fresh oysters, clams, mussels, crab, and Pacific salmon.

Gastown, the charming cobblestoned area that surrounds Maple Tree Square—the city's original core—at the end of Water Street, is a fun place to stroll and shop. A block away from Gastown is **Chinatown**, the second largest outside of San Francisco. Needless to say, there are many choices of Chinese restaurants.

9

*Windjammer
Cruises*

Does the thought of dressing for dinner and being six stories above sea level leave you feeling alienated from the ocean? If it does, then a windjammer cruise may be the sailing trip you want to try. Windjammers follow the winds and anchor in small harbors off coastal islands. These tall-masted ships give passengers a special sense of the sea. Although all vessels are equipped with modern navigation equipment and radios, windjammers are powered the old-fashioned way—by the wind. You don't have to navigate, rig the masts, or swab the decks, but you can help if you want. Many wanna-be first mates come aboard to get the feel of a big ship and to literally learn the ropes.

What is a windjammer? The term is a generic name for a fore- and aft-rigged sailing ship that carries passengers on overnight cruises. Schooners, while not technically windjammers, are sometimes employed on these cruises. Just for the record, schooners are a type of sailing rig, a two-masted vessel on which the forward mast is shorter than on windjammers. But for our purposes, the distinction doesn't matter because the back-to-sea, bit-of-old-salt experience is the same.

Who should go on a windjammer cruise? "Passengers," notes one ship's owner, "should not expect the Cunard line with all [those] creature comforts, but they can expect camaraderie, a reasonably priced vacation, and a chance to go to places cruise ships cannot even think about [going]."On board a windjammer, don't look for a deck chair (a mistake we made). You sit wherever you find space, often on the rim of a hatch or on the floor. Cabins are cozy in the truest sense of the word. There's little headroom and sometimes less storage space. Take "packing light" seriously; no wonder sailors took only one small duffel bag to sea. Generally, only a few cabins have private baths, but most have sinks with running water. Evening entertainment is what you make of it. There are no lavish stage shows, glitzy nightclubs, or ever-present cabin stewards. The amenities are simple: three meals a day with little choice of entree and a clean cabin.

So what is there? The allure that has drawn sailors and explorers for centuries—the feel of the salt spray, the stars at night, the thrill of being under full sail, the friendliness of a small group (most ships hold twenty to forty-five passengers), and the allure of sailing nineteenth-century style.

Note: Because prices for these cruises are fixed and don't vary as much as other cruise prices do, we've included the fees here; fees are current as of press time. The windjamming season is from May to October.

A WINDJAMMER PRIMER

Old or New Ships

Some people prefer older ships because they feel that the older timbers, rail, and decking bring them closer to an authentic experience. These ships often have smaller cabins with less headroom, and private baths can be hard to find. Newer ships, built as reproductions, often feature a few more comforts: some cabins have private baths and a bit more space

Clothing

Dressing up is putting on a clean T-shirt for dinner. There is no need for ties, jackets, or dresses. Rubber-soled shoes (sneakers) are highly recommended for the

Dozens of schooners participate in the annual Great Schooner Race. Photo by Vanderwarker.

deck. Pack lightly, preferably with soft luggage that can be easily stowed. Bring shorts and swimsuits, but also sweaters, jeans, and foul-weather gear.

Seasickness

Some people do get seasick on windjammers, but old salts say there's much less of this on sailing ships than on traditional cruise ships because the wind in the sails lessens the ship's rolling. Generally, sailing is smooth and gentle in the protected waters of islands off the coast. But if you are prone to seasickness, take precautions. Consult your physician and bring along the appropriate medication.

THE LINES

Maine Windjammer Association

One of the largest groups of windjammers plies the coastal waters of Maine: the Maine Windjammer Association. Eleven ships, individually owned, participate in this marketing association. These vessels, most of which carried lumber or fruit in the early part of the century, now carry passengers. Most were specifically constructed as reproductions of nineteenth-century windjammers, but the *Lewis R. French* and the *Grace Bailey* date to the era of tall ships. The eleven vessels also include the *Angelique, Timberwind, J & E Riggin, Nathaniel Bowditch, Mary Day, Victory Chimes, Mercantile, Roseway,* and *Mistress.* All of these are schooners except for the *Angelique,* which is a ketch. How does a ketch differ from a schooner? A ketch has two masts but the forward mast is taller. (Now you know.)

Life aboard a windjammer is simple but fun. Meals are cooked in the ship's galley, and although the selection is limited, the food is both hearty and healthy. Menus generally consist of staples such as fresh-baked muffins and breads, soups, stews, and, of course, seafood. A lobster bake is held one night on the majority of these cruises. Fresh lobster, clams, and corn are cooked over a driftwood fire on the beach of one of the coast's many islands.

All of the cruises have a minimum age requirement. One ship does offer family cruises. While the children's programs aren't the drop-you-off-in-the-morning-pick-you-up-later type, the activities are designed to engage children and to encourage a fascination with the sea. A crew member teaches kids sea shanties, how to tie sailors' knots, what to look for in the night sky, and how to site a whale. Children, like adults, can join in and learn. For pre-teens and teens, the hands-on experience in hoisting sails, tying knots, navigating, and other activities is often the highlight of the cruise.

All of the ships take part in special sailing events. Windjammer Days in June mark the beginning of a new season when a bevy of these sailing beauties gather in Boothbay Harbor. Around the Fourth of July, the Great Schooner Race takes place. Passengers can help steer their vessel across the finish line. In late July at the Schooner Gam, ships are roped together to give passengers the opportunity to tour other vessels and party with other passengers. Early August brings the Sweet Chariot Music Festival at Swan's Island where shore treats include New England folk singers and music. Labor Day at the Camden Windjammer Weekend marks the beginning of fall with a windjammer sail parade, fireworks, music, and dancing. The mid-September Wooden Boat Sail-In in Brooklin, Maine, is the final fall gathering of the fleet and brings autumn colors under full sail.

North End Shipyard Schooners

This company offers windjammer cruises on three ships, *Isaac H. Evans*, *American Eagle*, and *Heritage*. The *Isaac H. Evans* also offers special family sailings; P.O. Box 482, Rockland, ME 04841; (207) 594-8007 or (800) 648-4544.

Windjammer **Mystic Whaler**

The *Mystic Whaler* offers both day and evening sails as well as extended trips; P.O. Box 189, Mystic, CT 06355; (800) 697-8420.

Best Bets

Pick one of the shorter cruises for a first outing or a special event sailing that appeals to your family, such as the Great Schooner Race or the Sweet Chariot Music Festival.

Best windjammers for families with children ages five through nine:
Day trips on the *Mystic Whaler* or special family sailings on the *Timberwind*

Best windjammers for families children ages ten through sixteen:
Family sailings on the *Timberwind*, *Isaac H. Evans*, and *Mystic Whaler*

Best windjammers for families with children ages sixteen and older:
Pick one of the more comfortable, modernized windjammers such as *Angelique* or *Mary Day*

THE SHIPS

Maine Windjammer Association

Angelique: Yankee Packet Co., P.O. Box 736, Camden, ME 04843; (207) 236-8873 or (800) 282-9989. Departs from and returns to Camden.

Length overall: 130 feet

Passenger capacity: 31

Cabins: 14 doubles, 1 triple

Minimum age: sixteen

Built in 1980 by Imero Gobatto specifically for windjamming vacations, the 95 foot ketch-rigged *Angelique* is modeled after the older sailing vessels but offers a slightly more modern and comfortable setting. All of the cabins have sinks and enough headroom for standing. Passengers share two hot-water showers and three toilets (heads). All cabins have reading lights and linens. Cruisers gather in the deck house, which is protected from the elements, and go ashore via two rowboats that the ship carries.

Three-day cruises range from $350 to $425 per person. Weekly cruises range from $580 to $700 per person. Special events include:

The Great Schooner Race ($700 per person),

The Music Cruise and Windjammer Gam ($700 per person),

The Sweet Chariot Music Festival on Swan's Island ($700 per person), and

The Fall Foliage Three-Day Getaway ($350 per person).

Grace Bailey: Maine Windjammer Cruise, P.O. Box 696, Camden, ME 04843; (207) 236-4449 or (800) 255- 4449. Departs from and returns to Camden.

Length overall: 123 feet

Passenger capacity: 29

Cabins: 12 doubles, 2 singles, 3 Pullman berths

Minimum age: ten

The *Grace Bailey* was built in 1882 and was used to transport timber and granite to the West Indies until the 1940s. There is one hot freshwater shower below deck and four heads. All cabins have windows or portholes for ventilation. Six-day cruises on *Grace Bailey* range from $595 to $685 per person.

J & E Riggin: P.O. Box 571, Rockland, ME 04841; (207) 594-2923 or (800) 869-0604. Departs from and returns to Rockland.

Length overall: 120 feet

Passenger capacity: 26

Cabins: 10 doubles, 2 triples

Minimum age: sixteen

Built in 1927 for the oyster dredging trade, the *J & E Riggin* was originally known for her speed. This schooner won the first oyster schooner race ever held on the Delaware Bay. In 1974, she was found off Cape Cod and rebuilt by her current owners. Each cabin has linens, overhead and reading lights, a sink with cold running water, and a window that opens. Heads are located above deck as is the hot freshwater shower.

Three-day cruises range from $370 to $400 per person. Six-day cruises range from $580 to $675 per person. Special events include:

Great Schooner Race ($650 per person),

Schooner Gam ($665 per person), and

Wooden Boat Sail-In ($585 per person).

Lewis R. French: P.O. Box 992, Camden, ME 04843; (207) 236-9411 or (800) 469-4635. Departs from and returns to Camden.

Length overall: 101 feet

Passenger capacity: 22

Cabins: 9 doubles, 4 singles

Minimum age: sixteen

Built in 1871, *Lewis R. French* is the oldest of the windjammers and a national historic landmark. The cabins have freshwater sinks, portholes, reading lights, linens, and a vase of fresh wildflowers. Two heads are located nearby, and there is one hot freshwater shower on board. Two rowboats take passengers ashore; one of the rowboats is also rigged for sailing. Portable radios, telephones, and televisions are strictly forbidden, as is smoking.

Most six-day cruises head to Acadia National Park on Mount Desert Island. The three- and four-day cruises explore Penobscot Bay.

Three-day cruises range from $325 to $410 per person. Four-day cruises range from $395 to $505 per person. Six-day cruises range from $595 to $700 per person.

Mary Day: P.O. Box 798, Camden, ME 04843; (800) 540-2750, in Maine, or (800) 992-2218, in U.S. and Canada. Departs from and returns to Camden.

Length overall: 90 feet

Passenger capacity: 30

Cabins: 10 doubles, 2 triples, 2 singles

Minimum age: fifteen

Constructed in 1962, the *Mary Day* was the first schooner built specifically for windjammer cruising. All cabins have windows that open as well as skylights. All linens are provided. There are kegs of fresh water for washing in each cabin, and there are two heads and a hot freshwater shower on deck. Auxiliary power is provided by the yawl boat, which though small, can push the schooner if there is no wind. A salon above deck, complete with fireplace and parlor organ, serves as a gathering place at night or during inclement weather. Smoking is only permitted on deck.

Three-day cruises range from $295 to $435 per person. Four-day cruises range from $410 to $510 per person. Six-day cruises range from $620 to $670 per person. Special events include:

Boothbay Harbor Windjammer Days ($635 per person),

The Great Schooner Race ($665 per person),

The Sweet Chariot Folk Music Festival ($660 per person), and

Photography Workshop ($430 per person).

Mercantile: Maine Windjammer Cruises, P.O. Box 617, Camden, ME 04843; (207) 236-2938 or (800) 736-7981. Departs from and returns to Camden.

Length overall: 115 feet

Passenger capacity: 29

Cabins: 14 doubles, 1 single

Minimum age: ten

The *Mercantile*, built in 1916 in Deer Isle, Maine, was used for shipping fish and firewood to Rockport. It has three heads below deck and one hot freshwater shower. There are portholes and full-standing headroom in every cabin.

Four-day cruises range from $365 to $485 per person. Weekend cruises range from $135 to $405 per person.

Mistress: Maine Windjammer Cruises, P.O. Box 617, Camden, ME 04843; (207) 236-2938 or (800) 736-7981. Departs from and returns to Camden.

Length overall: 60 feet

Passenger capacity: 6

Cabins: 3 doubles

Minimum age: sixteen

The *Mistress* was also built in Deer Isle, but in 1960. Each of her three double cabins has its own toilet and lavatory, a rarity on windjammers. Because of the size of this vessel, it is only available for bookings of either one double cabin or the entire boat.

Nathaniel Bowditch: P.O. Box 459, Warren, ME 04864-0459; (207) 273-4062 or (800) 288-4098. Departs from and returns to Rockland.

Length overall: 108 feet

Passenger capacity: 24

Cabins: 11 doubles, 2 singles

Minimum age: sixteen if unaccompanied, ten with an adult

The *Nathaniel Bowditch* was built as a racing yacht in 1922. After winning many honors, it was used by the Coast Guard during World War II and has been employed as a cruise vessel since the 1970s. All the cabins have running water and linens. Heads and showers have running water and are located below deck.

Three-day cruises range from $325 to $395 per person. Four-day cruises are $500 per person. Six-day cruises range from $500 to $665 per person. Special events include:

Windjammer Days ($595 per person),

Great Schooner Race ($625 per person), and

Camden Windjammer Weekend ($650 per person).

Roseway: Yankee Schooner Cruises, P.O. Box 696, Camden, ME 04843; (202)236-4449 or (800) 255-4449. Departs from and returns to Camden.

Length overall: 137 feet

Passenger capacity: 34

Cabins: 11 doubles, 3 quads

Minimum age: sixteen

Built in 1925, the *Roseway* is the only member of the Windjammer Association to have sailed internationally. She began sailing as a windjammer in 1975. Her cabins have reading lights, fans, and linens. There are two heads and hot freshwater showers. Three-day cruises cost about $400 per person, and six-day cruises cost about $700 per person.

Timberwind: Rockport Schooner Cruises, Box 247, Rockport, ME 04856; (207) 236-0801 or (800) 759-9250. Departs from and returns to Rockport.

Length overall: 100 feet

Passenger capacity: 20

Cabins: 7 doubles, 2 triples

Minimum age: sixteen

Family cruise minimum age: five

Classified as a schooner, the *Timberwind* (built in 1931), served as a pilot boat for Portland Harbor. After thirty-eight years, she was converted to a cruise schooner and has never left the waters of Maine. The cabins have windows that open, electric lamps, and linens. Heads are located below deck near the cabins, and there is a fully enclosed freshwater shower on deck. The minimum age is sixteen, but during the summer family cruises, the minimum age drops to five.

Three-day cruises range from $250 to $365 per person. Four-day cruises are $400 per person. Six-day cruises range from $599 to $675 per person. Special events include:

The Family Cruise for families with kids five and older ($365 per person; kids are priced as adults),

The Sailing & Hiking Cruise ($665 per person),

The Folk Music Cruise ($665 per person), and

The Lighthouse Cruise ($665 per person).

Victory Chimes: P.O. Box 1401, Rockland, ME 04841; (207) 594-0755 or (800) 745-5651. Departs from and returns to Rockland.

Length overall: 170 feet

Passenger capacity: 44

Cabins: 16 doubles, 1 triple, 1 single, 1 quad

Minimum age: around ten, but negotiable depending on the maturity of child

The *Victory Chimes* is the only remaining three-masted ship in use today. Built in 1900, she is also one of the last "ram" schooners, which were used to carry lumber on the Chesapeake Bay. Cabins have both hot and cold running water, reading lights, and linens. There are two hot freshwater showers and three heads located near the cabins.

Half-week cruises range from $400 to $465 per person. Six-day cruises range from $675 to $700 per person. Special events include:

Great Schooner Race ($700 per person),
Schooner Gam six-day cruise ($700 per person), and
Camden Windjammer Festival ($675 per person).

North End Shipyard Schooners

Not affiliated with the Maine Windjammer Association, this company offers windjammer sailing aboard three ships. Write P.O. Box 482, Rockland, ME 04841; or call (207) 594-8007 or (800) 648-4544.

American Eagle:

Length overall: 122 feet

Passenger capacity: 33

Cabins: 14 doubles

Minimum age: fourteen

A national historic landmark, the *American Eagle* was first launched in 1930. Each cabin has a sink with fresh water, lights, and linens. Heads and a hot freshwater shower are located below deck.

Three-day cruises range from $375 to $395 per person. Six-day cruises range from $545 to $685 per person. Ten-day cruises to New Brunswick are $1,195 per person. Special events include:

Great Schooner Race ($645 per person),

The Schooner Gam ($395 per person),

Sweet Chariot Music Festival at Swan's Island ($645 per person), and

Fall Foliage cruises (from $545 to $565 per person).

Heritage:

Length overall: 140 feet

Passenger capacity: 33

Cabins: 13 doubles, 2 triples, 1 single

Minimum age: sixteen

The *Heritage* was built in 1983, but is designed like a nineteenth-century merchant vessel. Each cabin has cold running water, and all linens are provided. There are three heads located above deck and hot freshwater showers. Although there is no engine, a yawl boat provides auxiliary power if needed. Two rowboats take passengers ashore.

Week cruises range from $565 to $645 per person. Special events include:

Windjammer Days ($645 per person),

Sweet Chariot Music Festival at Swan's Island ($645 per person), and

Fall Foliage cruises (from $565 to $585 per person).

Isaac H. Evans:

Length overall: 99 feet

Passenger capacity: 22

Cabins: 11 doubles

Minimum age: sixteen, except family cruises when kids age ten and older are welcome

Built in 1886 as an oyster boat, the *Isaac H. Evans* is a national historical landmark. Rebuilt in 1973 as a passenger vessel, the ship now has windows that open, sinks with fresh running water, and electric lights in each cabin. Linens are provided. There is one hot freshwater shower on board. Two rowboats are used to take passengers ashore, and a yawl boat is available as a source of auxiliary power should there be no wind.

Three-day cruises range from $325 to $375 per person. Weeklong cruises range from $615 to $645. Special events include:

Three-day Family Cruises for children ten and up ($345 per person),

Great Schooner Race Family Cruises ($375 per person), and

Sweet Chariot Music Festival at Swan's Island ($645 per person).

Windjammer Mystic Whaler

Not associated with the MWA, this company has been offering windjammer cruises out of Connecticut for years; P.O. Box 189, Mystic, CT 06355, (800) 697-8420.

The Mystic Whaler:

Length overall: 110 feet

Passenger capacity: 65 on a day sail; 38 overnight

Minimum age: ten on overnight cruises; five on day and evening sailings

A modern version of the schooners of the past, the *Mystic Whaler* was built in 1967. With a variety of accommodations and seven heads with showers, this whaler is far more comfortable than the original vessels. The ship has five different types of cabins. An auxiliary diesel engine is used when leaving from and returning to port. Each cruise begins with a tour of the Mystic Seaport Museum and a scenic sail down the Mystic River.

Cabins come in several classes. A Clipper Class cabin comes with a double bed, private toilet, and shower. The other cabins have bunk beds and share a bath. The Great Room sleeps eight (good for all the young cousins in a family reunion). Sloop Class cabins have upper and lower bunk beds, hot and cold running water, and room for only one person to stand at a time. All linens are provided. Children ten and older are permitted on the two-, three-, and five-day cruises. Children ages five to ten are welcome on the day sails and evening cruises.

Day-sail cruises (9:30 A.M. to 3:30 P.M.) are $60 per person, $30 children ages five through ten. Overnight day-sail cruises range from $70 to $100 per person. Evening cruises (5 to 8 P.M.) are $30 per person, $15 children ages five through ten. Two-day cruises range from $200 to $310 per person. Three-day cruises range from $300 to $420 per person. Five-day cruises range from $500 to $620 per person. Special events include:

Treasure Hunts,

Full Moon Cruises,

Maritime History Cruises, and

Lighthouse Cruises.

ON SHORE

One of the pleasures of windjamming is not having a set destination. The ships go wherever the wind takes

them, sailing during the day and anchoring somewhere in the late afternoon. The vessels sometimes
anchor near small towns so that passengers can stroll
the streets and browse the shops. More often, the ships
anchor off a small island, allowing plenty of time for
swimming. (Yes, the water is cold.) Some of the longer
cruises in Maine go to Acadia National Park on Mount
Desert Island. On the *Mystic Whaler*'s two- and three-
day trips, possible ports of call are Block Island, Shelter Island, Sag Harbor, and Stonington. Five-day
cruises may end up in Cuttyhunk, Martha's Vineyard,
or Newport.

Best Bets

Because the itineraries vary in length and these ships
follow the wind, we have not listed best bets for shore
tours. Some not-to-be-missed sites if you're sailing in
the area include: Acadia National Park, Mystic Seaport Museum, and Mystic Marine Life Aquarium.

Windjammers have no set itinerary because of their
reliance on the wind. But that's not a problem because,
for sailing fans, simply being on the sea is part of the
experience. The ships do anchor at a few ports of call.
Here are highlights of some of them.

Maine

In Rockland, Maine, before or after you cruise, visit
the **William A. Farnsworth Library and Art Museum** at 19 Elm St., (207) 596-6457. Open daily June
through September. The museum features work by
American artists, including Thomas Cole, Fitz Hugh
Lane, Rockwell Kent, Maurice Prendergrast, and
Willard Metcalf. There is also a permanent exhibit

Passengers are invited to participate in all aspects of running a tall ship, including furling the canvas after a full day's sail. Photo by Nina Kennedy.

entitled *Maine in America* that follows the development of Maine landscape paintings. You can also visit **The Farnsworth Homestead**. Built in 1850, it is full of lavish Victorian furnishings.

   Acadia National Park (P.O. Box 177, Bar Harbor, ME 04609-9702, 207-288-3338) is a large national park in the northeastern U.S. It gets attention with its rocky coasts, cliffs, mountains, and off-shore islands. Cormorants, gulls, ducks, rock crabs, starfish, and green sea urchins are among the shore life. Sand Beach's fifty-degree saltwater and Echo Beach's freshwater are popular for swimming (if you can handle cold water). Both areas have lifeguards in summer. To get away from the crowds, try the less-visited western side of Mount Desert Island or hop a mail boat to Isle Au Haut. Walk or bike along the fifty miles of carriage roads. Carriage rides are offered by Wildwood Stables, (207) 276-3622. Pick wild Maine blueberries along Summit Trail. Before fishing, check with the park rangers because some fish contained mercury last season.

Isle au Haut is part of Acadia National Park, and there are more than eighteen miles of trails that are maintained by the National Park Service. The beaches are rocky but picturesque. Part of Captain Kidd's treasure is supposedly buried in one of the coves along the shore. There is an operating lighthouse, whose Keeper's House provides the only lodging or dining on the island.

Mystic, Connecticut

Mystic Seaport Museum is an indoor/outdoor educational maritime museum that was built as a nineteenth-century coastal village on seventeen waterfront acres; 50 Greenmanville Ave.; (203) 572-5317. Though several of the twenty-two historic buildings—including homes, shops, and workplaces—remain on their original sites, many were brought from other New England locations. There are three ships to explore as well. Check the schedule of performances, crafts, and sailing demonstrations. Children love acting as sailors in a play, helping the barrel maker, and lending a hand to hoist boats. There are more than 130 programs and special events held throughout the year.

Mystic Marinelife Aquarium is at 55 Coogan Boulevard; (203) 536-3323. According to the Mystic

Tourist Board, more people visit here than any other admission-based attraction in Connecticut. With six thousand marine creatures displayed in fifty exhibits, there's plenty to see. The outdoor Seal Island complex on 2.5 acres re-creates New England, Alaskan, and Californian habitats and features four species of seals and sea lions. Highlights include watching sharks swim in a thirty-thousand-gallon tank behind a sixteen-window display, the largest fish exhibit at the aquarium. There are daily dolphin, whale, and sea lion demonstrations in the aquarium's Marine Theater, and everybody loves to watch the penguins' antics above and below water in an outdoor pavilion. *The Deep Frontier*, shown on a large screen in the aquarium's main building, explores marine life twenty-seven hundred feet below the ocean's surface using footage provided by scientists in a submersible.

Denison Pequotsepos Nature Center is at Pequotsepos Road; (203) 536-1216. About two miles from the Seaport Museum, this 125-acre wooded wildlife sanctuary offers seven miles of hiking trails that traverse ponds and meadows. There's also a small natural history museum, but the real attraction is the chance to enjoy country trails and quiet not far from the city. Bring a picnic lunch and stay awhile.

10

Eco-Adventure Cruises

Ecuador's Galápagos Islands

The Galápagos Islands, six hundred miles off the shore of Ecuador, sport a dreamlike aura. Famous as a wildlife sanctuary, this archipelago of thirteen major islands and scores of minor ones not only sustains some unique species but the critters here, having evolved without predators, have no fear of people. Thus, island walks and beach outings can bring close encounters with wildlife. On our first morning at sea on one of these cruises, we awoke to a frigate bird perched captain-like atop the mast, a pelican on the bow, and a school of luminescent pink groupers floating starboard.

This cruise offers an adventure for families who are interested in wildlife. The ships, while comfortable, are simply a means of getting to the various islands. We thoroughly enjoyed this experience.

"Mom, look!" is one of our favorite traveling phrases and a standard by which we judge an outdoor vacation. By that measure, our four-day, three-night voyage through the Galápagos Islands proved to be a record breaker. From the very beginning, this adventure elicited delighted squeals from my thirteen-year-old daughter, Alissa. After all, a trip that starts with a welcome squad of sea lions packs a great deal of "wow" power.

We found groups of these slick animals at San Cristóbal's dock. Some, balanced like acrobatic clowns on the sterns of moored dinghies, barked at our arrival. The younger among us mimicked back throaty greetings, eliciting a comic dialogue of "gulps" and "arfs." With that we began our sea-life safari.

Before the trip, we worried that Alissa, a devotee of large cruise ships with elaborate kids' programs, might be bored on a ten-cabin motor yacht whose only entertainment was watching the wildlife. But much to her own surprise, she found the voyage a nice break and a new opportunity to interact in ways not possible on a mega-liner. She liked to hang out with the captain and the crew and share such U.S. cultural icons as *Seventeen* and *Teen* magazines and such songs as "Dookie" by Green Day.

But the best "cross-cultural" treat for us was swimming with the sea lions. One afternoon, soon after we jumped in the water, a pair of playful sea lions slid off the rocky slopes and joined us. They frolicked nearby, diving under us, cutting quick loops behind our backs, and then suddenly appearing yards down the beach. Another afternoon, as we sat in the shallows on another island, one curious pup with friendly brown eyes and fluttering whiskers came jiggling over to us. When we kicked our legs and splashed, he wiggled his flippers and barked. We kept doing this and he kept responding, much to our amazement.

From such simple encounters, we gained a powerful sense of peace and joy. This proved to be the special, unforgettable magic of the Galapágos Islands.

TIP: Because there are fewer variations in the types and number of cruise options and combinations, there are few cruise-only agencies that discount eco-adventure tours. Specific price ranges are listed throughout this chapter. As always, however, prices can change at a moment's notice. Always check with the individual tour operator for the latest ports and prices.

FAMILY VOYAGES

Two companies—Wildland Adventures and Natural Habitat Adventures—offer special family departures.

Activities

What do you do each day on an eco-adventure cruise? Walk, look, wonder, and sometimes swim and snorkel. Generally twice a day, in the morning and after a shipboard lunch, passengers travel from the yacht to an island by small boats called *pangas*, similar to Zodiac rafts. Multilingual guides lead hikes and explain the island's diverse wildlife. After dinner each night, guests are briefed about the next day's landing and schedule.

Island walks follow marked paths that are determined by the season and nesting areas. Most of the hikes are relatively easy, though a few of the more strenuous hikes require maneuvering over and around lava rocks. Because of this and the need to get in and out of the *pangas*, most companies suggest that children be at least seven years old (some require them to be eight), and that visitors be in reasonably healthy condition. But if a passenger decides the walk is too tough, he or she always has the option to stay on board where there are videos and a library.

No one on our voyage ever stayed on board. Most of the passengers we saw on our island hikes were forty, fifty, sixty, and seventysomething. With the exception of one woman who fell when she ventured off the trail and onto some slippery rocks, young and old alike found the trails do-able if also a bit muddy and slippery after it rained. Special treats were the afternoons that brought us to swimming and snorkeling locations.

When to Visit

Decide which is more important to your family— swimming without wet suits or seeing abundant wildlife. You'll have to make a choice. We visited during Ecuador's summer (our winter), a season known for intermittent rain, sparse colonies of animals, an absence of albatross, but seas warm enough for snorkeling and swimming in just a bathing suit. We liked this trade-off because the lazy afternoons of unstructured beach fun gave us welcome time-outs from the organized hikes.

Health Precautions

Call your physician, a travel clinic, and also the Centers for Disease Control in Atlanta, (404) 639-3311 or (404) 332-4555. Although not required, many health experts recommend updating your typhoid and measles inoculations and gamma globulin to prevent against hepatitis. Depending on the areas you visit, some experts suggest taking a malaria preventative, too. Check with your pediatrician about appropriate dosages.

Vessels

Smaller vessels, those with fewer than twelve passengers, can visit more sites because new park regulations somewhat limit the access of bigger ships. The larger the ship, though, the more facilities it may have, including more public lounge space and decks. Consider which is more important to your family.

Most of the cabins are small but efficient. That is, the cabins will suffice as a place to sleep and change clothes if you don't bring too much.

Generally, these ships do not offer children's menus although most kids will be happy enough with the pasta, chicken, and rice entrees and grateful for the array of cold cereals for breakfast.

If your children are fussy eaters, do two things: Call the cruise line well ahead of time to ask if any special meals can be arranged, but don't ask for elaborate changes. Request simple alternatives, such as grilled cheese at lunch or hamburgers and broiled chicken for dinner. Chances are the cruise line will be more than happy to accommodate.

Then, assume that despite everybody's good intentions, the special meals never arrived on board. (How often has this happened to you on an airline?) Be prepared. Don't leave port without peanut butter and jelly (jams and jellies are in the ship's galley, but these are not typically the brands your kids are accustomed to), a box of favorite cold cereal, cookies, and several boxes of two easily transportable kid staples such as macaroni and cheese mixes and cans of tuna. Explain the routine to the cook. These items, combined with the on-board stuff, should keep your children fed and happy.

Extra Fees

The cruise typically includes accommodations, meals, island sightseeing, guides and lectures, taxes, transfers in the islands, and transfers from hotels in

Guayaquil or Quito to the airport. Generally not included is the $80 per person entrance fee for the Galápagos National Park. Be prepared to pay this fee at the airport in the Galápagos or sometimes in the Quito or Guayaquil airports. (Natural Habitat Adventures, however, does include the park fees in its rates.)

Travelers under twelve pay $40, but students over twelve with an identification card (we saw one seventh-grader use her school library card) also pay the reduced rate of $40. Inquire about this rule; it may or may not be posted near the window where you pay.

There is also a $25 per person departure tax from Ecuador that is paid at the airport or point of departure.

CRUISE LINES AND SHIPS

Children's Programs

None of the following companies offer formal children's programs on any of their cruises nor do they have special children's playrooms, baby-sitters, or counselors. But don't count these voyages out. Several family-friendly companies cruise the Galápagos Islands, a wondrous destination for nature-loving kids and adults, and two companies offer special family departures—Natural Habitat Adventures and Wildland Adventures.

The Galapágos Network

The *M/Y Eric*, *Flamingo*, and *Letty*, three identical ten-cabin motor yachts, offer three-, four- and seven-night voyages round-trip from San Cristóbal as

The M/V Corinthian. Photo courtesy of NRS Communications.

does the line's larger *M/V Corinthian*, a forty-eight-passenger ship. Each of the four ships has one three-berth cabin.

The three-night (Tuesday to Friday) itinerary includes Leon Dormido (Kicker Rock Island); Gardner Bay, Española (Hood Island); Punta Suarez, Española (Hood Island); Punta Cormorant, Floreana; and Puerto Ayora and Darwin Station, Santa Cruz. The four-night (Friday to Tuesday) itinerary includes Lobos Island or Ochoa Beach; Darwin Bay, Tower (Genovesa Island); Prince Phillip's Steps; Puerto Egas, Santiago (James Island); Bartolome; Puerto Ayora and Darwin Station, Santa Cruz; Puerto Baquerizo Moreno, San Cristóbal.

The seven-night cruises combine the three- and four-night itineraries and add El Junco Lake, in good weather.

The *M/S Sea Cloud*, the line's smaller vessel, accommodates eight to ten people and is available for group charters of at least one week or longer. Families looking for a memorable reunion or a multigenerational vacation should consider this option. The itinerary can follow the line's regular seven-night schedule, or stops can be customized.

Rates on the motor yachts range from about $700 per person for a three-night cruise to about $1,850 per person for a seven-night cruise. Children ages seven to twelve travel for 50 percent of the adult fare. The recommended minimum age is seven.

This line runs a good cruise. We can personally vouch for this one—our trip aboard the *M/Y Letty* proved to be especially memorable. Well appointed, the *Letty*, is all teak and polished brass. The cabins are small but functional, and all have private baths. The partially covered sun deck proved to be the place where most guests lounged between shore excursions.

All meals are served in the dining area, a series of booths for four or six people. Because no formal seats are assigned, it's easy to mix and mingle with other passengers. Except for breakfast when several cold cereals are offered, there's no choice. You eat what you are served, not usually a problem because most of the food is good, tending toward continental preparations of chicken, beef, and fish. We would, however, have preferred to sample more Ecuadorian fare.

Two naturalist guides on board lead the shore tours. The twenty passengers are divided into two groups at random. The first half in the *pangas* go with one guide; the rest go with the other guide.

On the larger *M/V Corinthian*, cruisers are assigned to permanent groups that tour with the same guides on each outing. The *Corinthian* looks somewhat plain next to the sleeker, smaller, and newer *Letty* and her sister ships, but it does have certain advantages. First of all, there's more public space, including Darwin's Hideaway with a big-screen television (good for evening VCR movies), a cafe, dining room, and bar. Meals are served buffet style so there's more choice for picky eaters. The *Corinthian* also has a Jacuzzi and an on-board infirmary with a full-time doctor. Although the *Letty* doesn't have these medical facilities, her schedule closely parallels that of the *Corinthian*, so a doctor is within easy reach should a problem arise.

Metropolitan Touring

This well-known Galapágos tour operator employs several ships.

Isabela II has three-, four-, and seven-night cruises year-round of the Galápagos, round-trip from San Cristóbal or Baltra, stopping at Hood, Floreana, Santa Cruz, Tower, Isabela, and Fernandina islands.

M/V Santa Cruz has three-, four-, and seven-night cruises year-round of the Galápagos, round-trip from Baltra Island. Three-night cruises of the northern islands include Santa Cruz, Bartolome, Tower, and Fernandina. Four-night cruises of the southern islands include Seymour Island; Punta Suarez on Hood Island; Punta Cormorant on Floreana Island; Puerto Ayora on Santa Cruz; and Jervis, James, and Baltra Islands. Seven-night cruises combine these itineraries.

Delphin II offers a four-night variation of the typical Galápagos cruise: passengers lodge on shore at the Hotel Delfin in Santa Cruz and take daily cruise excursions aboard the 120-foot yacht. The Wednesday to

Sunday program features trips to the islands of Daphne, Santa Fe, and Floreana, as well as to Puerto Ayora and Dragon Hill on Santa Cruz. The Sunday to Wednesday program tours Daphne Island; Puerto Ayora, Santa Cruz; Plaza Island; and Rabida Island.

Rates per person range from about $600 for a three-night cruise to about $1,500 per person for a seven-night cruise. The recommended minimum age is seven. There are triple and quad cabins. Kids under twelve receive a 50 percent discount.

For twenty-five years, this line has been organizing voyages to the Galápagos Islands. Planned itineraries include in-depth nature tours of each island with a licensed naturalist guide. Visitors fly into Quito or Guayaquil in Ecuador and are then transferred to Baltra Island by air (airfare is included in the cost).

The *Isabela II* was built in 1989; it is 166 feet long, 1,083 gross tons, and has twenty outside twin cabins, most with two lower berths. Metropolitan claims that the *Isabela II* is the largest deluxe yacht cruising the Galápagos. This carpeted and air-conditioned ship accommodates forty passengers in twenty outside cabins that are equipped with private shower and toilet. The dining room accommodates all the passengers in one sitting. The twenty-seven-person crew always includes two licensed, multilingual naturalist guides. This ship is in dry dock in October.

The *M/V Santa Cruz*, at 1,500 tons, accommodates ninety passengers. It was built for touring the Galápagos, has sun decks, large lounges, a comfortable dining room, and observation decks for whale and dolphin watching. In addition to a cocktail lounge and bar, a small gift shop sells crafts, books, and personal items (just in case there's something you forgot).

The cabins have lower berths, private showers, and toilets; there are some triple—and quadruple—occupancies available. There is a forty-eight-person crew, including naturalists, and two small boats for ferrying passengers to the islands. This ship is in dry dock in September.

The *Delphin II* is used specifically for day trips. Passengers in the *Delphin II* program sleep on shore at the Hotel Delfin on Academy Bay in Santa Cruz. By day they use the thirty-six-passenger *Delphin II*, a 120-foot-by-302-foot, motorized yacht to visit the other Galápagos islands.

The ship is air-conditioned, and travels with a crew that includes two naturalist guides. Lunch is served buffet style and there is a sun deck with partial cover. The *Delphin II* program provides an interesting option, especially for families who are unsure about how much they or their children will like—or be able to stomach—life on board. Those who remain uneasy or queasy at the thought of a week on board anything smaller than a 35,000-ton ship with state-of-the-art stabilizers might consider this. The beachfront Hotel Delphin has twenty rooms with twin beds, private bathrooms, and showers with hot water as well as a dining room where breakfast and dinner feature international and Ecuadorian cuisine. Guests can swim in the pool or sun on the nearby private beach.

On board the *Isabela II* and the *M/V Santa Cruz*, passengers choose breakfast and lunch items from a buffet while dinner is served nightly in the dining room. Meals feature continental cuisine with some Ecuadorian items. None of the ships or the Hotel Delphin have children's menus; most likely, though, your kids will find something they like. On all three ships, bar items, including wine, beer, and sodas, are extra.

Natural Habitat Adventures

This eco-tour operator offers voyages on the *Galápagos Adventure*. The ship, a ten-cabin, twenty-passenger, air-conditioned yacht built in 1992, offers eleven-day cruises of the Galápagos Islands round-trip from Baltra with a stop in Quito. Ports include South Plaza, Hood, Floreana, Charles Darwin Research Station on Santa Cruz Island; James, Bartolome, Tower, and North Seymour Islands (five trips per year).

The company offers special family departures of nine to seventeen days on six- to nineteen-passenger ships. Recommended minimum age is eight, but inquire. Cost for an eleven-day cruise, including park fees and flight from Quito to the Galapagos Islands, is $2,895. Inquire about children's pricing.

Wildland Adventures

Wildland Adventures offers the Galapágos Wildlife Odyssey (or Galapágos Family Odyssey), eleven-day, year-round, round-trip voyages from San Cristóbal. Wildland Adventures primarily uses yachts owned by Quasar Nautica S.A., including *Parranda*, *Mistral*, *Nortada*, *Resting Cloud*, *Lammer Law*, and *Sandpiper*. Ports include Hood, Floreana, Santa Cruz , Bartolome, Jervis, and Santa Fe islands.

Costs start at about $2,000 per person for an eleven-day trip. The recommended minimum age is eight. Children younger than twelve receive a 20 percent discount off the adult fare, and teens ages twelve through fifteen receive a 10 percent discount. The company offers free airfare to anyone organizing a group of

> **TIP:** Because the trips accommodate small groups, they offer more intimate experiences, and can often depart with as few as four passengers. As a result, these trips are rarely canceled and passengers are not likely to be shuttled onto larger ships at the last minute.

fifteen persons or more, a nice touch if you are planning a family reunion.

Wildland Adventures, which books yachting charters to the Galápagos, has been dubbed by *Conde Nast Traveler* as one of the world's top eighteen eco-tourism companies both for their service to cruisers and for their commitment to conservation. Groups are generally kept small, mostly yacht tours that sleep ten to twelve passengers.

The primary ships include *Resting Cloud* and *Nortada. Resting Cloud*, an 85-foot yacht that can be motored or sailed, sports beautiful teak interior and sleeps up to ten people in its five cabins. On board there are five crew members plus a guide. The 66-foot, speedy *Nortada* is the best boat if passengers would like to travel the distance to see Isabela and Fernandina. The five cabins sleep ten guests; on board are five crew members and a guide.

Sometimes Wildland employs the twelve-passenger *Lobo del Mar* which, unlike the others, has no air-conditioning. Also at times, Wildland books the twenty-passenger *Galápagos Adventure*, also employed by Natural Habitat Adventures (see description above), and the *M/Y Letty* and *Eric*, also used by the Galápagos Network (see description above).

Wildland Adventures' Galápagos Wildlife Odyssey offers eleven days of traveling these volcanic islands. Special departures for families, the Galápagos Family Odyssey, are scheduled once a year or by request.

South American Fiesta

South American Fiesta (SAF), specialists in cruises and tours to South and Central America, offers both seven-night motor yacht and sailing cruises to the Galápagos Islands on a variety of vessels, primarily on six- to sixteen-passenger ships. Larger ships are sometimes available. This company, in business since 1979, will also create special itineraries and do group charters. The recommended minimum age for children is seven. In addition to swimming and snorkeling, many vessels offer fishing and diving.

ON SHORE

Quick Facts

Currency: U.S. dollars, travelers checks, and the Ecuadorian sucre are good, but remember that there are no exchange facilities on the islands and credit cards are not accepted. About 2,000 sucres equals one U.S. dollar.

Language: Spanish

Tourist Information: The Government Tourist Office, Corporación Ecuatoriana de Tourismo (CETUR), is in Quito, Reina Victoria 514 y Roca 527-002.

Emergency Numbers: In an emergency, your captain will be in radio contact with medical personnel. Because there are many ships in a port at once, one of them generally has a doctor or nurse aboard.

Main Towns: About 2,800 people live in Puerto Baquerizo Moreno on San Cristóbal Island (Chatham). Most planes land at Puerto Ayora, Santa Cruz, which has a population of about 3,400.

Transportation: A few of the larger ships leave from Guayaquil, but most Galápagos visitors fly into either Quito or Guayaquil where they board planes to the islands. Small Zodiac rafts tender passengers from their ship to the islands where all tours are by foot.

Best Bets

For families with children ages seven through eleven:

Swimming with sea lions at Ochoa Beach; hiking to the boobery on Hood Island; peering at pink flamingoes on Floreana Island

For pre-teens, teens, and adults:

Swimming with sea lions at Punta Suarez; hiking to the boobery on Hood Island; snorkeling at Devil's Crown

Beaches

Not all of the islands have beaches suitable for swimming. One of the loveliest beaches, a great wide swath of soft sand on Floreana Island at Playa Picona, is not for swimming because the large sting ray population makes the waters dangerous. The beach is well worth a walk—you are likely to see figure-eight tracks carved in the sand by the flippers of green sea turtles in search of nests. Playa Ochoa on San Cristóbal has calm waters and often a colony of sea lions as does Punta Suarez.

Nature and the Environment

This type of cruise leads you through an exploration of nature and the environment. To some extent, the season you choose to travel determines what you see on each island.

We traveled in Ecuador's summer, and Hood Island proved to be the favorite of the four we visited because of its abundant population of creatures. Sea lion pups frolicked in the tide pools and full-grown sea lions lounged head-to-belly on the sand. Scores of red-and-green-dotted Christmas lizards that were fat as house cats hugged the gray rocks, soaking up the sun. Flashy red crabs scuttled agilely from crevice to crevice, moving like a beach-bred Addams Family "Thing."

Following the naturalist guides, we hiked through knee-high vegetation, and even stepped over a sea lion pup who'd wiggled her way into our path. Swallow-tailed gulls swooped overhead, doves cooed, and the salt bush was full of finches. Where the cliffs met the sea in a spray of waves and a blowhole spewed rainbows, we discovered the boobery. Scores of masked birds, named for the black lines on their faces, favor these heights. We delicately maneuvered ourselves around their eggs and delightedly eyed the famed blue-footed boobies who really do sport neon blue feet, the envy of any teenage grunger.

TIP: If you want to see the Galápagos tortoise in the wild, visit Isabela and Fernandina, islands that have giant tortoise populations. Fernandina also sports another favorite Galápagos site—flocks of penguins. Penguins can also be found on Bartolome and Santiago.

Sea lions frolick on the shore. Photo courtesy of NRS Communications.

Most of the other islands we visited had far fewer fauna. Floreana Island boasted only a few sea lions rather than the usually large colonies lying belly-to-belly on the beach in Ecuador's winter (our summer). But we were never bored. Being close to these creatures in their natural environment creates a special sense of freedom.

Outdoor Sports

On a Galápagos cruise, most of what you'll do is hike. In Ecuador's summer, the warm waters are fine for snorkeling and swimming without a wet suit. Most ships keep a variety of snorkeling masks and fins on board and provide them for free. To be sure that your children have gear that fits, it's prudent to bring your own masks, fins, and floating vests. Wetsuits are not provided.

Some lines, such as Metropolitan Touring, operate special diving-only cruises that feature two dives a day. Other companies, such as Wildland Adventures, can arrange trip extensions to Ecuador's Andes, a tour not to be missed. At several *haciendas*, you can enjoy horseback riding through the high mountain valleys and shopping at local craft markets.

Historic Attractions and Museums

The Charles Darwin Research Center in Puerto Ayora on the island of Santa Cruz is a must, not because it's so interesting (although it is) but because cruise companies are required to make this facility a port stop. The center researches and rears many species of Galápagos tortoise, repatriating them to their original islands. A nature trail takes you past hatchlings and various species to an enclosure where several of these huge giants, which were once pets, live. Children love having their picture taken next to these friendly five-hundred-pound behemoths.

Other Activities

Bring binoculars—these islands are good spots for bird watching. When we were in Floreana Island, the thick green bushes were aflutter with some of the islands' thirteen species of Darwin's finches, varieties discovered by the scientist. Also unique to the islands are the

Darwin mockingbirds, the Galápagos dove, and the Galápagos hawk. Most kids, however, find little excitement in focusing on flighty specks that fly away almost as soon as you see them. The islands' answer to that is huge frigate birds and pelicans that swoop close to the water and like to perch on the top masts on ships. A special treat: rise early in the morning and throw some pieces of bread to the gulls who practically want to eat out of your hands.

Best Eateries and Snacks

You'll be eating on board. In the few small towns you'll encounter, such as Puerto Baquerizo Moreno on San Cristóbal Island and Puerto Ayora on Santa Cruz, you'll want to bring money for sodas and snacks.

Shopping

There's not much shopping in the Galapágos. The best bet for the die-hard shopper is to book a cruise extension to the Andes and shop to your heart's delight at the native market in Otavalo. Here you'll find embroidered bags, llama-wool blankets, alpaca shawls, and handknit sweaters for about one-third to one-fourth of the prices in fancy boutiques at home.

Puerto Ayora in Santa Cruz does have some shops that cater to tourists. The Travel Company and Iguana Bananas, for example, sell some interesting T-shirts. Simply walk the road that winds between the Charles Darwin Research Center and the dock.

11

*More Eco-
Adventure
Cruises*

*Costa Rica, Belize,
Peru, Chile, and
Patagonia*

COSTA RICA

Nestled between the Caribbean Sea and Pacific Ocean and serving as a land bridge between North and South America, Costa Rica boasts an incredible diversity of ecological zones from cloud forests to mangrove swamps, rain forests, marshes, and coral reefs. Such areas create an abundance of plant and wildlife riches. In Costa Rica, nature lovers hike through jungles where macaws cry, monkeys chatter, and parrots screech. You can also drive by a spewing volcano or raft down rivers flanked by macadamia nut plantations.

There are enough wildlife encounters and scenic wonders to bring out the child in even the most burned-out city dweller. This ecologically sensitive country, about the size of West Virginia, protects more than 21 percent of its land as national parks, refuges, and reserves. With 850 species of birds—more than in all of North America—and hundreds of species of mammals and reptiles, Costa Rica offers lots to see in a relatively small area. A visit here enables you to teach your children to value nature by experiencing it.

Costa Rica is also eminently family-friendly. It is safe (the *ticos* like Americans), nearby (about a 2½-hour flight from Miami), and affordable (hotel rooms and restaurants cost less than in many U.S. cities and Caribbean islands).

An ecological cruise offers families a special bonus: an easy way to reach many of the country's less accessible, and therefore less visited, Pacific parks. Once here you'll see fewer people and more wildlife than in most of Costa Rica's other parks. Instead of having to maneuver long, windy stretches of country road in a foreign land, a cruise allows parents and children to sit

back in a deck chair while the captain easily gets
everyone to the next port.

With a cruise, you avoid a common mistake made by
many of Costa Rica's visitors—setting a too ambitious
itinerary. Because Costa Rica is relatively small, the
actual distances between parks don't appear too great
until you head out in a rental car. To reach many of
the reserves and wildlife regions by land, you need to
creep up, over, or down a mountain on windy switch-
backs, a scenic but time-consuming process. With a
cruise, travel time is easy and enjoyable. Rather than
long stints in a van, you have leisure time on deck,
effortlessly combining exploring with relaxing.

LINES AND SHIPS

Temptress Cruises

Temptress Cruises is the primary company offering
extended voyages to Costa Rica's Pacific parks. And
Temptress does a very good job, indeed. Tomás
Pozuelo, Temptress' vice president, notes, "Since our
inception in 1991, we have really crested the wave of
the soft adventure market. We are responding to current trends and increased demand with greater capacity and with programs that appeal to the family
traveling together."

In the summer of 1995, Temptress inaugurated
Temptress Family Adventures, cruises that feature an
organized children's program, from June through
mid-September.

The *M/V Temptress Explorer*, a 185-foot, ninety-
nine-passenger, fifty-cabin ship built in 1995, takes the
place of the *M/V Voyager*, which repositions to offer

TIP: If you have limited time and can only cruise for three nights, pick the Curu voyage. This itinerary offers the most varied topography, the best chance for seeing wildlife, and the best beaches, including a visit to Manuel Antonio National Park.

similar voyages in Belize. The *Explorer* offers three- or six-night voyages year-round. The three-night Curu Voyage (Saturday to Tuesday) embarks from Puntarenas, goes to Curu National Wildlife Refuge, Tortuga, Corcovado National Park, and Manuel Antonio National Park, and disembarks at Golfito. The three-night Cano Voyage embarks from Golfito, stops at Cano, visits Golfito National Wildlife Reserve and Corcovado National Park, and returns to Puntarenas where a day trip by bus takes guests to Carara Biological Reserve before returning them to San José. Passengers on the Cano voyage have the option of flying from San José to Golfito.

The six-night Pacific cruise, which leaves from and returns to Puntarenas, combines the Curu and Cano itineraries and offers the option of visiting Casa Orquidea, a private botanical garden.

Rates for the Temptress family package for the six-night Pacific voyage are about $1,350 per person based on double occupancy. This includes all meals, guided nature tours, port charges, taxes, national park entrance fees, soft drinks, well-brand liquors, and watersports. Children up to seventeen years old cost about $550, double or triple occupancy.

Several tour companies use Temptress Cruises for part or all of their trips in Costa Rica. Wildland

Adventures, for example, typically includes Temptress' three-night Cano Voyage as part of their Costa Rican Rain Forest and Ocean Adventure. South American Fiesta also books guests on seven-night Temptress cruises.

Temptress Cruises' Costa Rica Voyage surprised us. We expected to be awed by flocks of scarlet macaws and the sight of a beak-heavy toucan trying to land on a tree limb, but what we didn't expect was how much we liked the small ship and the lack of glitz, glamour, and entertainment. One reason: the exceptional, friendly, and accommodating crew. (We don't say this lightly.) Whether we were sitting in a dinghy, walking in the rain forest, or dining on board, the staff went out of their way to be attentive, helpful, and fun.

This proved important to our multi-generational family's needs. Before embarking, we wondered whether our thirteen-year-old would find enough friends and activities to be happily occupied, and if the hikes would be challenging enough for my husband (who thinks nothing of jogging eight miles) but also paced to please my seventy-six-year-old mother-in-law.

Not to worry. Temptress offers options. On land tours (most of which take place in the morning), choose either a hike, which may involve a bit of uphill trekking, or a nature observation walk, which follows relatively easy terrain. Both offer numerous opportunities to see the region's wildlife. Even though the daily itinerary lists these treks as 2½ hours, none feel like forced marches. Whether you traverse flat terrain or hilly landscape, the naturalist guides pause frequently to speak about the local vegetation. Listen, learn, and catch your breath.

Another nice touch: the guides carry high-powered telescopes. When a brown-crested flycatcher or a

TIP: Binoculars are a must for bird and wildlife viewing. Bring your own or rent them from Temptress for a nominal charge. Rain gear and boots are advised because the terrain is sometimes muddy. Old sneakers will often do. The ship has a range of mid-calf rubber boots that passengers borrow free of charge. A nice touch: leave your muddy, wet shoes on deck after a hike and they will be returned dry and clean the next day. Also, don't forget insect repellent, sunblock, and a wide-brimmed hat for strolling the deck or the beaches.

sac-winged bat is spotted in a tree, the guides expertly hone in on them. You don't have to squint endlessly or fuss with your binoculars; just step right up to the telescope for a good view. Children especially appreciate this.

Continental breakfast is served on deck, and a full breakfast is served in the dining room. Temptress takes advantage of the scenic locale to sometimes host lunch and dinner beach buffets as well as luncheons on the sun deck. The dining room accommodates all the passengers and one night on board—the captain's dinner—requires nicer attire. No gowns or cocktail dresses needed, a summer dress will do.

You won't go hungry. The food ranges from okay to very good. Buffets offer ample choices and some kid pleasers such as pizza, chicken nuggets, or burgers. If you or your children have special dietary needs, tell the staff.

Initiated in the summer of 1995, Temptress' Family Adventure is designed to offer activities for ages three through seventeen on board and on shore from June through mid-September. The children's coordinator works hard at engaging the children, even going out of her way to encourage "too cool" teens to participate. Be sure your children of whatever young age go to the junior briefing held the first evening on board. Encourage (force?) your teens. They'll meet other children and teens, and the camaraderie will make the cruise that much more enjoyable for them.

The structure of the children's program changes depending on the ages of those participating. With younger kids, activities include sand castle building contests, coloring, crafts, and separate early dining. When more teens and pre-teens are signed up, the program is appropriately flexible. The teens can join adult walks and dinners, but there are separate beach activities, kayak races, and evening movies. The new ship is said to have a designated activities room for children, which will be a plus. The ship has child-sized life jackets and snorkel gear.

We witnessed a fairly homogenous, though tough-to-please group enjoy this program. The teens ranged from thirteen to seventeen, and a ten-year-old came on board mid-week. The counselor adjusted the activities to engage everyone. Those who participated had great fun. Supposedly, the program works as well when participants range from five-year-olds to teenagers. We're told that the older ones befriend the younger ones and even carry them over difficult parts

---

TIP: Check on how the program keeps track of younger children. Older ones simply come and go as they please. If you don't want your child to have that freedom, make it clear to the counselor.

of the trail. The teens we spoke to said they'd certainly help out with the youngsters, but none of the teens felt the program would be as much fun if the pace slowed down to accommodate little kids, too. Hopefully, as Temptress' program catches on and more families come on board, the staff will increase so that children can always be divided into appropriate age groups. Still, the program works and young children and teens all come away with new friends and an appreciation for Costa Rica's natural beauty.

The old ship, the *Temptress Voyager*, proved to be surprisingly comfortable, and the new ship, the *Temptress Explorer* should be even more so. On the *Voyager*, each cabin had two twin beds, so a child or third person slept on a rollaway cot that was folded during the day. The *Explorer* should have some cabins with upper berths that accommodate third passengers.

South American Fiesta

This line offers a cruise to Costa Rica's prime dive spot. The *Okeanos Aggressor*, a 120-foot cruiser, features ten-day cruises for up to eighteen divers. After a thirty-two-hour voyage, the ship anchors 260 miles off Costa Rica's coast at Coco Island, one of the country's top dive spots. Hikes take you through tropical rain forests to waterfalls. Families with older teens and adult children who are dedicated divers might want to consider this tour.

ON SHORE: COSTA RICA

Quick Facts

Currency: The unit of currency is the colón. The current rate of exchange is about 180 colones to the dollar.

Language: Spanish is the official language, but many Costa Ricans, especially in San José, speak English.
Tourist Information: Call (800) 343-6332 for brochures. The embassy of Costa Rica can also provide some information: 2114 S St., N.W., Washington, D.C. 20008; (202) 234-2945.
Emergency: For an ambulance, call 215818.
Transportation: Taxis are available in San José. Rental cars are the best bet for extended day trips. Reserve these ahead and go for as much time as possible. Check the U.S. companies and the Costa Rican Elegante Rent-A-Car, (800) 283-1324, (800) 582-7432, or (305) 871-4332. Request air-conditioning (not all vehicles come equipped) and bring car seats for small children (these are not available).

Best Bets

For families with children ages two through six:

Frolicking in the waters on Tortuga Island; seeing the white-throated Capuchin monkeys in Manuel Antonio Park

For families with children ages seven to eleven:

Water fun at San Josecito Beach; hiking in Corcovado National Park in search of toucans and scarlet macaws

For families with pre-teens and teens:

Kayaking near the village of Drake Bay; banana boat rides and waterskiing; hiking to a river waterfall in Corcovado's rain forest; water fun at any of the beaches

For adults:

Walking along the beautiful beaches of Manuel Antonio; admiring the laid-back sloths in Manuel

Antonio; sitting deckside and enjoying being sloth-like and lazy.

Beaches

Most afternoons feature beach stops with plenty of swimming. You might want to bring a beach blanket (Temptress doesn't seem to have any of these) and a backrest because Temptress brings along only a few. Snorkeling gear is available for free (although there's not much to see), and there are free banana boat rides and waterskiing, a teenager's dream. Some ports feature river kayaking, which is also free. The only extras are for deep-sea fishing and diving excursions for certified divers only.

The beaches on **Tortuga Island**, **Manuel Antonio Park**, and **San Josecito Beach** are especially nice. Because of the remoteness of many of these parks, Temptress passengers will generally be the only ones on the beach, though occasionally you'll encounter visitors from a private ship or another tour. The exception is at popular Manuel Antonio National Park. To enjoy more space here, walk past the first beach to the less crowded ones. If you haven't seen the monkeys yet, Manuel Antonio National Park is your best bet for watching troops of white-throated Capuchin monkeys as they swing from branches traveling through the dense forest canopy.

Nature and the Environment

Costa Rica's rain forests feature many wonders. This isn't Kenya where you see scores of large animals such as zebras and giraffes. Costa Rica's pleasures come in smaller packages, but are just as intriguing. Whether you opt for a nature observation walk or a hike, you'll step into the rhythms of the rain forest.

Curu is a tropical dry forest noted for having five of the world's seven species of mangrove trees. On a hike here, look for woodstorks, egrets, spoonbills, and frigate birds as well as howler monkeys. Even when a walk leads to spotting only a few birds, the sounds and senses of the forest delight. Listen to the distant screeches of the howler monkeys, the twittering of parakeets, and the flap of fish splashing in a brook. We fell in love with the extraordinary, flute-like sound of the very ordinary looking rufous and white wren.

Corcovado is a highlight. Favorite sightings here include the scarlet macaw—bold red, brilliantly feathered, and long-tailed—and toucans, big-beaked flashes of black and yellow. A walk in Corcovado, because of its remoteness, delivers on the promise of wildlands. Except for paths that are cut from the dense undergrowth, Corcovado presents a pristine rain forest. As you hike, be careful to avoid the droves of leaf cutter ants that troop together, bearing a leaf as wide as a human hand on their backs.

After the cruise, and before returning to San José for your departure, Temptress takes cruisers by land to **Carara Biological Reserve**, a moist rain forest that serves as a transitional area between the humid shore and the Guanacoste region's dry climate. Carara, a native Indian word, means "place of the crocodiles." Clusters of toothy crocs are likely to be smiling up at

---

TIP: Always bring along a canteen of water and a sun hat. The earlier the hike, the more birds you're likely to see. (Some hikes leave as early as 7 A.M.) Another bonus if you make these early hikes: it's appreciably cooler at 7 A.M. than it is at 9 A.M.

> **TIP:** After the remoteness of Corcovado and Curu, Carara may seem like a bit of a let-down when you enter off a highway. If you have to choose between more time for day trips from San José and seeing Carara, go to San José.

you from the nearby canal. Inside the forest, ferns, massive trees, and tall banyans with intricately fingered roots and thick, leafy branches form a dense green canopy. With luck, you'll catch sight of Carara's jewel, the scarlet macaw.

Other Activities

Of necessity, you'll be flying into San José before being picked up by chartered bus to meet the ship in port. If possible, allow some extra time for sightseeing either before or after you cruise. Although San José is a plain, cinder-block city, it's well located for a variety of day trips. The following are some suggestions for day trips in the area.

Explore a volcano: **Irazú**, Costa Rica's highest volcano, whose summit reaches eleven thousand feet, is within easy reach of San José. The 1½-hour drive to the summit takes you along cultivated slopes—potato and cilantro farms, cattle pastures, patches of purple wildflowers, and tall eucalyptus trees. At the top, the moon-like crater seems barren and eerie.

Another volcano, also about a 1½-hour drive (fifty-seven kilometers) from San José is **Poas Volcano National Park** (57-0922). The winding roads offer scenic valley views of coffee plantations with dark green, bushy fields outlined by willowy palms and

Horseback riding along the shore in Costa Rica. Photo courtesy of Temptress Voyages.

slopes lush with mango and guanacosta trees. Poas' crater steams with sulfurous waters.

Raft a river: This proved to be one of our favorite day trips. Several companies offer all-inclusive daylong raft trips on the **Rio Reventazón**, a swift-moving river with some notable white water and jungle scenery. Tour leaders pick you up, take you for breakfast, teach you some safety pointers, and guide you on a three-hour trip followed by late lunch at the takeout point. Paddle by coffee plantations and slopes green with tall poro and huge ceiba trees. Swirl under bamboo bridges and listen to flocks of parakeets chirp overhead. Watch for kingfishers, swallows, and the occasional pair of toucans. We liked our trip with Rios Tropicales Adventure Specialists, (506) 33-6455.

Visit a butterfly farm. **The Butterfly Farm** is located in La Guacima de Alajuela, (506) 48-0115, a rural area with small sugar cane and coffee farms about fifteen minutes from the San José airport. If you haven't visited one of these butterfly havens in the U.S., come here. This place presents a fantasyland of winged color and slowly creeping critters.

In this netted garden luxuriant with tropical plants, hundreds of butterflies hover like angels above orchids and other fragrant blossoms. A delicately feathered caligo flits by and a blue Morpho lands on a visitor. The naturalist leading the tour describes the butterfly life cycle, allows kids and adults to handle the wriggly worm-like larvae and touch the rows of pupae that hang like so many dried brown leaves and are ready to be shipped to zoos and centers all over the world.

San José has many modern hotels. A real find, with big hotel amenities but boutique hotel charm, is the **Hotel Grano de Oro**; Calle 30, between Ave 2 and 4; (506) 255-3322. This pink Victorian grande dame, reminiscent of San Francisco's restored bed and breakfast inns, is actually composed of several buildings connected by interior covered walkways that feature fountains and lots of potted plants. The thirty-three rooms all have private and modern baths. They are comfortably furnished and have televisions. Many of the rooms are large enough to accommodate a family of three or four.

The staff is friendly and the property is manageable, providing a nice welcome to a foreign country—more so than you're likely to get at a big, impersonal hotel. The dining room, which is open for breakfast, lunch, and dinner, serves good food at reasonable prices. Try the black bean soup, the chicken fajitas, or the beef and tortillas. Such American staples as hamburgers and tuna salad are served as well. The wicker and chintz dining room is charming, as is the outdoor garden courtyard, available for breakfast or lunch. Tots under two are free. Children are $5 extra when sharing a room with parents.

Extend your trip on land. Several companies offer family-friendly guided land excursions in Costa Rica. **Family Explorations, Inc.** offers a trip that visits rain forests, beaches, and the central valley. There are special cross-cultural activities for parents and kids to do together as well as a kids' counselor for some afternoons and all evenings. No minimum age. Call (800) WE-GO-TOO or (610) 543-6200. **Wildland Adventures** features a Costa Rica Family Odyssey that visits several parks and nature reserves. Minimum age is five; (800) 345-4453 or (206) 365-0686.

Other companies that have featured land-based family Costa Rica trips in the past include **Journeys**, (800) 255-8735 or (313) 665-4407, and **Rascals in Paradise**, (800) U-RASCAL or (415) 978-9800.

MORE CENTRAL AND SOUTH AMERICAN CRUISE ADVENTURES

Belize

Belize, a slice of a nation about the size of Massachusetts, occupies only 8,866 square miles. But its land and seas draw nature-loving travelers. They come to hike the rain forests, explore the Mayan ruins, and dive and snorkel the spectacular coral reefs. Belize boasts the second largest barrier reef in the world. The island's interior intrigues as well. Crocodiles slither along river banks and dense rain forests shelter monkeys and toucans as well as jaguars and tapirs. This is a country well placed for eco-tourism, and a cruise here offers a convenient and comfortable way to explore.

The *M/V Temptress Voyager*, a sixty-three-passenger, 163-foot vessel, offers three- or six-night tours of Belize. The Manatee Voyage, a three-night journey embarks from Belize City, disembarks from Placencia and visits Goff's Caye, the Southern Lagoon at Gail's Point, Rendezvous Caye, Hopkins, and Bird's Caye Sanctuary. The three-night Laughingbird Voyage embarks from Placencia, disembarks from Belize City, and visits Monkey River, Laughingbird Caye, Wild King Caye, Snakes Caye, and Punta Gorda. Day tours from Belize City go to either the Baboon Sanctuary or Altun Ha. The six-night voyage round-trip from Belize City combines both three-night itineraries.

Temptress Cruises takes its Costa Rican winning formula and cruise ship and transplants it, ship and all, in Belize. Cruises began here in December 1995. Children's programs, based on anticipated demand, are slated to start the summer of 1996.

Although the *Voyager* lacks the sleek silhouette of a yacht and the sundry public rooms of a mega-liner, it offers surprising comfort and a first-rate crew. Each of the good-size cabins has twin beds, a sink in the main area, and a private bath with a large (for a cruise ship) shower. There's adequate storage space with six bureau drawers, but only if you pack light. Just three hangers dangle from the small rack that substitutes for a closet. We had trouble obtaining two more.

> **TIP:** Bring fewer clothes and more hangers.

Because the cabins have only twin lower beds, a roll-away is brought in to accommodate a third passenger, generally a child. This just fits squeezed between the two twin beds, providing little or no floor space. With two children, families need two cabins. Depending on the occupancy of the sailing, you may be able to get a second cabin at the children's rate. Inquire.

Comfortable sofas and chairs are in the lobby, which serves as a briefing area and living room. When others are out snorkeling or hiking, this offers a quiet place to read. Feel free to borrow the wildlife books on the shelves and relax with a cup of coffee which, along with tea, sodas, and cookies, is always available here for free.

The Belize voyage emulates the rhythms of the Temptress' Costa Rican forays. Mornings feature organized tours while afternoons generally offer less structured time to enjoy the beaches. The six-day trip begins Sunday with a beach barbecue. The next day, you observe manatees near **Gail's Point**, dubbed Manatee Lagoon, and swim at the palm-lined beaches of **Rendezvous Caye**. The ship cruises at night to the **Sittee River**. Small boats take you exploring between the foliage-lined banks where you're likely to see toucans, monkeys, ospreys, and alligators. Sunset finds the *Voyager* at **Bird's Caye Sanctuary** in time for the evening return of huge flocks of frigate birds. At **Tabacco Caye**, snorkelers and divers delight in the schools of rainbow-colored fish. There's time to explore land at Placencia, a small village. The remaining days include dinghy tours of Monkey River and Laughing-bird Caye. Once back in Belize City, guides take you to the Baboon Sanctuary or to Altun Ha, whose ruins attest to an ancient civilization.

South American Fiesta

South American Fiesta (SAF), a wholesale tour operator, specializes in cruises and tours to South and Central America. One of their most popular cruises sails to the fjords of Chile. Others explore **Peru's Amazon River** as well as the remote regions of **Tierra del Fuego** and **Patagonia**. These cruises may appeal most to families with adult children who want to explore different realms but still savor creature comforts of cabins and good cuisine. On some journeys, ties and jackets are requested for dinner. Many of these itineraries offer little or no swimming, a fact that could prove frustrating for some elementary and teenage passengers. The following sections discuss the ships and destinations of the line.

Chile

From September to May, the *M/V Skorpios II*, a 1,210-ton vessel with a capacity for 130 passengers and thirty-four crew members, offers six-night voyages round-trip from Puerto Monttonea thousand kilometers south of **Santiago**, Chile's capital. The ship cruises southern Chile's Pacific channels and fjords that combine spectacular glacial scenery with opportunities to explore port-side villages. Highlights include navigating the icebergs of the **San Rafael Glacier**, indulging in the thermal baths at **Quitralco**, and strolling the fishing hamlet of **Chonos**. Children

A fishing adventure in Belize. Photo courtesy of Temptress Voyages

especially like the welcome greeting by local school children in Puerto Aguirre.

All the cabins, paneled with Chilean wood, have private baths. Cabins with third and fourth bunks are available, as are suites. Children age one to five sail free. Ages six through eleven receive a 50 percent discount when sharing a cabin with parents. Rates start at about $750 per person for a six-night cruise, including all meals, regularly scheduled tours, soft drinks, and alcohol.

The Amazon

Say the name "Amazon" and you conjure up images of a hot, dense jungle teeming with wildlife. South American Fiesta offers several different cruises that enable you to make those images real. Through **Amazon Lodge and Safaris**, SAF offers three-night voyages on the *Amazon Explorer*, a 150-ton, 80-foot, two-deck, steel-hulled ship. Built in 1978 with a shallow draft so it can better navigate the Amazon, the ship was refurbished in 1988. The eight cabins, each with an upper and a lower berth, are air-conditioned and have sinks. The passengers share four bathrooms, each with a shower and toilet.

This ship cruises round-trip from Iquitos in Peru's northwest. Naturalists lead passengers on guided hikes through the jungle and on canoe jaunts along the **Nahuapa River** and inland lagoons to view dolphins, toucans, parrots, owls, horned screamers, and blue, yellow, and red macaws, as well as a variety of monkeys, including squirrel, howler, and Capuchin. Fishing enthusiasts may angle for bullfish and white river bass.

Through Amazon River Adventures, SAF offers five itineraries on two boats plus land options to stay overnight in the jungle at lodges and camps. Among the more comfortable ships are the *M/V Rio Amazonas* and the *M/V Arca*. The *M/V Rio Amazonas* has twenty-six cabins, twenty of which feature air conditioning and private baths. Mercifully, the dining room and the library are air-conditioned, and the open deck has some shade and hammocks. The Downriver Cruise departs from Iquitos and returns opposite **Leticia, Colombia,** and **Tabatinga, Brazil**. Passengers visit the Bora and Huitot Indian villages on the Ampiyacu River, hike the Shishita River area, and go on a piranha fishing expedition. The Upriver Cruise picks passengers up from either the Leticia or Tabatinga airports, cruises the Ataquari River, and spends the last afternoon at the Bora and Huitot Indian villages before returning to Iquitos.

The *M/V Arca*'s Downriver Cruise and Upriver Cruise offer three-night itineraries similar to that of the *M/V Rio Amazonas*. All of the fifteen twin-bedded cabins and the one single cabin are air-conditioned, but none has a private bath. Guests share five bathrooms.

Patagonia and Tierra del Fuego

Yes, you can cruise to the ends of the Earth, or to at least what Magellan and other early explorers thought to be land's end. The *M/V Terra Australis* offers seven-night cruises round-trip from Punta Arenas, Chile, through the **Strait of Magellan** to **Patagonia** and **Tierra del Fuego**. The vessel has fifty cabins, including two suites, all with private bathrooms, heat, and air-conditioning. Some cabins are large enough for a rollaway cot. Guides focus on the region's history, flora, and fauna as you cruise by icy blue glaciers, schools of porpoise and sea lions, and nesting penguins. Search the sky for condors and count waterfalls. Land excursions take you to national parks and duty-free shopping.

12

Additional Family Cruise Alternatives

Steamboats, Barges, and River Cruise Ships; Mini Cruise Ships; and Eco-Educational Adventures

This chapter, a kind of catch-all of *other* cruise experiences, focuses primarily on several types of river trips: plain and fancy, domestic and foreign, and on large and small vessels. Steamboats, barges, and small luxury ships that ply rivers are discussed in detail, but we also discuss a hybrid that we've labeled "eco-educational" trips. Our example is a tour of Turkey that includes a six- or seven-day cruise of the Aegean Sea plus land visits to ruins, palaces, mosques, bazaars, and Turkish homes.

While definitely not river trips, these eco-educational voyages by Wildland Adventures seem to fit best into this chapter following a description of a Nile River cruise. Both trips explore the culture of ancient civilizations by touring their symbols and ruins. But Wildland's journey also explores the natural environment with hikes and snorkel trips, which Nile cruises are generally not equipped to do. That's why we've labeled these eco-educational adventures. Why didn't we describe this voyage in one of the eco-adventure chapters? We could have, but most of those trips emphasize wildlife rather than ancient stones, fortifications, and archaeological sites. In any case, all of the cruises presented here offer great trips that your family will long remember.

Rivers have an allure all their own. Whether winding through farmlands and pastures or cutting a bold swath through a town, rivers connect directly to the heartland of a nation, revealing the soul of its cities and the charm of the countryside. River trips, including steamboat, barge, and yacht cruises, are alternatives for families searching for cruise vacations. No matter what vessel or itinerary you choose for your trip, the river is just as important as any port. River-watching is a time-honored sport. The waters change with the light, the width of the channel, the skyline, and the greenery on the banks.

In the sweet quiet of night on the Mississippi, you hear frogs croaking and water lapping just as Mark Twain described the experience in his novels. In the early morning on the Columbia River, you sense the excitement of discovery as did the early explorers. At dusk on the St. Lawrence, the maze of oak and pine tree islands sparkle like enchanted beads in a string of new land promises.

Like other water vacations, river cruises come in all sizes. Steamboats range from authentic midsized vessels to small reproductions to big, brassy modernized ships. Rent-your-own barges are basic and just big enough for eight people. One company, Kemwel, offers half-board charter boats equipped with a skipper and a cook/housekeeper who prepares breakfast and lunch (you are on your own for dinner). For full pampering, you can book a deluxe vessel where sophisticated service and meals are as important as the sights.

This chapter details some of these river choices. Although most companies don't have special family departures, a few do. While many don't attract families with school-aged children, some do, and those that have traveled this way love it. Barge trips, whether basic or deluxe, offer families a unique way to sample Europe. When thinking "cruise," consider all your options.

TIP: For those prone to seasickness, river cruises, whether on steamboats, barges, or yachts, offer relatively calm waters and little swaying of the sort that causes seasickness.

STEAMBOATS

Along with interesting ports, steamboats offer cruisers the lore and magic of river travel. With their relatively shallow drafts, easy maneuverability, and good capacity for freight and passengers, steamboats became an important means of transportation in the nineteenth century. Now these vessels, whether gussied-up reproductions, toned-down working ships, or paddle-wheel originals with all the gingerbread trim, evoke a turn-of-the-century élan when ladies played bridge, gentleman passed the time with port and cigars, and more than a few rogues gambled their way from town to town. Devotees love these cruises for their charm and the chance to sense the America and Canada of long ago.

Three major companies offer steamboating today: American West Steamboat Company travels America's northwest rivers; St. Lawrence Cruise Lines cruises the St. Lawrence River; and the largest company, the Delta Queen Steamboat Company, traverses the Mississippi River system, steaming along such tributaries and branches as the Cumberland, Ohio, Arkansas, Missouri, Chippewa, Quachita, and Tennessee rivers.

The Lines

American West Steamboat Company
Queen of the West offers two- to seven-day cruises round-trip from Portland, Oregon, on the Willamette, Columbia and Snake rivers from March to December.

The Delta Queen Steamboat Company
The Mississippi Queen, Delta Queen, and *American Queen* offer three- to sixteen-night, year-round cruises

on the Mississippi River and its many tributaries. Cruises originate in New Orleans, Lousiana; St. Louis, Missouri; Louisville, Kentucky; Cincinnati, Ohio; St. Paul, Minnesota; Little Rock, Arkansas; Tulsa, Oklahoma; Galveston, Texas; and Chattanooga, Nashville, and Memphis, Tennessee. A typical five-day cruise leaves from New Orleans and visits St. Francisville, Baton Rouge, and Natchez before arriving back in New Orleans or Memphis.

The *Delta Queen* operates from February to late December, and the *Mississippi Queen* operates from January through November. For her inaugural season, the *American Queen* sailed from June through December. In 1996, she is slated to cruise nearly year-round.

St. Lawrence Cruise Lines

Canadian Express offers four-night cruises on the upper St. Lawrence River from Montreal to Kingston or from Kingston to Montreal (June to October). Six-night cruises on the St. Lawrence River go from Quebec City to Kingston or from Kingston to Quebec City (May to October). Five-night cruises on the St. Lawrence and Ottawa rivers travel from Ottawa to Kingston or from Kingston to Ottawa (June to September).

Best Bets

Best cruises for families with children under twelve:

The *American Queen* combines historical flare with such nice-to-have modern conveniences as a swimming pool and movie theater

Best cruises for families with teens and older children:

Look at the itinerary and the length. Try towns and places your teens have always wanted to visit, and keep the trip relatively short (three to four days). That said, most of the applicable ships will do. Still can't pick? Then opt for the ship with the most modern conveniences because teenagers sincerely like their creature comforts unless, of course, they are totally roughing it. Good choices include *Queen of the West* and *American Queen*.

Steamboat Companies and Ships

American West Steamboat Company

The American West Steamboat Company is a brand-new cruise line that debuted in July 1995 with the *Queen of the West*. Cruises, which leave and return to Portland, Oregon, travel on the Willamette, Snake, and Columbia rivers, exploring the west side of the Oregon Trail, Native American culture, and the route of Lewis and Clark's journeys. On this line all regularly scheduled on-shore excursions are included in the price.

Queen of the West: entered service in 1995; 230 feet; 163 passengers; 73 cabins

Though completed in 1995, the *Queen of the West* is a replica of the paddle wheel steamboats of the turn of the century except, of course, modern conveniences have been added. The ship's paddle wheel is twenty-six feet tall (almost three stories high) and is the vessel's sole means of propulsion. The wheel is powered by diesel engines that are cleaner burning and more efficient than the era's steam engines.

Other updates: all cabins are outside staterooms with picture windows. Many cabins have private verandahs, and all have private baths, color televisions, and VCRs. Suites also have refrigerators. A video library holds a selection of movies in case you want to spend a quiet evening in your cabin.

In case you don't, this steamboat line offers entertainment that's more formally organized—music, dancing, and singers—than the impromptu sessions on some small ships, but the shows are still less glitzy than those on big cruise vessels. On *The Queen of the West*, historians conjure up the era for you and naturalists tell you about the river, gorges, and surrounding scenery and wildlife. Showboat theme cruises add special touches. On the River Jazz Fest, listen to the rhythms of Dixieland, ragtime, boogie-woogie, and modern jazz. Theater on the River cruises feature extra entertainers: sometimes mimes, celebrity guests, or murder mystery plays. Like other steamboats, the American West Steamboat Company probably attracts an older clientele, but don't count these trips out for teens, especially the theme and holiday cruises. These could be great grandparent/grandchild voyages and multi-generation family vacations.

The Queen of the West's decor has the distinctive look of the steamboat era with Victorian pieces and a modified turn-of-the-century decor. Some cabins accommodate third and fourth passengers who cruise for 50 percent off the regular rate.

Sample Itineraries
All cruises depart and return to Portland, Oregon.

- Oregon Coast Route (two nights)
  Head down the Willamette River to the falls at Oregon City—the end of the Oregon Trail. Then

continue on the Columbia River to Astoria. Prices from $279 per person.

- Window on the West (three nights)
  Cruise down the Willamette River to the end of the Oregon Trail. Shore excursions include the Mount Hood Railroad, Bonneville Dam and the Multnomah Falls, Astoria, and Lewis and Clark's Fort Clatsop. Prices from $439 per person.
- Heartland of the Pacific Northwest (four nights)
  To the three-day itinerary, this trip adds a visit to the Multnomah Channel, a picturesque nineteen-mile-long channel. Shore excursions from the port of Longview lead to the blast zone of Mount St. Helens. Prices from $589 per person.
- Three Great Rivers Lewis & Clark Exploration Route (seven nights)
  To the four-night itinerary, this trip adds a day of cruising on the Snake River past wheat fields and rolling farm country. The focus shifts to Native American culture. Shore excursions visit Nez Perce Indian territory and the national historical park. On the Columbia River, the boat travels near Hat Rock State Park for explorations and a day in Pendleton, Oregon, to see its wool mills, round-ups, and western art galleries. Prices from $945 per person.

The Delta Queen Steamboat Company

The Delta Queen Steamboat Company offers three- to sixteen-night cruises on three vessels: *Delta Queen*, *Mississippi Queen*, and *American Queen*.

These steamboats cruise the Mississippi River and its tributaries. Itineraries are generally the same for all steamboats except that, because of its smaller size,

382 Cruise Vacations with Kids

the *Delta Queen* is the only steamboat to travel the Arkansas River. None of these ships has an organized children's program.

"People love to be on the Mississippi River," says Delta Queen spokesperson Patti Young. "It's a very powerful, strong, magical kind of river. There's a whole spirit and mystery to it that is something that you just don't get by looking at the river from the shore. You have to experience being on the river." Steamboats probably appeal most to elementary-aged children and teens who enjoy history and want to sample a taste of something different. (With a teen onboard, we'd pick a short cruise.) That said, children and willing teens like the regularly scheduled kite flying, trivia and bingo games, shore towns and sites, and, of course, the special cruises. "Kids love the boats with their Victorian decor, the freedom of being on the boat and the chance to see America," Young says. But she cautions, "There are no televisions on the boats and no kids' programs. Families need to be ready for a vacation with a lot of togetherness." The Good ol' Summertime departures feature a miniature street carnival on board complete with hot dog stand (on the *American Queen* and the *Mississippi Queen*). Mardi Gras is celebrated with a Huck Finn costume party, and late-fall cruises feature pumpkin carving contests.

A "riverlorian," a historian who details facts and legends about the river, is aboard every departure. The bigger the ship, the more entertainment choices there are. The *Delta Queen* has dancing, a pianist, comedians, singers, and movies, but not all at once because most activities take place in the dining room after dinner. The *Mississippi Queen* and the *American Queen* have more space for ragtime and Dixieland bands as well as musical shows and movies. Don't

> **TIP:** Rates do not include shore excursions. In 1996, children sixteen and under, when sharing with two full-fare adults, cruise free in certain cabin categories. Check with your travel agent for details and conditions.

expect to find current movies on these cruises, however. To keep the period feel, you're likely to see such classics as *Gone With the Wind* or *Showboat*. Occasionally, a flick like *Forrest Gump* or *Parenthood* might be shown.

Rates vary with the length of cruise, the vessel chosen, and the time of year. The Delta Queen Steamboat Company offers these guidelines: Seven-night cruises on the *Delta Queen* or the *Mississippi Queen* start at about $145 per person per night. Fares for the newest ship, the *American Queen*, start at about $227 per person per night.

American Queen: entered service in 1995; 3,707 gross tons; 436 passengers; 222 cabins

The company's goal when constructing this ship was to combine the look, feel, and excitement of traditional steamboats with some big cruise ship comforts. This ship is touted as the world's largest sternwheeler and America's largest paddle-wheel steamboat.

So as not to lose the period élan, the ship's decor is high Victoriana inside and out. The *American Queen* sports detailed fretwork, towering fluted stacks, and a sixty-ton, bright red paddle-wheel.

Typical of the 1870s, the ship features reproduction turn-of-the-century light fixtures, gilt-framed floor-to-ceiling mirrors, and carved mahogany, cherry, and walnut sofas, armoires, and headboards. Old musical instruments, including an antique Steinway upright piano, an 1895 Edison roll phonograph, and a melodium, add to the period ambiance. More authentic era tunes emanate from the ship's calliope, a masterpiece of thirty-seven brass and copper whistles.

The Ladies' Parlor, where in the 1890s "spittin' and cussin' [were] forbidden," and the Gentlemen's Card Room, where the above-mentioned behaviors were condoned and even welcomed, add more charm. Decorative touches in the Ladies' Parlor include an antique silver tea set, and the Gentlemen's Card Room features a mounted black bear, stuffed fish, and antique tackle rods and reels. The six-hundred-volume library of nineteenth-century books is another nice touch. Children especially like perusing the kids' books and cookbooks, with instructions that are significantly more complicated than "microwave on high for one minute."

Children and adults are happy to know that modern touches include a swimming pool and a movie theater. Nine cabins are wheelchair accessible. There are three- and four-berth cabins.

Delta Queen: entered service in 1927 and refurbished in 1946; 3,360 gross tons; 174 passengers; 87 cabins

This authentic steamboat is protected as a national historic landmark. Built in 1926 as a steamboat for the Sacramento River, the *Delta Queen* operated as a U.S. Navy ferry in San Francisco during World War II and came to the Mississippi River in 1947. The Delta Queen Steamboat Company refers to this ship as "the only authentic, fully restored, overnight steamboat in

The Delta Queen. Photo © The Delta Queen Steamboat Company.

the world." As such, she exudes the feel of history from her hardwood floors to her solid brass appointments, grand staircase, and Tiffany crystal chandelier.

On the negative side, the cabins are small (in some cases "cozy" is a polite word). But they sport wood paneling and period decor. No cabins, however accommodate third or fourth passengers, and none is wheelchair accessible. Evening entertainment takes place in the dining room. Because this ship is small and because the cabins are all doubles, most families would feel more comfortable on either the *American Queen* or the *Mississippi Queen*.

Mississippi Queen: entered service in 1976 and renovated 1989 and January 1996; 3,364 gross tons; 420 passengers; 207 cabins

This modern version of a steamboat just recently reappeared after a refurbishment that got the boat ship-shape with new carpets, drapes, and other decorative items. Public lounges are more spacious than on the *Delta Queen*, and there are more of them. The *Mississippi Queen* sports a showroom and several lounges as well as a library, pool, movie theater, and exercise room. The decor is still Victorian with gingerbread fretwork, crystal chandeliers, a grand staircase, and period furnishings.

Staterooms are bigger than those on the *Delta Queen*, but some cruisers feel they lack the charm of the *Delta Queen*'s wood-paneled cabins. Other passengers are simply happy with the extra space. All cabins have telephones, individually controlled thermostats, and an intercom/radio on which you can hear the riverlorian's talk, in case you can't work up the energy to attend in person. Some cabins accommodate more than three passengers. One cabin is wheelchair accessible.

St. Lawrence Cruise Lines

The *Canadian Empress* offers four-, five-, and six-night river cruises departing from Kingston, Montreal, Quebec City, and Ottawa. The ship travels the St. Lawrence and Ottawa rivers from May through October. The minimum age permitted on board is twelve years old.

Canadian Empress: entered service in 1981; 66 passengers; 32 cabins

This ship, a replica of a 1908 steamboat, is a pleasant hybrid that combines the steamboat allure of scenic rivers with small ship camaraderie and some big cruise line comforts. The *Canadian Empress* offers an easy way to tour several of eastern-central Canada's major cities and sites. Depending on your itinerary, you savor the tiered skyline of Quebec City, sample the seaway's locks, and admire the scenic maze of the pine- and oak-dotted shores of the Thousand Islands, some of which are crowned with the opulent summer estates built by such rich and famous figures as Mary Pickford, George Pullman, the Astors, and Irving Berlin.

As on most river cruises, life on board follows a relaxed pace. River-watching is the prime activity with on-deck pursuits ranging from games of Trivial Pursuit to shuffleboard contests, skeet shooting, and reading about the river, the land, and Canadian-American history. Evening entertainment may be either folk singers, piano sing-alongs, or costumed interpreters telling tales.

The ships's decor evokes a turn-of-the-century atmosphere. The Grand Saloon, which functions as a dining room, gathering place, and theater, is appointed with a grand staircase, pressed tin ceiling, and tulip-glass fixtures. The comfortable but small cabins have maple furnishings and private bathrooms. The cabins are air-conditioned, and two staterooms accommodate a third passenger on a cot. Cabins have double or twin beds. The price includes fees for regularly scheduled shore tours.

Sample Itineraries
- Heritage Waterway Cruises (five days)
  Cruise on the Upper St. Lawrence River from Kingston to Montreal or from Montreal to Kingston. Highlights include the Thousand Islands, the

locks of the International Seaway, the Frederic
Remington Art Museum in Ogdensburg, New York,
and Fort Wellington. Prices start at about $800 per
person.

- Canada's Capital Cruises (six days)
Cruise on the St. Lawrence and Ottawa rivers
departing from Ottawa or Kingston. Highlights
include the Thousand Islands, Montreal, Upper
Canada Village (a living history museum circa
1850), and Ottawa. Prices start at about $995
per person.

ON SHORE

Here are some shore highlights for itineraries em-
ployed by American West Steamboat Company, the
Delta Queen Steamboat Company, and St. Lawrence
River Cruises.

Memphis, Tennessee

Tourist Information: The Memphis Visitors Information Center, 340 Beale St., (901) 543-5333, is open
Monday through Saturday from noon to 6 P.M.

Transportation: Memphis Area Transit Authority
(MATA) at Goodwyn and Institute Building at Second
and Madison, (901) 274-6282, operates trolleys and
subways throughout the city. Obtain a pass for the
MATA Showboat, which stops at scores of attractions
and hotels. Many taxi companies operate, including
Yellow Taxi Cab, (901) 577-7700 or (901) 526-2121.

Okay, so you're in Memphis. You might as well make
the pilgrimage to Graceland as millions of visitors do

each year. Besides the virtual obligation, your teens may be interested in the rock legend who was somehow connected to their parents' youth. Graceland rewards the faithful with a 1½-hour guided tour through the King of Rock and Roll's mansion. View his gold records, his gardens, his (questionable) taste in furnishings, and his grave. Reservations are recommended; I-240, exit 5B at Elvis Presley Boulevard. Call (901) 332-3322 or (800) 238-2000.

For younger kids, the **Children's Museum of Memphis** at 2525 Central Ave. (on the grounds of Liberty Bowl Stadium) is worth a stop. In warm weather, head for **Adventure River** where kids cool off in a play pool and on slides and flumes, off I-40, exit 14, at 6880 Whitten Bend Cove; (901) 382-WAVE.

Mud Island, on Libertyland Fairgrounds, (901) 576-7241, is another favorite outdoor retreat. This fifty-two acre island river park has replicas of old steamboats, a tow boat, a World War II bomber, and American Indian artifacts. Stroll along the River Walk, a five-block replica of the lower Mississippi. Children especially like the beach and pool. North of the city near Millington, the **Meeman-Shelby Forest State Park**'s outdoor fun includes swimming, boating, and horseback riding.

Memphis reputedly boasts the largest pedestrian mall in America. Located between Civic Center Plaza and Union Avenue on Main Street, this mall is adorned with fountains, trees, and sculptures and offers great browsing, people-watching, and some inexpensive eateries.

Minneapolis/St. Paul, Minnesota

Tourist Information: There are two information centers for the city of St. Paul: City of St. Paul, (612)

298-4012, and St. Paul Convention and Visitors Bureau, (612) 297-6985. For Minneapolis information, call the Minneapolis Convention and Visitors Bureau, (612) 348-4313.

Transportation: Public transportation is good and operates between the Twin Cities and the Mall of America. Call the Metropolitan Transportation Commission, (612) 827-7733.

Because the Twin Cities are surrounded by more than twelve thousand lakes and bodies of water, outdoor recreation is part of the daily routine. Take a walk or bike ride along the **Mississippi Mile**, Plymouth and Hennepin avenues in Minneapolis, (612) 348-9300.

Both cities love children and theater, and there's lots to see. The **Minnesota Children's Museum** at 1217 Bandana Blvd. North in St. Paul, (612) 644-5305, is great for ages eight and younger. Four- to seven-year-olds explore a child-size Main Street with an ice cream parlor, a recording studio, and a bank. In the warm months, browse through the garden. The **Minnesota History Center** at 345 Kellogg Blvd. in St. Paul, (612) 296-6126, has lots of artifacts and hands-on exhibits from an 1890 fire engine and vintage Betty Crocker radio broadcasts to pioneer clothing.

The **Children's Theater Company** is an award-winning theater associated with the Minneapolis Institute of Arts that attracts both children and adults, 2400 Third Ave. South, Minneapolis; (612) 874-0499.

The **Minnesota Valley Wildlife Refuge** at 3815 East 80th St. in Bloomington, (612) 854-5900, has interactive exhibits and computer games that allow children to explore jobs such as wildlife manager of a deer herd or fire boss on a fire burn. Naturalist-led programs, and spectacular slide shows are held as well. The **Minnesota Zoological Gardens** is 485 acres and houses two thousand animals, 13000 Zoo Blvd., Apple Valley; (612)431-9200. Take the Sky Trail, a monorail that runs above tigers and camels, or view Japanese snow monkeys on the Discovery Trail.

If you have the time, you don't want to miss this city unto itself: the **Mall of America**, Interstate 494 and Highway 77 in Bloomington; (612) 851-3500. This complex is huge. There are more than four hundred specialty shops, eight nightclubs, fourteen movie theaters, a miniature golf course and, in the middle of it all, Knott's Camp Snoopy, a seven-acre indoor amusement park. Needless to say, inexpensive eateries abound.

Montreal, Quebec

Montreal offers families many options. For culture, the city boasts a bevy of good museums, and for outdoor fun, there are beautiful parks and gardens.

Tourist Information: Infotouriste, 1001 Square-Dorchester, has brochures. Write ahead to the Greater Montreal Convention and Tourism Bureau at Les Cours Mont-Royal, 1555 Pell St., Suite 600, Montreal H3A 1X6; or call (800) 363-7777 or (514) 873-2015.

Transportation: Use the Metro subway. One- and three-day passes are available. Call (514) 288-6287 for information.

This island city at the confluence of the St. Lawrence and Ottawa rivers has much to offer. **Vieux Montreal**, the Old City, is a ninety-acre historic area. Even kids who roll their eyes at the thought of touring a cathedral (instead of Rollerblading, for example) are impressed by the beauty of **Basilique Notre-Dame-de-Montreal** with its facade and stained glass windows. *Then*, take them Rollerblading in **Vieux Port** (Old Port), 333 de la Commune St. West, a federal park between McGill and Berri streets in the Old Montreal Harbour. Street performers enliven the scene, and teens especially enjoy browsing the boutiques. Also in Old Port, **Expotec** at Saint Laurent Boulevard and de la Commune Street, (514) 496-7678, piques the entire family's interest with its hands-on scientific exhibits and IMAX theater.

Looking for more roaming space? The **Jardin Botanique de Montreal** (Botanical Garden of Montreal) at Rue Sherbrooke Est, (514) 872-1400, blooms with acres of flowers in thirty gardens when in season. Out of season, the ten greenhouses add interest as does the Insectarium with butterflies and bugs from around the world.

An amusement park, **La Ronde**, on the Ile Ste-Helene, (514) 283-5000, pleases young children and elementary kids with its old wooden roller coaster, simulated volcano ride, and Biosphere, a remnant of the American Pavilion Expo in 1967 that is now an interactive river and lakes learning and observation center.

Among the many museums, the **Centre Canadien d'Architecture** (Canadian Center for Architecture), 1920 Rue Baile, intrigues older children and teens with exhibits on urban planning and building, and the **Musée des Beaux Arts de Montreal** (Montreal Museum of Fine Arts), 1379 Rue Sherbrooke Ouest, has a vast collection. Turn this into a search for treasured examples of silver, furniture, period paintings, or anything else your children admire.

For lunch, enjoy the atmosphere and the inexpensive food (good croissants and pastries) at one of the city's many outdoor cafes and bistros. Another good bet: the bagels (that's right—the bagels in Montreal are said to rival New York's.)

Nashville, Tennessee

Tourist Information: The Nashville Area Chamber of Commerce, 161 Fourth Ave. North, (615) 259-4702, is open weekdays from 8 A.M. to 5 P.M.

Transportation: Metropolitan Transit Authority (MTA), (615) 242-4433, is Nashville's public bus service. Taxis include Checker Cab, (615)256-7000, and Nashville Cab, (615) 242-7070.

Nashville has become synonymous with country music, and the heart of Nashville's entertainment is **Opryland USA**, 2802 Opryland Drive; (615) 889-6611. This southern version of Disney World spreads over 120 acres. The fun includes a theme park, roller coasters, water rides (try the Grizzly River Rampage and the Screamin' Delta Demon), and lots of musical performances. Three favorites: **The Grand Ole Opry**, **Country Music USA** (a toe-tapping tribute and for children), and the **Opryland Kid's Club** where singers ages nine through twelve perform.

For country music memorabilia, visit the **Country Music Hall of Fame**, 4 Music Square St.; (615) 256-1639. Get a glimpse of Elvis' gold Cadillac, see Garth Brooks' stage outfits, and watch a film about Patsy Cline.

Younger kids enjoy visits to the **Nashville Zoo**, 1710 Ridge Road Circle, Joelton, (615) 370-3333.

Wildlife includes Siberian tigers, Vietnamese pot-bellied pigs, and a petting zoo with Capuchin monkeys and an elephant.

Carolyn's Homestyle Kitchen, 330 Charlotte Ave., (615) 255-1008, serves southern food. For a unique way to visit Nashville, hop on the **Broadway Dinner Train**, First Avenue South and Broadway; (615) 254-8000. This train winds through downtown Nashville as you dine. (This is best for pre-teens and teens; there are no meals specifically priced for young children or high chairs.)

New Orleans, Louisiana

Tourist Information: The Greater New Orleans Tourist and Convention Commission, Inc., 1520 Sugar Bowl Drive, (504) 566-5011, offers New Orleans for Kids, a family guide. The Welcome Visitor Center, 529 Saint Ann St., (504) 566-5031, is open daily.
Transportation: The Regional Transit Authority (RTA), 101 Dauphine St., (504) 569-2700, is a public bus and streetcar service. For unlimited rides on all buses and streetcars, ask for the VisiTour Pass.

There's more to New Orleans than Mardi Gras and adult nightlife. Families enjoy the **Louisiana Science and Nature Center**, 11000 Lake Forest Blvd. in Joe Brown Memorial Park, (504) 246-5672, an eighty-six-acre wildlife preserve with trails that wind through wetlands and forests. When it's time to sit, children like the planetarium with its IMAX theater and laser show to music. Don't miss the **Aquarium of the Americas**, 1 Canal St., a recreation of freshwater and saltwater habitats. Highlights include the Coral Reef, with schools of rainbow-colored fish, and the Amazon

Rain Forest, with waterfalls and rare orchids. Watch the paddle wheel and rest for a spell on benches shaded by oaks and magnolias at the adjacent **Woldenberg Riverfront Park**. Nature lovers should also visit the **Audubon Park and Zoo**, rated as one of the top zoos in the U.S. Along with other critters, the Louisiana Swamp Exhibit is home to a rare white alligator.

The town has lots of history, some of which may even interest your kids. The visitor's center at **French Quarter Unit**, 916 North Peters, (504) 589-3719, has free tours including ones that highlight women's landmarks, African American art, and architecture. Because of liquor laws, one of the few places your children can enjoy live jazz is **Preservation Hall**, 726 Saint Peter St.; (504) 522-2841.

The city is renowned for its food. For a taste of the local Cajun specialties, **Ralph and Kacoo's Seafood Restaurant** has charcoal-broiled redfish, crawfish, and large crab. But go early, because this popular spot accepts no reservations, 519 Toulouse St.; (504) 522-5226. Along with antique stands and shops, the 250-year-old **French Market**, along Royal and Chartre in the French Quarter, has casual eateries.

For upscale shopping, browse **Canal Place**, 365 Canal St., (504) 522-9200, where fifty shops include Gucci, Brooks Brothers, and Saks.

Portland, Oregon

Tourist Information: Portland/Oregon Visitors Association, 26 Southwest Salmon; (503) 222-2223 or (800) 962-3700.

Transportation: Use Tri-Met bus and trolley. The main station is at 701 Southwest Sixth Ave.; (503)

233-7433. A large portion of downtown is fareless. Metropolitan Area Express (MAX), although under construction for 1998, will provide a light rail for the fifteen-mile stretch from downtown to Gesham, the gateway to Mount Hood.

Several attractions in Portland delight young and old alike. The **Oregon Museum of Science and Industry** (OMSI) has six halls of science fun, 1945 Southeast Water Ave.; (503) 797-4000 or (800) 955-6674. Live through a (simulated) earthquake and tornado and explore a real submarine. A scenic zoo that is great for walking is the **Metro Washington Park Zoo**, 4001 Southwest Canyon Road, (503) 226-1561, which has more than one thousand animals. Fish and wildlife of the region are represented in the Cascade exhibit. From the zoo, it's enjoyable to ride the Washington Park and Zoo Railway to the **International Rose Garden**, a site not to be missed (in season) when a terraced hillside blooms with hundreds of varieties of roses. The view of the city's skyline is spectacular from here.

For scenic day trips, take the **Mount Hood Railroad** to the base of Mount Hood, which is the highest peak in Oregon (11,235 feet). The train winds through the Hood River Valley, Oregon's largest fruit growing district. The **Columbia Gorge** offers several scenic choices. Exhibits at the Columbia Gorge Interpretive Center depict the area's natural history. At the **Bonneville Dam Visitor Center**, you can view massive turbine generators and watch fish jump up the stream on a fish ladder. The **Multnomah Falls**, the second highest falls in the United States, are "awesome" at 620 feet high.

In **Pendleton**, the location of the famed Pendleton Round-Up and the Pendleton Woolen Mills, *The Queen of the West* offers designated shore tours. Visit a saddle maker, tour historic "underground" Pendleton known for its brothels and speakeasies, and gather for lunch at the Pendleton Rodeo grounds for barbecue and a performance by the Confederated Tribes of the Umatilla Indian Reservation. Some cruises provide an opportunity to see **Mount St. Helens National Volcanic Monument**. This is the volcano that erupted in 1980 leveling 230 square miles of forest and reducing the height of the mountain by thirteen hundred feet. At the Coldwater Ridge Visitor Center you look right into the volcano's crater. **Hell's Canyon National Recreation Area**, the deepest canyon in North America, features abundant wildlife, interesting earthen formations, and ancient Indian petroglyphs. In **Astoria**, the first American settlement on the Pacific Coast (1811), historic sites include the Columbia River Maritime Museum, and the Lightship Columbia, a national historic landmark.

Quebec City, Quebec

The city of Quebec charms children with its French flair, historic areas, and modern museums.

Tourist Information: Open daily, the Maison du Tourisme de Quebec, 12 Rue Sainte-Anne, has information and assistance, or write to Tourisme Quebec, Case Postale, 979 Montreal, Quebec, Canada H3C 2W3.

Transportation: Buses run regularly. Call the Commission de Transport de la Communaute Urbaine de Quebec (CTCUQ) at (418) 644-3704.

A stroll through Old Quebec is a must. Whether or not your children will remember all the historical facts of forts, French explorers, and battles with the British, they will remember the city's Old World feel. To get oriented, stop by the **Parc de l'Artillerie**, near the Porte St-Jean gate. The interpretation center, once the arsenal foundry, briefs visitors with an orientation film that details three centuries of Quebec history. Young children can try on a soldier's life at the Officers' Quarters by dressing up in costumes and preparing for battle.

Visit **La Citadelle** (the Citadel) on the cap diamant promontory (entrance on Rue St. Louis); (418) 694-2815. For great views from the boardwalk, the Citadel is impressive, especially at 10 A.M. from mid-June to Labor Day, when the pomp includes the changing of the guard. Nearby, **Parc des Champs de Bataille** (Battlefields Park), between Grande Allee and Champlain Boulevard, delights with 250 acres for romping.

Especially appealing to younger children when in Sainte-Foy is the **Aquarium du Quebec**, 1675 Avenue des Hôtels; (418) 659-5264. The aquarium features fishy finds, seal shows, and splendid St. Lawrence River views.

If your children are frustrated because there's water everywhere but noplace to swim, then take a fun time-out at **Villages des Sports**, 1860 Boulevard Valcartier, Saint-Gabriel-de-Valcartier; (418) 622-0312. Swim in a wave pool, watch acrobatic diving shows, roller skate, and play miniature golf.

Chute Montmorency in Beauport-Boischatel is a nice day trip. These scenic falls, at 270 feet, are higher than Niagara Falls. The park-like setting has trails, lookouts, and picnic tables, so bring a snack with you.

The St. Louis skyline. Photo courtesy of the St. Louis Convention & Visitors Commission.

St. Louis, Missouri

Tourist Information: The St. Louis Convention and Visitors Bureau can be reached at (314) 421-1023 or (800) 325-7962. For information on special events, call Fun Phone at (314) 421-2100.

Transportation: Metro Link, (314) 231-2345, is a light-rail transportations system that connects some major attractions within the city, such as the airport, Busch Gardens, and Union Station. Transportation is free weekdays from 10 A.M. to 3 P.M. However, rental cars are a good option. Taxis are also available: Yellow, (314) 361-2345; Country, (314) 991-5300; and Allen, (314) 241-7722.

Don't miss the **St. Louis Science Center** at 5050 Oakland Ave., (800) 456-SLSC, one of the new breed of interactive science centers. Children love the four-story OMNIMAX theater, and the hundreds of hands-on exhibits. At the **St. Louis Zoological Park**, (314) 781-0900, go "ape" over the gorillas in the Jungle of the Apes tropical rain forest. The zoo's halls, the Living World, offer high-tech exhibits and computers and video screens for hands-on learning about animals, fish, and ecology.

If your family loves taking in the symbols along with the sites, visit St. Louis' trademark, the 630-foot stainless steel **Gateway Arch**, (314) 982-1410. The first level houses a museum commemorating westward expansion.

In spring and summer, enjoy the **Missouri Botanical Gardens**, 4344 Shaw Blvd., (314) 577-5100, which blooms with acres of lily ponds and rose gardens and features an especially splendid Japanese garden complete with meditation huts and stone paths.

St. Louis also has lots of good eateries. **St. Louis Union Station**, Market Street between 18th and 20th streets, (314) 421-6655, is a reno-vated train station that sports several restaurants and inexpensive eateries as well as chain stores and boutiques.

RIVER BARGES, BOATS, AND RIVER CRUISE SHIPS IN EUROPE

Cruise through eighteenth-century canals past medieval villages, vineyards, fields of wildflowers, and thick forests. At night, float past cities with spectacular sunsets and evening twinkling lights. Tour country castles and cathedrals and peruse sophisticated European capitals at your own pace.

Barges provide all this plus the welcome family conveniences of cruising—no packing and unpacking and no struggling to get to your destination. Because most barges are relatively small, you can request special stops or design your own itinerary on a trip chartered for your own family.

Several companies offer barge vacations in Europe suitable for families. Some are staffed and some are self-skippered vacations where you play captain (and crew and cook) after the company explains the basics. Barges may be small eight- to ten-person boats suitable for one or two families to share, fifteen- to twenty-passenger boats, or even 180-passenger deluxe river ships.

Whatever style you choose—from country comfortable to dress-for-dinner—the daytime scenery and the languid pace is the same. "We're not selling entertainment. We're selling scenery, good food, and service," notes J. F. O'Rourke, president of KD River Cruises of Europe. "It's more of a hotel concept. In our case it's like going down the middle of a parkway except that our parkway is a river and we're pulling over to check out a castle, cathedral, or vineyard."

On most barge trips, especially the smaller ones, the itinerary is somewhat flexible. If you pass a particularly lovely riverbank path, the captain may pull over to let you bike under the lush canopy of trees or photograph a field of wildflowers. The key is to pick a barge with a style, either formal or casual, that's right for your family.

The Companies and Itineraries

The Barge Lady

This travel company has an inventory of thirty-two barges in various price ranges that travel through France and England. On a non-charter basis, these welcome ages sixteen and older. But, if you charter the whole barge, the captains and chefs aim to please even tots. (March through October.)

Families Welcome

This family-friendly tour agency also books guided barge trips in France. They book *La Belle Aventure* as well as six-night cruises on the *Geneviève*. Families Welcome also represents several self-skippered barges that travel the canals and waterways of England and Wales.

KD River Cruises of Europe

KD offers three- to eight-day guided cruises aboard eleven luxury river cruise ships. The ships travel along the Rhine, Moselle, and Main rivers in Germany, Holland, and Switzerland; the Danube in Germany, Austria, Slovakia, and Hungary; the Elbe in the Czech Republic to Germany; and also float along the Seine, Rhone, and Saone in France. (April through October.)

Kemwel's Premier Selections

This line offers three-, six- and nine-night trips on deluxe vessels, most of which cruise in France through Burgundy, Alsace, and Lorraine; some barges tour England and Holland. (March through October.)

Rascals in Paradise

This travel company offers a thirteen-day tour of France that includes a six-day barge trip in Burgundy on *La Belle Aventure*. (Selected summer departures.)

The Lines and Ships

The Barge Lady

Most of the barges represented by this company welcome families with children age sixteen or older and, of course, families traveling with adult children. However, four of the Barge Lady's vessels (those described below) welcome families with younger children if the families charter the entire barge. Each barge has its own style. Three cruise in France and one cruises in England, but all offer six-night voyages.

Avenir: six-night cruises on the Canal Du Midi in southwest France from Sète to medieval Carcassonne, stopping at villages such as Languedoc, Somail, Paraza, and Roubia; ten-passenger capacity; five cabins, each with a private bath. A charter of eight to ten people costs approximately $21,000.

This barge travels through the picturesque French countryside. The *Avenir*, a former coal-carrying vessel, still looks a bit like the working barge she was for fifty years. On board she has a splash pool, bicycles, board games, kites, and a library. Children's bicycles and cribs are available for rent, and special excursions can be arranged for the children. Ellen Sack, "the Barge Lady," says that "the unique, after-dinner musical programs are what differentiates this barge from the others. The children are invited to play the piano and operate the hurly-gurly." The barge's mini-bus takes you to shore sites.

Clementina: six-night cruises in England on the Avon River between Gloucester and Stratford-upon-Avon, visiting Slimbridge, Tewkesbury, Pershore, Bidford-on-Avon, and Worcester on the River Severn; five-passenger capacity; two cabins and two bathrooms. One cabin sleeps three. This is a self-catering vessel on which you do the cooking and cleaning.

This barge floats along the Avon River through England's Shakespearean country. You explore market towns, historic castles, and gothic abbeys. With bedrooms on opposite ends of common living quarters, the *Clementina* works well for two families with small children who want to share the trip. This boat can be rented with her pilot for $3,100 per week; a guide and shore vehicle are an additional $1,000 per week.

La Belle Aventure: offers a wide variety of itineraries on several canals in Central France. Families of six to eight persons are invited aboard this vessel that has three two-person cabins, a couch bed in the salon that can accommodate two, one full bath and one half bath.

The pilot of *La Belle Aventure*, John Bassett, is a father of four who knows just the right restaurants and auberges along the way that are family-friendly. Although a cook prepares breakfast and lunch, which is included, you are on your own for dinner, so you have an opportunity to sample more of the region. The ambiance is informal; the pilot leads outings and can help arrange baby-sitting. Rowboats, children's bicycles, tandem bicycles, and two sailing boats let you explore the land and the water on your own. In addition, the barge packs tents that you can pitch on shore for more privacy and shore breezes. The cost ranges from $800 to $1,000 per person.

Saint Louis: six-day cruises in France, primarily on the Canal de Bourgogne in central Burgundy in an area north and west of Dijon with stops at vineyards, ancient towns, and chateaux. Refurbished in 1994, the *Saint Louis* is billed as an elegant barge; three cabins, each with twin beds and a private bath, accommodate six passengers.

With the new refurbishments, the *Saint Louis* features central air-conditioning and heating and cellular phone service. Three options are available. On the Gourmet Cruise, you dine at five Michelin-rated restaurants on shore and must dress for dinner. On the Connoisseur Cruise, the focus is on wine. Food is served aboard the vessel, but regional wines are specially selected and guest speakers talk about various aspects of wine. Both of these cruises are suitable for families with adult children. The Classic Cruise features meals on board and suitable wines. This is the cruise for families with younger children.

The *Saint Louis* has six adult-size bikes for exploring the countryside and also has children's bikes on board (double check to be sure). All cruises include meals, liquor, and shore excursions led by the captain in an air-conditioned minibus. The captain can arrange tennis and golf, meals at area restaurants, and even a hot air balloon ride. The Classic Cruise for a party of six is $18,000. The Connoisseur and Gourmet cruises range about $24,000 for six people.

Families Welcome

Families Welcome, a travel company specializing in group and individual tours for families, represents two guided barges in France: *La Belle Aventure* (also represented by the Barge Lady and Rascals in Paradise) and the *Geneviève*. Families Welcome also represents three self-skippered boats, the *Stort*, *Nene*, and *Chiltern*, which all cruise in England.

Barges

La Belle Aventure: See the description under The Barge Lady
Geneviève: entered service in 1912 and refurbished in 1984 and again in 1994; eight to ten passengers; three cabins, each with private bath

The *Geneviève* accommodates a family of six with possible room for two more small children on rollaway beds. Continental breakfast and buffet lunch are provided. You are on your own for dinner. The barge carries bicycles and a dinghy for guests. The price includes excursions, beverages, breakfast, and lunch. The cost is $1,250 per person for a family of six for six nights.

Self-Skippered Boats

Stort: 33 feet; accommodates a family of four in two cabins (one is a double and two are singles)
Nene: 37 feet; accommodates a family of four to six in two cabins (one double and two single bunks)
Chiltern: 41 feet; accommodates a family of six in three cabins (3 doubles)

All three boats cruise the canals and waterways of England, Scotland, and Wales. They are fully equipped with kitchens, bed linens, and towels. Choose from fixed itineraries or be adventurous and set your own. Families Welcome can arrange Mix N' Match packages that let you combine three- and four-night self-skippered boat holidays with stays at small inns and guest homes. You may also add a car or train option.

A sample package: three nights in London in a two-bedroom apartment with maid service; three nights in the Cotswolds in a family suite at Woolley Grange, a country manor home with a children's program; plus a self-skippered narrowboat for a three- or four-night cruise on the Stratford Canal. Families Welcome rate, based on a family of two adults and two children, is $2,800. Car and train segments are extra. Call Families Welcome at (800) 326-0724.

KD River Cruises of Europe

With eleven luxury river cruise ships traveling many itineraries through Germany, Holland, Switzerland, Austria, Slovakia, Hungary, the Czech Republic, and France, KD River Cruises of Europe offers its clientele lots of options. Tour sophisticated cities, centuries-old villages, majestic cathedrals, renowned museums, and well-known vineyards. Most cruises, depending on length, visit one or two major cities and several smaller towns. These ships generally cruise at night and call at different ports every day. Folk dancers and singers entertain in the evenings on the ship, but many passengers prefer to enjoy the city sites at night because the ship often stays in port until late in the evening.

For older elementary-age children and teens intent on experiencing a few European cities in several days, these ships provide a welcome alternative to the hassles of driving and switching hotels. The focus on these cruises isn't the on-board activities, which mostly consist of eating and drinking, but the sites themselves, which offer excitement enough for most pre-teens and teens.

The ships depart from Amsterdam, Basel, Strasbourg, Cologne, Frankfurt, Dusseldorf, Rotterdam, Trier, Wurzburg, Budapest, Vienna, Berlin, Prague, Dresden, and Hamburg.

The ships range in capacity from 104 to 184 passengers. The *Britannia* and the *Deutschland* have heated outdoor swimming pools, and the *Heinrich Heine* has a heated indoor pool. Triples are not available on the French cruises (the *Arlene* and the *Normandie*), but all other vessels have three-passenger cabins. Children under four cruise free. A child age four to fourteen sharing a triple cabin with parents cruises for 25 percent of the full fare. A child age four to fourteen sharing with one adult cruises for 50 percent of the regular fare. Shore excursions are not included in the cruise fare. Call KD River Cruises of Europe: (800) 346-6525 in the eastern U.S., or (800) 858-8587 in the western U.S.

Sample Itineraries

(Unless otherwise indicated, the ships cruise mid-April to mid-October.)

Arlene

- Seven-night, round-trip cruise from Geneva and visiting Seurre, Macon, Lyon, Tournon, Viviers, and Avignon

Austria

- Three-night cruise from France through Germany and Holland visits Strasbourg, Rudesheim, Speyer, Cologne, and Dusseldorf
- Four-night cruise from Holland through Germany and France visits Rotterdam, Dusseldorf, Braubach, Cologne, and Speyer

Britannia

- Four-night cruise from Germany through France to Switzerland and visiting Dusseldorf, Koblenz, Speyer, Cologne, and Strasbourg
- Three-night cruise from Switzerland through France and Germany visits Basel, Strasbourg, Cologne, and Boppard

Clara Schumann

- Seven-night cruise from Hamburg to Dresden and visiting Lauenburg, Magdeburg, Wittenberg, Torgau, and Meissen (April, May, and June)
- Three-night cruise from Dresden to Wittenberg and visiting Bad Schandau, Dresden, and Torgau (May and June)
- Five-night cruise from Wittenberg to Prague visits Torgau, Meissen, Dresden, and Decin (mid-May to mid-October)
- Six-night cruise from Prague to Hamburg visits Velke Zernoseky, Dresden, Meissen, Wittenberg, and Magdeburg (April, May, and June)
- Five-night cruise from Prague to Wittenberg visits Velke Zernoseky, Bad Schandau, Dresden, and Torgau (end of July to mid-October)

Deutschland

- Four-night cruise from Switzerland through France and Germany to Holland with visits in Basel, Strasbourg, Koblenz, and Dusseldorf; stops in Konigswinter and Cologne
- Four nights from Holland through Germany and France with visits to Amsterdam, Dusseldorf,

Boppard, and Speyer, and stops in Cologne and Linz
- Two-night cruise from France to Germany visits Strasbourg and Rudensheim with a stop in Speyer
- Four-night cruise from Germany through France to Switzerland and visiting Cologne, Rudensheim, Speyer, and Strasbourg, plus a stop in Mainz

Heinrich Heine

- Seven-night cruise from Nuremberg to Budapest on the Main-Danube Canal and downstream on the Danube River to Vienna and Budapest (mid-May to mid-October); reverse itinerary available
- Seven-night cruise from Nuremberg to Vienna through the Main-Danube Canal and downstream on the Danube to Vienna (May, July, August, October)

Helvetta

- Seven-night cruises from Basel to Amsterdam and visiting Strasbourg, Rudesheim, Cologne, and Nijmegen (June, July, August, and September); reverse itinerary available

Italia

- Two-night cruise on the Middle Rhine from Cologne to Frankfurt with visits in Cologne, Braubach, Mainz, and Rudesheim
- Three-night cruise from Frankfurt on the Main, Rhine, and Moselle rivers to Trier and visiting Frankfurt, Alken, Bernkastel-Kues, Rudesheim, Koblenz, and Cochem

- Two-night cruise from Trier on the Moselle and Rhine rivers to Cologne and visiting Cochem, Bernkastel-Kues, and Zell

Normandie

- Seven-night, round-trip cruise from Paris to visit Vernon, Les Andelys, Rouen, Caudebec, and Honfleur

Theodor Fontane

- Seven-night cruise on the Main, Rhine, and Moselle rivers, from Trier to Wurzburg

- Sixteen-night cruise on the Moselle, Rhine, and Main rivers, the Danube Canal, and Danube River from Trier to Vienna (May, July)

- Fourteen-night cruise on the Danube, Main-Danube Canal, Main and Rhine rivers (May and August)

- Six-night cruise on the Rhine and Neckar rivers from Cologne via Heidelberg to Stuttgart (June and August)

- Six-night cruise on the Neckar, Rhine, and Moselle rivers from Stuttgart to Trier (June and August)

- Seven-night cruise from Wuzburg to Stuttgart on the Main, Rhine, and Neckar rivers (June to September); reverse itinerary available

Wilhelm Tell

- Six-night cruise from Nuremberg to Vienna visiting Berching, Regensburg, Passau, Linz, and Durnstein (mid-May to mid-September)

Kemwel's Premier Selections

Kemwel offers nearly twenty luxury barges that cruise throughout France, as well as a few that cruise in England and Holland. These voyages, like other river cruises, explore historically and culturally rich urban and rural regions. Where the *Litote* cruises, Caesar defeated an army of Gauls in 52 B.C., and *La Joie de Vivre* takes you to the remains of Roman baths.

Cruise fares include meals, wine, excursions, and bicycles. The barges range in size from 100 to 128 feet long and carry eight to fifty passengers. They have air-conditioning and alfresco dining, and all cabins have private baths. The barges provide bicycles for towpath riding (English barges do not offer bicycles for this purpose because the rocky towpaths are not recommended for bicycles). Except for private charters, guests should be at least fifteen years old on the *Litote* and the *Luciole*, and at least sixteen years old on *La Joie de Vivre*.

Sample ships and itineraries:

- *La Joie de Vivre*: six-night cruises on the Upper Loire; ten passengers; five cabins, all with private baths. Fares from about $2,500 per person.
- *Litote*: six-night cruises along the Burgundy Canal from Venarey-Les Laumes to Tonnerre; twenty passengers; ten double cabins, each with private bath. Fares from $1,990 per persons.
- *Luciole*: six-night cruises along the Burgundy Canal and Canal du Nivernais; fourteen passengers; six twin cabins and two singles, all with private baths. Fares from $1,800 per person.

Rascals in Paradise

Rascals in Paradise, a tour operator that specializes in arranging individual and group family trips, books six-day barge trips aboard *La Belle Aventure* as part of their suggested thirteen-day tour of France. Call (800) U-RASCAL.

See the description of the barge under the listing for The Barge Lady. The rate for the Rascals in Paradise thirteen-day trip to France, including three days in Paris and two days at a Burgundy Estate, is $8,195 for one family of two adults and two children, or $5,695 per family if two families travel together.

MINI CRUISE SHIPS

Mini cruise vessels are in a class by themselves. These ships resemble traditional cruise ships, but on a miniature scale. A main dining room offers one seating; a lounge or salon constitutes a social room for mingling; and most, if not all, of these ships feature sun decks, and some even have swimming pools. Because of the small size of the ships and the small number of passengers on board, the atmosphere is generally casual and intimate. These ships can also travel rivers and other destinations that are unreachable to traditional cruise ships. On these cruises, the boats and ships function more as a means to explore an area than as an end in themselves. A cruise aboard one of these ships with well-behaved older children could be a great vacation for your family.

The Lines and the Ships

Alaska Sightseeing CruiseWest
Alaska Sightseeing CruiseWest is dedicated to small ship cruising because they believe that "smaller is

better." Cruises emphasize the geology, culture, wildlife, and history of the region. There are no beer guzzling parties here (none that are officially scheduled
anyway). For a more detailed description of the 101-
passenger ship and this line, which offers several voyages in Alaskan waters, refer to chapter eight.

Spirit of '98: entered service in 1984; 192 feet; 96 tons;
101 passengers. Offers eight-day round-trip cruise
from Portland on the Columbia and Snake rivers.
Ports and excursions include Astoria, Columbia River
Gorge, Bonneville Dam, Hood River, Ice Harbor Dam,
Lower Monumental Dam, Little Goose Dam, Lower
Granite Dam, and Lewiston, Idaho (April, May, Sep-
tember, and October).

American Canadian Caribbean Line

American Canadian Caribbean Line has expanded a
great deal since their beginning in 1966. Once cruising only New England and Canada, the line now has
voyages in the Great Lakes, along the intracoastal waterways of eastern North America, and in the Bahamas and Venezuela. The line caters generally to
older clientele or to families with adult children. Children under fourteen are not permitted.

Refer to chapters two and three for more details
about this cruise line. (For on-shore ideas in Montreal,
New Orleans, Nashville, Portland, Quebec City, and
St. Louis, see the On Shore section that follows Steamboats in this chapter.)

Mayan Prince: entered service in 1992; 175 feet;
92 passengers. Offers a fifteen-day intracoastal waterway cruise from Warren, Rhode Island, to Palm Beach
Gardens, Florida (reverse itinerary available). Ports

include Norfolk, Virginia; Savannah, Georgia; and Titusville, Florida (May, June, and November). Six-day cruise from College Point, New York, to Hyannis and Nantucket, Massachusetts (July). Six days round-trip from Warren, Rhode Island, visiting Cuttyhunk, Block Island, Newport, Martha's Vineyard, and Nantucket (July). Twelve-day cruise from Warren, Rhode Island, to Quebec City with visits in New York Harbor, Little Falls, Oswego, Upper Canada Village, and Pointe Aux Pic (August through October).

Niagara Prince: entered service in 1994; 175 feet; 84 passengers. Offers a twelve-day cruise from New Orleans to Chicago (reverse itinerary available). Ports include Biloxi, Mobile, Columbus, Shiloh, Nashville, Paducah, St. Geneviève, St. Louis, Peoria, and Joliet (May, June, and November). Sixteen-day cruise from Chicago to Warren, Rhode Island (reverse itinerary available). Ports include Mackinac Island, Wyandotte, Cleveland, Erie, Buffalo, Niagara Falls, Welland Canal, Rochester, Oswego, Sylvan Beach, Troy, and the Hudson River (July, August, September, October). Twelve-day cruise from Warren, Rhode Island, to Buffalo (reverse itinerary available). Ship stops in New York and Vermont (August and September).

Caribbean Prince: entered service in 1984; 156 feet; 78 passengers. Fifteen-day intracoastal waterway cruise from Warren, Rhode Island, to Palm Beach Gardens, Florida (reverse itinerary available), and visits ports such as Norfolk, Virginia; Savannah, Georgia; and Titusville, Florida (May and November). Twelve-day cruise from Warren, Rhode Island, to Quebec City, visiting ports such as New York Harbor,

Little Falls, Oswego, Upper Canada Village, and
Pointe Aux Pic (July through October).

Sonesta Nile Cruises

Each ship accommodates about seventy passengers.
Nile Goddess and *Sun Goddess* offer four-night Egypt-
ian cruises to and from Luxor and Aswân, visiting
Esna, Edfu, and Kôm Ombo, and six-night Egyptian
cruises to and from Luxor and Dendera or Luxor and
Aswân, visiting Dendera, Abydos, the West Bank,
Edfu, and Kôm Ombo.

Children, especially elementary-age kids, love seeing the Egyptian temples and tombs. When asked by
a major museum to name environments and eras that
most fascinated them, this age group put the mum-
mies, pyramids, and pharaohs of ancient Egypt at the
top of their list. As a result, the museum created an
exhibit based on ancient Egypt. But with a Nile cruise
from Aswân to Luxor (or the reverse), you and your
children can enjoy the real thing.

We know from experience that a Nile River cruise
truly fascinates children. While we were hesitant to
take our daughter (then nine years old), on this trip,
the adventure proved to be one of her most memorable.
Also, the Egyptians love children, and having one with
us made for instant friendships and warm conversa-
tions. We were invited into homes for tea, given private
camel rides, and taken on special tours of native
markets.

These cruises take you back to a time when
pharaohs ruled Egypt. Bilingual guides explain the
history of such sites as the Temple of Karnak, the
Temple of Luxor, the Temple of Horus, the Valley of
the Kings, and the Valley of the Queens. We learned
the meaning of a few hieroglyphics before arriving in

Egypt so we could make a treasure hunt (and some sense) of the hieroglyphics we found. This added to the fun.

Both ships feature five decks, deluxe accommodations, and ample buffets. Each cabin is equipped with air-conditioning, telephone, television, music, and a big picture window that makes watching the palm trees and fields along the Nile easy. It's wonderful to wake up to these soothing sites. Suites are available. Each ship has a sun deck and a pool, a welcome place to cool off after a land tour. This is definitely not roughing it; the creature comforts are first-rate. Cabins can accommodate three people.

The cabin rate for two people is about $1,300 for a four-night cruise on the *Nile Goddess*, and the rate is about $1,500 per couple on the *Sun Goddess*. Children under six cruise free. On a package plan, the additional fee for a child age six to twelve is about $180 on the *Nile Goddess* and about $210 on the *Sun Goddess*. Call (800) SONESTA. (Many companies in addition to Sonesta offer Nile cruises, and many tour companies also incorporate Sonesta's Nile cruise into their tour packages of Egypt. Check with your travel agent for the best deals.)

ECO-EDUCATIONAL YACHT ADVENTURES

Wildland Adventures

This educational and adventure travel company aptly employs the subtitle "authentic worldwide explorations." In their group trips that journey to Alaska, Costa Rica, the Galápagos Islands, Nepal,

Belize, Kenya, Turkey, and other places, Wildland covers some of the well-known sites, but also visits off-the-beaten-path locales and creates opportunities for cross-cultural exchange.

Conde Nast Traveler listed Wildland as one of the top eighteen eco-tourism companies in the world. These trips aren't look-and-point bus tours. Wildland works hard at getting their clients involved in experiences that reveal the social fabric and special history of a locale.

Kurt Kutay, president of Wildland Adventures, calls the Turquoise Coast Odyssey through Turkey "the best trip we do because of the diversity of experiences. We visit the coast, ancient ruins, stay in a village with a family, swim, hike, snorkel and stroll along shore towns." Six days of this nineteen-day trip concentrate on cruising the Aegean Sea aboard a traditional Turkish *gulet*, a twelve-passenger yacht. Another variation is Wildland's Ancient Aegean Voyage, which Kutay recommends for families with elementary-age children. This features a shorter, seven-day cruise and easier hiking shore trips; it is also less expensive than the Turquoise Coast Odyssey.

Turquoise Coast Odyssey: This nineteen-day, round-trip tour from Istanbul includes a six-day yacht cruise of the Aegean Sea to Myra, Kekova Bay, Aperlae,

---

TIP: If you aren't concerned with taking children out of school (yours may be too young or too old) or if your school system operates on a twelve-month cycle (and long breaks are not just in summer), then the best time to cruise Turkey is spring and fall when temperatures are more mild.

> **TIP:** The seas are calmest from May through October, so problems with motion sickness are minimized. But do come prepared with any preventatives suggested by your physician and pediatrician.

Gemlier Island, Turquoise Cove, Caunos, and Marmaris. Land stops include Istanbul, Cappadocia, Goreme, Konya, Urunlu, Antalya, Termessos National Park, and a two-night stay with a Turkish host family (May to October).

Ancient Aegean Voyage: This fifteen-day, round-trip tour leaves from Istanbul and provides seven days of cruising and seven nights in hotels. Visit Izmir, Pammukale, Fethiye, Kalkan, Myra, Simena, Finike, and Antalya (May to October).

To enhance the cross-cultural experience, Wildland Adventures employs traditional Turkish *gulets* on these cruises. These six-cabin yachts sleep up to twelve people in six double cabins, each of which have private bathrooms with showers. A sailboard and a paddle kayak are available, but cruisers should bring their own snorkeling equipment. Ogle sponges, fish, and octopus in the sunken baths of Cleopatra in Turquoise Cove, an inlet in Fethiye.

You get to explore little-traveled places because these yachts can anchor in places inaccessible to big ships. Hike rarely used trails to Hellenistic and Roman theaters, baths, and aqueducts. Climb to crusader fortifications, stroll through picturesque coastal towns, and explore sunken ruins that are easily visible through the clear Aegean waters. To enhance the experience, the cook prepares traditional Turkish meals.

A bilingual local guide with a command of Turkey's history accompanies the group.

Both trips depart from and return to Istanbul, an intriguing city of markets, mosques, and palaces. Bargain at the Grand Bazaar for carpets and jewelry and explore the impressive Topkapi Palace. On the Turquoise Coast Odyssey, in addition to Istanbul and a six-day yacht cruise, land tours take you to sample wine at local vineyards, hike through canyons, and tour underground cities that served as havens for the early Christians; this also includes a two-night stay with a local family. Visit Aspendos, a well-preserved Roman theater, and travel to the forests of mythological legend. Land tours on the Ancient Aegean Voyage include strolling the Mediterranean village of Kalkan, browsing for handicrafts in the village of Kas, walking the streets of a Greek ghost town called Kaya Koy, and exploring the ancient mythological sites in Arycanda and Olympos.

The Turkish *gulets* can also be chartered with a crew for groups of six to twelve people for weeklong trips along Turkey's Turquoise Coast. Contact Wildland Adventures at 3516 N.E. 155th St., Seattle, WA 98155; (800) 345-4453 or (206) 365-0608.

Appendix

Directory of Cruise Lines

Traditional Cruise Lines

American Hawaii Cruises
2 North Riverside Plaza
Chicago, Illinois 60606
(800) 765-7000
(312) 466-6000

Big Red Boat (Premier Cruise Lines)
400 Challenger Road
Cape Canaveral, Florida 32920
(800) 327-7113
(407) 783-5061

Carnival Cruise Line
Carnival Pl.
3655 N.W. 87th Avenue
Miami, Florida 33178
(800) 327-9501
(305) 599-2600

Celebrity Cruises
5200 Blue Lagoon Drive
Miami, Florida 33126
(800) 437-3111
(305) 358-7325

Costa Cruises
World Trade Center
80 S.W. 8th Street
Miami, Florida 33130
(800) 462-6782
(305) 358-7325

Cunard
555 5th Avenue
New York, New York 10017
(800) 528-6273 for Cunard Crown and
    QE II, and
(800) 458-9000 for Cunard Royal
    Viking

Holland America Line
300 Elliott Avenue West
Seattle, Washington 98119
(800) 426-0327
(206) 281-3535

Norwegian Cruise Line
95 Merrick Way
Coral Gables, Florida 33134
(800) 327-7030
(305) 445-0886

Princess Cruises
10100 Santa Monica Boulevard
Los Angeles, California 90067
(800) 421-0522
(310) 553-1770

Royal Caribbean Cruise Line
1050 Caribbean Way
Miami, Florida 33132
(800) 327-6700
(305) 539-6000

Steamboats and River Cruise Vessels

America West Steamboat Company
520 Pike Street, Suite 1400
Seattle, Washington 98101
(800) 434-1232
(206) 621-0913

The Delta Queen Steamboat Company
30 Robin Street Wharf
New Orleans, Louisiana 70130-1890
(800) 543-7637
(504) 586-0631

St. Lawrence Cruise Lines
253 Ontario Street
Kingston, Ontario
Canada, K7L 2Z4
(800) 267-7868
(613)549-8091

Windjammers

The Angelique
Yankee Packet Co.
Box 736 Camden, Maine 04843
(800) 282-9989
(207) 236-8873

Grace Bailey, Mercantile, & The
  Mistress
P.O. Box 617
Camden, Maine 04843
(800) 736-7981
(207) 236-2938

J & E Riggin
Box 571
Rockland, Maine 04841
(800) 869-0604
(207) 594-2923

Maine Windjammer Association
P.O. Box 1144
Blue Hill, Maine 04614
(800) 807-WIND

Mystic Whaler Cruises
P.O. Box 189
Mystic, Connecticut 06355
(800) 697-8420
(860) 536-4218

Nathaniel Bowditch
Box 459
Warren, Maine 04864-0459
(800) 288-4098
(207) 273-4062

North End Shipyard Schooners
P.O. Box 482
Rockland, Maine 04841
(800) 648-4544
(207) 594-8007

Schooner Lewis R. French
P.O. Box 992
Camden, Maine 04843
(800) 469-4635
(207) 236-9411

Schooner Mary Day
P.O. Box 798
Camden, Maine 04843
(800) 992-2218

The Timberwind
Rockport Schooner Cruises
Box 247
Rockport, Maine 04856
(800) 759-9250
(207) 236-0801

Victory Chimes
P.O. Box 1401
Rockland, Maine 04841
(800) 745-5651
(207) 594-0755

Barges and River Cruises

The Barge Lady
101 West Grand Avenue
Suite 200
Chicago, Illinois 60610
(800) 880-0071
(312) 245-0900

Families Welcome
Woodcroft Shopping Center
4711 Hope Valley Road
Durham, North Carolina 27707
(800) 326-0724
(919) 489-2555

KD River Cruises of Europe
2500 Westchester Avenue
Purchase, New York 10577
(800) 346-6525
(914) 696-3600

or

323 Geary Street
San Francisco, California 94102
(800) 858-8587
(415) 392-8817

Kemwel's Premier Selections
106 Calvert Street
Harrison, New York 10528
(800) 234-4000
(914) 835-5555

Rascals In Paradise
650 Fifth Street #505
San Francisco, California 94107
(800) U-RASCAL

Small Cruise Ships

Alaska Sightseeing/CruiseWest
4th & Battery Bldg.
Suite 700
Seattle, Washington 98121
(800) 426-7702
(206)441-8687

American Canadian Caribbean
Line
P.O. Box 368
Warren, Rhode Island 02885
(800) 556-7450
(401) 247-0955

Sonesta Nile Cruises
4 El Tayaran Street
Nasr City, Cairo
Egypt
(800) 766-3782

World Explorer Cruises
555 Montgomery Street
San Fransisco, California 94111
(800)854-3835
(415) 393-1565

Eco-Adventure Cruises

American Wilderness Experience Inc.
2820-A Wilderness Place
Boulder, Colorado 80301-5454
(800) 444-0099

The Galapagos Network
7200 Corporate Center Drive
Suite 404
Miami, Florida 33126
(800) 633-7972
(305) 592-2294

Metropolitan Touring
in the U.S.: book through Adventure
Associates
13150 Coit Road
Suite 110
Dallas, Texas 75240
(800) 527-2500
(214) 907-0414

or in Ecuador:
Ave. Republica de El Salvador 970
Quito, Ecuador
(593) 2-46-47-80

Natural Habitat Adventures
2945 Center Green Court South
Boulder, Colorado 80301
(800) 543-8917
(303) 449-3711

South American Fiesta
910 West Mercury Boulevard
Hampton, Virginia 23666
(800) 334-3782
(804) 825-9000

Temptress Cruises
1600 N.W. LeJeune Road
Suite 301
Miami, Florida 33126
(800) 336-8423
(305) 871-2663

or in San José, Costa Rica
(506) 220-1679

Wildland Adventures
3516 N.E. 155th Street
Seattle, Washington 98155
(800) 345-4453
(206) 365-0686

Index